A Special Issue of
Cognition and Emotion

Appraisal and Beyond
The Issue of Cognitive Determinants of Emotion

Edited by

Nico H. Frijda

*Department of Psychology, University of Amsterdam,
The Netherlands*

 LAWRENCE ERLBAUM ASSOCIATES, PUBLISHERS
Hove (UK)   Hillsdale (USA)

Lawrence Erlbaum Associates Ltd., Publishers
27 Church Road
Hove
East Sussex, BN3 2FA
U.K.

British Library Cataloguing in Publication Data

Appraisal and Beyond: Issue of Cognitive Determinants of Emotion
I. Frijda, Nico H.
152.4

ISBN 0-86377-915-8

ISSN 0269-9931

Index by Sue Ramsey
Printed and bound in the United Kingdom by BPCC Wheatons, Exeter

Contents

*This book is also a special double issue of the journal Cognition and Emotion which forms issues 3 and 4 of Volume 7 (1993). The page numbers used here are taken from the journal and so begin with p.225

COGNITION AND EMOTION, 1993, 7 (3/4), 225–231

Appraisal and Beyond

Nico H. Frijda

Department of Psychology, University of Amsterdam, The Netherlands

Appraisal is a central notion in current emotion theory. A process of appraisal can be considered the key to understanding that emotions differ for different individuals. Assuming a process of appraisal that mediates between events and emotions is the clue to understanding that a particular event evokes an emotion in one individual and not in another, or evokes an emotion at one moment, and no emotion, or a weaker or stronger one, at another moment. A process of appraisal also explains that an emotionally charged event elicits this particular emotion, and not another one, in this particular individual, under these particular conditions. Appraisal is the clue for understanding the conditions for the elicitation of different emotions, as well as for understanding what makes one emotion different from another.

A process of appraisal accounts for the fact that the arousal of an emotion depends on the meaning of the event for the individual, and explains why the emotion that is evoked often depends on quite subtle aspects of that meaning. Arousal of emotions is determined by the interaction between events, the individual's conceptions or expectations as to what constitutes well-being for him or her, and the individual's expectations that he or she will be able to deal or cope with the event and, if so, in what manner or how effectively.

The notion of appraisal has been developed to deal with these issues, and it has been with us now for a considerable time. It was first used extensively in 1960 by Arnold when she proposed, in her influential book *Emotion and personality*, that emotions arise when events are appraised as harmful or beneficial, and that different emotions arise because events are appraised in different ways. The book provides a first attempt to describe these different ways of appraisal as the systematic variation in a small number of appraisal components or dimensions, thus systematically accounting for the conditions that lead to the different emotions. In fact,

Requests for reprints should be sent to N. H. Frijda, Department of Psychology, University of Amsterdam, Roetersstraat 15, 1018 WB Amsterdam, The Netherlands.

basic emotions were defined as those that correspond to the various combinations of those components that can occur.

The notion of appraisal was taken up by Lazarus in his extensive experimental work in which cognitive appraisal processes were manipulated. The experiments appeared to show that such cognitive processes indeed produce variations in the emotions elicited by particular events, and that this held both for the emotions as subjectively felt, and as manifest in physiological reactions. The work led to his seminal *Psychological stress and the coping process*, published in 1966, in which the considerable explanatory power of the concept of appraisal was elaborated. Lazarus analysed in detail how emotions and stress effects do not depend directly on the objective properties of stimulus events, but on their meaning for personal well-being as appraised subjectively. The distinction between primary and secondary appraisal made the relationships clear between the conditions for emotion arousal as such, and for the coping processes that shape particular emotions, and that form an integral aspect of emotions in general.

Then, towards the end of the 1970s, a torrent of theoretical and empirical work broke loose in which the cognitive variables involved were spelled out in great detail, and the cognitive structure of particular emotions was analysed. Solomon (1976) was an early pioneer, and De Rivera (1977) and Kemper (1978) worked on lines that have affinities with the appraisal notion; then came the large number of theoretical and empirical studies that Scherer (this issue) enumerates, and that forms what he calls "a highly cumulative body of research". What was surprising was the fact that so much work started almost simultaneously, without the investigators being aware of each other until years later, and with great similarity in content. I do not know what caused this diverse but almost simultaneous upsurge of interest. The emergence of cognitive psychology was of course important, as were the specific proposals of cognitive emotion theory, notably Arnold (1960) and Schachter and Singer (1962), and the revival of interest in emotion generally (e.g. Tomkins, 1962). Experimental work on cognitive emotion antecedents during that period also emerged from entirely different research traditions, as in the experiments on predictability and controllability (for instance, Glass & Singer, 1972; Seligman, 1975); and so did the development of cognitive behaviour therapy (Beck, 1976; Bandura, 1977). And of course the work had its predecessors, notably Spinoza (1677) with what was the first, and highly systematic, structural emotion theory (Frijda, in press).

Thus the studies proliferated, and along with that came critical voices. Zajonc (1980) objected to the important place given to cognitive processes in something as immediate as emotional reactions. Russell (1987) expressed strong reservations about what the empirical appraisal work was supposed to mean, and so too did Parkinson and Manstead (1991).

It is therefore about time to take stock. This Special Issue is one endeavour to do that. Fraser Watts suggested the idea of an issue on appraisal, and I agreed quickly with him that the idea was a good and timely one. The Special Issue is called "Appraisal and beyond", in order to invite state-of-the-art reports of appraisal research, critical comments, and suggestions that might carry the theory further. I have been lucky in receiving such reports, comments, and suggestions. A number of prominent contributors to the field have been willing to contribute. All of them have been working in the field before, several of them for a long time and some, in fact, belonging to the group that initiated this research endeavour.

The issue opens with a contribution by Smith and Lazarus. In their study they carry the notion of appraisal somewhat further than before, by introducing the notion of core relational themes and providing empirical evidence of its usefulness. Core relational themes describe the cognitive antecedents of specific emotions at a more molar and integrative level than that of patterns of appraisal components. Core relational themes link appraisal patterns to the transactions between the person and the environment in a more explicit fashion, and embody the hypothesis that particular emotions correspond to particular relational themes occurring in those transactions. Smith and Lazarus set out to test specific hypotheses with regard to the relationships between appraisals, themes, and emotions, framed within their version of structural emotion theory. They do this by making use of vignettes, constructed so as to vary systematically with respect to appraisal-relevant components, and by measuring appraisals, themes, and emotions separately.

Their study makes it clear that empirical and theoretical research has advanced far enough to propose and test specific hypotheses as to which appraisal patterns and core relational themes go with which emotions. At the same time, their article illustrates that the theory of appraisal-emotion relationships is still in flux. Not only do the specific appraisal components hypothesised by different authors differ somewhat, even the two authors of this paper have come to develop somewhat different views, in the time between conducting their study and its publication. Their differences in view reflect a basic but hidden issue in appraisal theory, namely whether the arousal of particular emotions is independent of the particular concerns involved in the person-environment encounter or, rather, whether particular emotions involve relevance to particular concerns. In the latter case, the concern, and not only harm or benefit to whatever concern, enters into the appraisal process.

Reisenzein and Hofmann, in the second paper, pose the important question of evaluating the predictive power of appraisal theory. How well does appraisal theory do, in predicting the occurrence of particular emotions? In some studies, patterns of appraisal make some 30% to 40% correct predictions, but one wonders whether that is a good or a poor result. As they argue, the question can only be answered if the maximum performance that is possible in discriminating emotions (or, rather, the differential use of emotion labels) is known. In other words, the performance of appraisal theories in predicting which emotion labels correspond with which appraisal patterns can only be evaluated if a base rate is known that reflects the prediction of emotion labels when all relevant information is available, including that on the specific nature of the eliciting situations. They investigate such a base rate by having subjects guess the emotion names for carefully selected and edited actual scenarios of events that had aroused particular emotions in some individuals. They find that, overall and certainly for selected scenarios, prediction on the basis of full information is appreciably better than that found in most appraisal studies, and on occasion is maximal.

In posing the question, and setting out to examine an answer, the authors signal a vital issue in appraisal theory, but one that has hardly been faced up to squarely, namely that of distinguishing appraisal from other emotion-relevant, situational information. No clear definitional line has been drawn by anyone in the literature. Apart from that, one may assume that the prediction of emotion labels profits from the latter information, quite independently from that of the former. Little appraisal information is needed to predict that the response to third-party threat of an intimate relationship will be one of jealousy. The authors' findings amply support this assumption. The issue is confronted more fully in the following article.

In this third article, Parkinson and Manstead take studies of appraisal inferences from stories as their targets, and direct arrows of sharp criticism at this research methodology. Their main target is vignette methodology; in writing their paper, they were familiar with a previous, and later the final, version of the Smith and Lazarus paper in this issue. But their critique reaches further, to self-report studies of appraisal generally, and to some of the assumptions that, in their view, underlie most of the theoretical and empirical work in this area. They question the roles of representation in emotion elicitation, the adequacy of methodologies that involve the subject as a distant observer rather than as a participant in an emotional transaction, and the representativeness of traditional narratives, and stories in general, as stimulus events for the study of emotional processes. These questions form the grounds for doubting whether the appraisal components found to be important in vignette studies might also be those that are relevant in real-life emotional encounters. These criticisms are added to those advanced earlier by the same authors

(Parkinson & Manstead, 1992). The major thrust of these earlier criticisms concerned the potential influence of knowledge and stereotyped scripts upon the subjects' reports of how they recall having appraised particular emotional events, or how they imagine they would respond to such an event. Recall studies as well as vignette studies may reflect social memory schemata rather than individual experiences. In other words, the authors express general doubt about the extent to which appraisal-relevant information gained from self-report studies reflects the real antecedents of the emotions. It might come from other sources.

Their main point is to emphasise the interactive, narrative, and social context of most relevant emotional situations. That context may be quite different from the context in stories, as in vignette methodology, or in retrospective accounts of one's experiences. The individualistic perspective, in particular, may hamper a view of the factors that are actually emotionally operative, because in relevant emotional situations emotions are part of a dialogue between the subject and others, a dialogue, moreover, that develops in time, and not the results of a unidirectional flow of information from the object to the subject, with fixed and stable meanings.

With all the research on emotional appraisal, analyses of the process of appraisal itself have been rare. That is one of three major problems in emotional appraisal theory, signalled by Scherer in the next paper. The other two problems concern the role of cognition in emotion elicitation, and the nature and number of the appraisal components that should be distinguished. After discussing the emotion-cognition relationship from a neurophysiological angle, he surveys the major appraisal components mentioned in the literature, and finds a fair degree of consensus. Then a process model of appraisal is sketched, in which emotions result from a continuously repeated or updated series of "stimulus evaluation checks"; each of those checks corresponds to one of the appraisal components.

The model has been reported before. Novel, however, is the fact that it is tested by means of a computer model of the appraisal process. An expert system has been constructed that links the outcomes of appraisal questions to emotion names. Subjects are asked to recall an emotional experience, and respond to evaluation check questions presented by the system. The system then translates the pattern of those responses into the most appropriate (or several appropriate) emotion names. The translations are made on the basis of prior hypotheses of the appraisal patterns that are theoretically supposed to correspond to the various emotions; the input patterns provided by the subjects are tested against these hypothesised patterns. The expert system thus tests the theory, with regard to both the sufficiency of the checks, and to the specific patterns for different emotions. The success rate of the system compares favourably with the predictions made by more conventional means. The paper represents a further specification of the process by which appraisals are supposed to operate, and a way to test aspects of the theory.

In fact, apart from providing overall success rates, Scherer's study leads to detailed suggestions about shortcomings of the appraisal model in its current form, and particularly with regard to the fact that it offers no way to catch the temporal development of appraisals, emotions, and the coping processes that the emotions motivate.

In this final paper, the author discusses several critical issues with regard to the concept of appraisal, and the process by which appraisal is supposed to operate in the generation of emotions. He suggests that "appraisal" has two meanings: that of an aspect of emotional experience, and that of an antecedent of emotions. Self-report may represent the former, rather than the latter. Discrepancies exist between what a person says he or she is emotionally upset about, and what is known, or can be surmised, about the actual causal factors. The analysis of what can be inferred on minimal conditions for emotions, including anger, guilt, and shame, leads him to the notion that emotional experience is the result of both antecedent appraisals and cognitive elaborations consequent upon emotion arousal. He then proceeds to detailed hypotheses concerning the nature of the process of appraisal, in a way that tries to do justice to the fact that all emotion is held to involve some appraisal process.

It is argued that the basic processes of appraisal, although belonging to the domain of cognition, represent cognitive processes of quite elementary kinds. Suggestions as to the nature of some of these processes are advanced, in an effort to bring the often automatic nature of emotion arousal, and its cognitive nature, closer to each other.

I am grateful for the contributions that the authors have been willing to provide, and for the quality of these contributions. I hope and I expect that the Special Issue will provoke thought, discussion, and new research.

REFERENCES

Arnold, M.B. (1960). *Emotion and personality*. Vols I and II. New York: Columbia University Press.

Bandura, A. (1977). Self-efficacy: Towards a unifying theory of behavior change. *Psychological Review, 84*, 191–215.

Beck, A.T. (1976). *Cognitive therapy and the emotional disorders*. New York: International Universities Press.

De Rivera, J. (1977). *A structural theory of the emotions*. New York: International Universities Press.

Frijda, N.H. (In press). Spinoza and current emotion theory. In Y. Yovel (Ed.), *Spinoza by 2000*, Vol 3. Haarlem: Brill.

Glass, D.C. & Singer, J.E. (1972). *Urban stress: Experiments on noise and social stressors*. New York: Academic Press.

Kemper, T.D. (1978). *A social interactional theory of emotions*. New York: Wiley.

Lazarus, R.S. (1966). *Psychological stress and the coping process*. New York: McGraw-Hill.

Parkinson, B. & Manstead, A.S.R. (1992). Appraisal as a cause of emotion. In M. S. Clark (Ed.), *Emotion. Review of personality and social psychology*, Vol. 13. Newbury Park, CA: Sage, pp. 122–149.

Russell, J.A. (1987). Comment on articles by Frijda and by Conway and Bekerian. *Cognition and Emotion, 1*, 193–197.

Schachter, S. & Singer, J. (1962). Cognitive, social and physiological determinants of emotional state. *Psychological Review, 63*, 379–399.

Seligman, M.E.P. (1975). *Helplessness: On depression, development and death*. San Francisco: Freeman.

Solomon, R.C. (1976). *The passions*. New York: Doubleday-Anchor.

Spinoza, B. (1677/1989). *Ethica*. Amsterdam: Rieuwertsz [English translation: G.H.R. Parkinson. London: Everyman's Library].

Tomkins, S.S. (1962). *Affect, imagery and consciousness*, Vol. 1. *The positive affects*. New York: Springer.

Zajonc, R.B. (1980). Thinking and feeling: Preferences need no inferences. *American Psychologist, 35*, 151–175.

COGNITION AND EMOTION, 1993, 7 (3/4), 233–269

Appraisal Components, Core Relational Themes, and the Emotions

Craig A. Smith

Vanderbilt University, USA

Richard S. Lazarus

University of California, Berkeley, USA

This study experimentally tests the contributions of specific appraisals, considered at both molecular (appraisal components) and molar (core relational themes) levels of analysis, to the experience of four emotions (anger, guilt, fear/anxiety, and sadness) using a two-stage directed imagery task. In Stage 1, subjects imagined themselves in scenarios designed to evoke appraisals hypothesised to produce either anger or sadness. In Stage 2, the scenarios unfolded in time to produce a second manipulation designed to systematically evoke the appraisals hypothesised to produce each of the four emotions under study. The results provided substantial support for the theoretically specified appraisal-emotion relationships for anger, guilt, and fear/anxiety. However, support for the predictions for sadness was weaker, partially due to ineffective manipulation of the relevant appraisals. Implications for the further development and testing of emotion theory are discussed.

INTRODUCTION

Recent evidence is consistent with a key premise of all cognitive theories of emotion (e.g. Frijda, 1986; Lazarus & Folkman, 1984; Leventhal, 1984; Roseman, 1984; Scherer, 1984), namely, that certain relational meanings concerning the implications of one's circumstances for personal well-being,

Requests for reprints should be sent to Craig A. Smith, Department of Psychology and Human Development, Box 512 Peabody, Vanderbilt University, Nashville, TN 37203, USA. Telephone: (615) 322-8141; Bitnet: SmithCA@VUCTRVAX.

The research described in this article was supported, in part, by a National Institute of Mental Health training grant to the first author, and, in part, by the Dean's Office of Peabody College of Vanderbilt University. We are indebted to Jill Novacek for her helpful input and advice on numerous facets of this article and the research it describes. We would also like to thank Helen Bateman, Laura Griner, Lothar Laux, Kelly Haynes, Anna Pecchinenda, Lois Pope, and Hannalore Weber for their helpful comments on earlier versions of the manuscript.

achieved via cognitive appraisal, are associated with specific emotions (e.g. Conway & Bekerian, 1987; Frijda, Kuipers, & ter Schure, 1989; Roseman, Spindel, & Jose, 1990; Shaver, Schwartz, Kirson, & O'Connor, 1987; Smith & Ellsworth, 1985).

Although this evidence contributes to a comprehensive theory of cognition and emotion, a number of problems limit the conclusions that can presently be drawn. One of the most important of these is the way appraisal is conceptualised (see Lazarus & Smith, 1988; Smith & Lazarus, 1990).

Appraisal is an evaluation of what one's relationship to the environment implies for personal well-being. Each positive emotion is said to be produced by a particular kind of appraised benefit, and each negative emotion by a particular kind of appraised harm. The emotional response is hypothesised to prepare and mobilise the person to cope with the particular appraised harm or benefit in an adaptive manner, that is, to avoid, minimise, or alleviate an appraised harm, or to seek, maximise, or maintain an appraised benefit. Whether a particular set of circumstances is appraised as harmful or beneficial depends, in part, on the person's specific configuration of goals and beliefs. Appraisal thus serves the important mediational role of linking emotional responses to environmental circumstances on the one hand, and personal goals and beliefs on the other.

We have proposed that two distinct but related types of cognition are involved in achieving this linkage, but that only one of these directly results in emotion (e.g. Lazarus, 1991a; Lazarus & Folkman, 1984; Lazarus & Smith, 1988; Smith & Lazarus, 1990; Smith, Haynes, Lazarus, & Pope, submitted). First, a well-developed construal of the factual nature of one's circumstances, reflecting one's *knowledge* or *beliefs* about what is happening, is necessary. However, we do not believe this construal by itself is sufficient to produce emotion. Instead, we propose that the "facts" as represented in this construal must be evaluated, or *appraised*, with respect to their significance for personal harm or benefit for emotion to result. The implications for personal well-being that emerge from this appraisal comprise the relational meaning that, we think, lies at the heart of emotion. In our usage, appraisal is meant to encompass the most proximal cognitive variables that directly result in emotion.[1] We consider appraisal

---

[1] In the present discussion we focus on the *contents* of adult appraisal rather than the formal cognitive processes underlying these contents or the precursors of these contents in infants. In particular, we do not mean to imply that appraisals are necessarily conscious or deliberate. Instead, we have consistently maintained that appraisal may often be unconscious and automatic (e.g. Lazarus, 1966, 1991a; Smith & Lazarus, 1990). Nor do we mean to imply that the appraisals relevant to emotion are necessarily identical for adults and infants. Although beyond the scope of the present article, we consider both the development of appraisal-emotion relationships and the formal cognitive processes underlying appraisal to be important research topics.

to be a sufficient condition of emotion, as well as a necessary one, although this latter position is clearly controversial (see Lazarus, 1991b).

Previous examinations of cognition and emotion have tended to treat knowledge and appraisal as interchangeable. The resulting models intermix components of appraisal with components of knowledge and the subjective properties of the emotional response, producing considerable theoretical and empirical unclarity (cf. Lazarus & Smith, 1988; Scherer, 1988). Thus, the main goal of the present research was to isolate appraisal (as we have defined it) as best we could, and to examine the relationships between it and emotion. Further, in developing our specific appraisal model, we attempted to maximise the model's theoretical coherence by explicitly integrating it into the more general theory of stress and coping previously developed by Lazarus and his colleagues (e.g. Lazarus, 1966; Lazarus & Folkman, 1984).

The present research tests predictions of our model for four emotions—anger, guilt, sadness, and fear/anxiety—commonly thought to be responses to (appraised) actual or potential harm. Therefore, a brief summary of the model's predictions for these emotions follows. More complete treatment of the model and its theoretical underpinnings can be found elsewhere (Smith, 1991; Smith & Lazarus, 1990).

In describing the model, we should point out that it differs in several respects from the one currently advanced by Lazarus (1991a,c). The discrepancies arise because in the time since the collaborative research reported here was performed, Lazarus has made changes in his analysis of the appraisal components and core relational themes postulated for several emotions. However, the present model is not obsolete. Smith continues to advance it, and it provides the foundation of his research programme (e.g. Smith, Ellsworth, & Pope, 1990; Smith & Pope, 1992).

The differences that have arisen do not involve fundamental premises about the relationship between appraisal and emotion, but reflect relatively minor disagreements about the nature of specific variables, the number needed for an adequate causal analysis, and their relationships to specific emotions. These disagreements are genuine, interesting, and potentially important. Therefore, to maintain clarity about our respective positions, we conclude this article with a brief postscript that highlights the most relevant differences between the present model and the one currently advanced by Lazarus (1991a,c).

Appraisal Components and Core Relational Themes

We describe the relational meaning underlying each emotion at two levels of analysis, which represent complementary ways of conceptualising and assessing this meaning. The first level is molecular, and describes the specific judgements made by a person to evaluate particular relational harms and benefits. The adaptational issues at this level are single *components* of appraisal, which correspond closely to appraisal dimensions described in previous work (e.g. Frijda et al., 1989; Roseman, 1991; Scherer, 1984; Smith & Ellsworth, 1985). We have attempted to refine the components to reflect more clearly our conceptualisation of appraisal (cf. Lazarus & Smith, 1988).

To this we have added a second, more molar level of analysis that combines the individual appraisal components into summaries, or perhaps more accurately, gestalts of relational meaning, referred to as core relational themes.[2] A *core relational theme* is simply the central (therefore core) harm or benefit that underlies each of the negative and positive emotions. Whereas the individual appraisal components describe the specific questions evaluated in appraisal, the core relational themes efficiently capture the central relational meaning derived from the configuration of answers to these appraisal questions, which differs in each emotion.

For example, the core relational theme for sadness is proposed to be irrevocable loss. This relational meaning draws on more than a single appraisal component. There must be an appraised loss which, in turn, stems from evaluating (1) a goal commitment as being (2) threatened or harmed in a manner that (3) cannot be avoided or repaired. In our analysis, there are, in effect, three separate and distinct appraisal components, each of which makes an essential contribution to the complex relational meaning hypothesised to produce the emotion, but none of which individually constitutes the whole meaning.

Notably, the answers to the appraisal component questions are not conceptualised as causing the core relational themes in a mechanistic sense. Instead, the relationship between the appraisal components and core relational themes is one of logical or analytic causality: Each core

---

[2] We are aware that Luborsky (1977, 1984) has used a similar term, "core conflictual relationship themes", with meanings that overlap but also differ from our core relational themes. His usage refers to the central and recurrent interpersonal scenarios of a troubled person. An example might be persons with a constant need to assert themselves with others, including loved ones, which, when enacted, leads to the vicious circle of rejection by the other, withdrawal by the needy person, and renewed but counterproductive efforts at assertion (see also Horowitz, 1988, on role relationship schemas). A major difference between Luborsky's usage and ours is the classic distinction between emotion traits and states. Because Luborsky is concerned with psychotherapy for dysfunctional people, his construct focuses on stable or recurrent themes, whereas ours focuses on the momentary themes of specific encounters.

relational theme is *defined* by a specific configuration of answers to several appraisal component questions. Thus, a specific configuration of appraisal components *implies* a particular relational meaning and vice versa— without any necessary causal ascription. In short, the appraisal components and core relational themes provide alternative ways of representing the *same* relational meanings associated with the various emotions. However, if one compares the appraisal components taken individually with the molar relational meanings as captured by the core relational themes, we would expect the latter to be more efficient in predicting emotion because they capture the meaning of the full configuration of appraisal components in a way that transcends the components' individual meanings—much in the way a sentence captures a complex idea that goes beyond the meanings of its individual words. The two levels of analysis have different properties, which, as we discuss later, provide for different uses in the study of emotion.

Specific Appraisals in Anger, Guilt, Fear/Anxiety, and Sadness

Each appraisal component addresses one of the two general appraisal issues originally proposed by Lazarus and his colleagues as relevant to well-being under stress (e.g. Lazarus, 1966; Lazarus & Folkman, 1984): *primary appraisal* concerns whether and how the encounter is relevant to the person's well-being; and *secondary appraisal* concerns the person's resources and options for coping with the encounter.

The model utilises six appraisal components, two of primary appraisal, and four of secondary appraisal. The components of primary appraisal are motivational relevance and motivational congruence (or incongruence). *Motivational relevance* is an evaluation of the extent to which the encounter touches upon personal commitments (issues the person cares about), and thus the degree to which the encounter is personally relevant. *Motivational congruence* refers to the extent to which the encounter is consistent or inconsistent with the person's desires or goals.

The four components of secondary appraisal are accountability, problem-focused coping potential, emotion-focused coping potential, and future expectancy. *Accountability* determines who or what (oneself or someone/something else) is to receive the credit (if the encounter is motivationally congruent) or the blame (if it is motivationally incongruent) for the outcome of the encounter, and therefore who or what should be the target of any subsequent coping efforts. The two components of coping potential correspond to the two main means of reducing discrepancies between one's circumstances and one's desires and motivations (cf. Folkman & Lazarus, 1988; Kimble, 1990; Smith & Lazarus, 1990):

TABLE 1
Appraisal Components and Core Relational Themes Associated with 4
Harm-related Emotions

Emotion	Core Relational Theme	Important Appraisal Components
Anger	Other-blame	1. Motivationally relevant 2. Motivationally incongruent 3. Other-accountability
Guilt	Self-blame	1. Motivationally relevant 2. Motivationally incongruent 3. Self-accountability
Fear/Anxiety	Danger/Threat	1. Motivationally relevant 2. Motivationally incongruent 3. Low/Uncertain (emotion-focused) coping potential
Sadness	Irrevocable loss Helplessness about harm or loss	1. Motivationally relevant 2. Motivationally incongruent 3. Low (problem-focused) coping potential 4. Low future-expectancy

problem-focused coping potential reflects evaluations of the person's ability to act directly upon the situation to bring or keep it in accord with the person's desires; and *emotion-focused coping potential* refers to the perceived prospects of adjusting pyschologically to the encounter by altering one's interpretations, desires, and/or beliefs. *Future expectancy* refers to the possibilities, for *any* reason, of there being changes in the actual or psychological situation which could make the encounter seem more or less motivationally congruent.

Specific patterns of appraisals along the above components, we suggest, shape each of the four emotions under study. The postulated appraisal components and core relational themes for each emotion are listed in Table 1. The four emotions under study are *all* associated with various types of harm, and thus are characterised by motivational relevance and motivational incongruence. The components of secondary appraisal further define and differentiate the core relational themes that produce these emotions, and thus determine which specific emotion(s) will be experienced in the harmful or threatening encounter.

To illustrate, the core relational theme for anger is "other-blame", which is defined by combining primary appraisals of motivational relevance and motivational incongruence with a secondary appraisal of other-accountability. Both the primary appraisals and other-accountability are necessary for an appraisal of other-blame, because accountability does not translate to blame in the absence of motivational incongruence. If one's circumstances are appraised as beneficial (i.e. motivationally relevant and motivationally congruent) an appraisal of other-accountability will contribute to a core relational theme of "other-credit" and a very different affective state, such as gratitude, will result (cf. Smith, 1991).

The core relational theme for guilt is "self-blame". This theme is also defined by combining primary appraisals of motivational relevance and motivational incongruence with accountability, but in this case the accountability is assigned to oneself. As with other-blame, both the primary appraisals and self-accountability are required to produce self-blame; under beneficial conditions the appraisal of self-accountability contributes to a core relational theme of "self-credit" and results in feelings of pride (Smith, 1991).

The core relational theme for fear/anxiety is "danger" or "threat"—the perception that one will not be able to psychologically adjust to a harm should it occur. In this theme, with its focus on the inability to adjust to potential harm, the primary appraisals of motivational relevance and motivational incongruence are combined with secondary appraisals of low emotion-focused coping potential. In contrast, for sadness the core relational theme is one of *irrevocable loss* or *helplessness about loss*, which emphasises the inability to restore the loss or eliminate the harm. This theme is defined by combining secondary appraisals of low problem-focused coping potential and negative future expectations with primary appraisals of motivational relevance and motivational incongruence.

METHOD

The present research was designed to provide an experimental test of the above appraisal model for anger, guilt, fear/anxiety, and sadness. We elected to examine four harm-related emotions because we believed manipulating appraisals associated with these emotions, which differ with regard to secondary appraisal components, would provide a more sensitive test of the discriminant validity of the model than could be obtained by contrasting one or two benefit-related emotions with one or two harm-related ones.

Our strategy was to manipulate the relevant appraisals twice. Once by systematically varying the conditions to which subjects were initially exposed, and a second time by systematically attempting to vary the subjects' appraisals during the experimental encounter. We think the second manipulation provides a more powerful test of the strength and specificity of the appraisal-emotion relationships than has been possible in most previous studies, which have relied more heavily on retrospective techniques. We reasoned that by dynamically manipulating specific appraisals during an encounter we would be able to rule out a host of third factor explanations for any observed appraisal-emotion relationships. A directed imagery task was employed because of the use of imagery appears to be a reliable technique for evoking emotion in the laboratory (e.g. Lang, 1979; Smith, 1989; Smith, McHugo, & Lanzetta, 1986), and it affords a high degree of experimental control.

Overview of Research Design

Four hypothetical scenarios, each involving multiple stages of an emotional encounter as it unfolded over time, were written to manipulate appraisal. These scenarios were administered in a between-subjects design. Two of the scenarios were designed to evoke initially appraisals of other-blame, theoretically associated with anger. One of these was learning that a friend had betrayed a confidence (the friend scenario); the other described being persecuted by a teaching assistant (the TA scenario). The remaining two scenarios were designed to evoke appraisals of irrevocable loss and helplessness, theoretically associated with sadness. One involved learning that a favourite relative had cancer (the cancer scenario); the other, learning that one had performed poorly in an important course (the course scenario).

The story of each scenario unfolded in two stages. The *first stage* established the motivational relevance for the central character (whose role the subject was instructed to assume), as well as both the motivational incongruence (or conflict) and the component(s) of secondary appraisal appropriate to the relational theme the scenario was intended to evoke. Thus the friend and TA scenarios emphasised other-accountability, whereas the cancer and course scenarios emphasised low coping potential and low future expectancy.

To allow a more explicit examination of the emotional effects of changes in appraisal over time, multiple versions of the *second stage* were written for each scenario, creating a second manipulation nested within the first. Whereas in Stage 1 each scenario was associated with a single appraisal condition, in Stage 2 different versions of each scenario were written to create four appraisal conditions: other-blame; self-blame; threat; and loss/helplessness. To provide closure, there was also a *third stage* in which subjects were asked to resolve the scenario.

Subjects sequentially imagined themselves in the events of their assigned scenario, and at the end of Stages 1 and 2 they reported on their appraisals and emotions in that stage. This allowed systematic manipulations of appraisals as the scenario progressed and assessment of how these appraisals affected the emotions experienced. Table 2 summarises the overall experimental design.

TABLE 2
Overview of the Experimental Design

Scenario Content	Appraisals Manipulated within Each Experiemental Cell		Cell N
	Stage 1	*Stage 2*	
Friend	Other-blame	Other-blame	12
		Self-blame	13
		Threat	12
		Loss/Helplessness	12
TA	Other-blame	Other-blame	12
		Self-blame	12
		Threat	13
		Loss/Helplessness	12
Cancer	Loss/Helplessness	Other-blame	12
		Self-blame	11
		Threat	12
		Loss/Helplessness	12
Course	Loss/Helplessness	Other-blame	12
		Self-blame	12
		Threat	12
		Loss/Helplessness	12

Subjects, Experimental Design, and Scenario Contents

Subjects were 193 University of California at Berkeley undergraduates (89 males, 104 females) who participated as part of an introductory psychology course requirement. Subjects were tested individually, and each was randomly assigned to one of 16 experimental cells, resulting in between 11 and 13 subjects being assigned to each cell (see Table 2).

The experiment was organised as a 2 (Stage 1 manipulation) × 4 (Stage 2 manipulation) between-subjects design. There were two scenarios for each condition, serving as replications, to yield the 16 experimental cells. Subjects sequentially imagined themselves within each stage to simulate the experience of the encounter as it unfolded. By varying the descriptions subjects received to guide their imagery, appraisal, at the level of both appraisal components and core relational themes, was manipulated in the first and second stages. All descriptions avoided any mention of emotional reactions to the depicted events to ensure that the subjects' reactions were guided by the provided contextual and cognitive cues.

For example, the first stage of the friend scenario established the subject's situation as important and motivationally incongruent, and suggested other-accountability:

You have a very close friend with whom you share much intimate detail about your life and emotions. This relationship is very important to you and the friend is your only confidant. You have revealed to him (her) that although you have an intimate, long-standing love relationship, you have also been seeing someone on the side. You impress upon your friend that it is very important to you that what you've revealed remains a strict secret, because you don't want your main lover to find out about the other relationship.

One day after class, you are talking to another student, who, in passing, indicates he (she) knows your secret.

Four distinct versions of the second stage for each scenario were used to create the Stage 2 manipulation. These versions correspond to the four appraisal conditions. Each version consisted of two parts. The first part was the same for each version, and simply added a factual development to the encounter. To illustrate, in the friend scenario:

You seek out your friend and confront him (her) with your suspicion that he (she) has revealed your secret. At first your friend denies being the source of the leak, but under intense questioning admits that he (she) told the other student and tries to make light of the whole incident.

The second part contained the appraisal manipulation and necessarily differed across appraisal conditions. In addition to motivational relevance and motivational incongruence, the four versions emphasised the secondary appraisal components defining the themes of other-blame, self-blame, threat, and loss/helplessness, respectively, as well as the themes themselves.

The other-blame version emphasised someone else's accountability. In the friend scenario:

You can't believe your friend betrayed your trust like this, especially since he (she) knew how important this secret was to you. You believe that for the first time you're seeing your friend for what he (she) really is, and that what he's (she's) done is totally inexcusable. You wonder why you ever liked him (her).

In contrast, the self-blame version emphasised the subjects' own accountability:

You realise that you've made a mess of things, and are largely to blame for what has happened. You now think that you were very wrong to cheat on your main lover in the first place, and you now see that the knowledge of your affair was simply too much of a burden to place upon your friend.

The threat version emphasised the subject's low emotion-focused coping potential by raising uncertainties about both the long-term implications of the encounter and the subject's ability to adapt to those implications:

> You wonder how far your secret has spread, who knows about your affair, and how much social harm you will suffer now that they know. You realise there is serious danger that you won't be able to salvage things if your main lover learns of your secret.

Finally, the loss/helplessness version emphasised both the subject's inability to alter the undesirable situation (low problem-focused coping potential) and the absence of any expectation for improvement (low future expectancy):

> You wish that you could change your friend so that he (she) wouldn't do things like this, but you know that there's nothing you can do. You realise that because of what's happened the close trust you once shared with this person is gone, and you're certain that you will never be able to feel the same way about this person again. The end of this trust and friendship is a great personal loss.

The complete text for the first two stages of the other three scenarios is presented in the Appendix. The third stage simply provided the subjects with an opportunity to resolve the episode.

Procedure

Subjects participated in the experiment as part of a study of "emotion, stress, and coping". They were provided with three clearly labelled envelopes containing the three stages of their assigned scenario. They were told that for each stage they should:

> Read through the description of the stage, and picture the situation that is described to you in your mind as best you can. Pretend that you are actually living through this experience . . . Try to mentally create the thoughts and feelings you would have if you were actually in this situation. When you . . . are experiencing the feelings it [the situation] evokes, please answer the questions that follow . . . as you think you would if you were actually experiencing the situation.

For each stage, subjects first imagined themselves in the described situation, and then to ensure engagement in the imagery task, they wrote a few sentences describing their reactions. Next, they completed three questionnaires designed to measure their appraisals of the stage (in terms of both components and relational themes) and their emotional reactions to it. The order in which the questionnaires were presented was counterbalanced across subjects, with each subject receiving the same order for all stages. After completing the questionnaires for a stage, the subjects repeated the entire procedure for the next stage, until all three stages had been completed. At that time, the research purposes were explained and any questions were answered.

Measures

Appraisal Components.   The subjects' appraisals for each stage were assessed with seven face-valid items designed to measure motivational relevance, motivational incongruence, accountability, problem-focused coping potential, emotion-focused coping potential, and future expectancy. A single item was used to measure each component, with the exception of two accountability items to measure self-accountability (i.e. "To what extent do you consider YOURSELF responsible for this situation?") and other-accountability (i.e. "To what extent do you consider SOMEONE ELSE responsible for this situation?"). Four items were rated on scales ranging from 1 (not at all) to 11 (extremely). The three scales measuring future expectancy and coping potential were bipolar and ranged from −5 (low coping potential, negative expectations) to +5 (high coping potential, positive expectations).

Core Relational Themes.   A second questionnaire contained 42 facevalid items representing the core relational themes hypothesised to be associated with a variety of emotions. Each item reflected a core relational theme for a particular emotion (e.g. two items measuring irrevocable loss/helplessness were: "I feel helpless"; and "Nothing can ever be done to fix this bad situation"). Subjects indicated on 9-point scales (1–9) the extent to which each statement characterised their thoughts during the stage they had just imagined. Four scales, measuring the core relational themes theoretically associated with anger, guilt, fear/anxiety, and sadness, were recovered for analysis. Scale scores were computed by taking the mean of the contributing items. Internal consistencies were estimated by computing the mean coefficient alpha for the first two scenario stages. The recovered scales and their estimated reliabilities were: other-blame (6 items: α = 0.89); self-blame (3 items: α = 0.89); threat (3 items: α = 0.69); and loss/helplessness (6 items: α = 0.89).

Emotions.   An emotion questionnaire (Ellsworth & Smith, 1988a) required subjects to rate on 9-point scales (1–9) the extent to which each of 33 emotional adjectives characterised their emotional state during the stage they had just imagined. Using the same procedures as for the core relational theme measures, scales were recovered to measure anger (6 items: $\alpha = 0.86$), guilt (3 items: $\alpha = 0.69$), fear/anxiety (3 items: $\alpha = 0.95$), and sadness (3 items: $\alpha = 0.73$).

Analytic Strategy

Two sets of analyses within each stage were conducted for each of the four emotions to examine the effectiveness of the manipulations in eliciting the desired appraisals, and to assess the effects of the appraisals on emotion. Multiple regression equations using a priori contrasts examined the overall effects of the appraisal manipulations (Cohen & Cohen, 1983, pp. 204–217; Rosenthal & Rosnow, 1985). Then, path analyses evaluated the hypothesised causal sequence from scenario to appraisal to emotion, for each emotion separately. In addition, two sets of follow-up analyses were conducted to examine further the discriminant and predictive validity of the appraisal model.

Stage 1 Manipulation.   The effects of the Stage 1 manipulation were measured by three orthogonal contrasts. Conceptually, this manipulation created two experimental conditions, other-blame and loss/helplessness, both with two replications involving different scenarios. The first contrast tested the main effects of the manipulation, and the second and third contrasts tested the replicability of any significant manipulation effects by testing for differences between the two scenarios within each condition.

Stage 2 Manipulation.   The effects of the Stage 2 manipulation were measured with 12 additional contrasts that completed the partitioning of the full 16-cell between-subjects design. To adequately test for the predicted effects, the set of contrasts differed for each emotion.

The first three contrasts tested the main effects of the Stage 2 manipulation. The first is of greatest theoretical interest, and pitted the condition hypothesised to produce the appraisal of interest (i.e. the other-blame condition for anger, the self-blame condition for guilt, the threat condition for fear/anxiety, and the loss/helplessness condition for sadness) against the other three combined conditions. To determine the next two contrasts the two conditions involving blame were paired, as were the ones involving loss-helplessness and threat. The remaining member of the pair split by the first contrast was pitted against the other two conditions to form the second contrast. The third contrast pitted these latter two conditions against each other. For example, the first three contrasts of the anger analysis were: (1) other-blame vs. the other three conditions; (2) self-blame vs. combined loss/helplessness and threat; and (3) loss/helplessness vs. threat.

The remaining nine contrasts always tested for interactions between the main effects of the Stage 2 manipulation (as coded by the first three contrasts of the set) and the effects of the Stage 1 manipulation (as reflected in the three Stage 1 contrasts).

For the analysis of each emotion (in both stages), the variables consisted of the emotion, its proposed core relational theme (other-blame for anger; self-blame for guilt; threat for fear/anxiety; and loss/helplessness for sadness), and the appraisal components hypothesised to define that theme. Motivational relevance and motivational incongruence were always included, but the components of secondary appraisal were limited to those most theoretically relevant to the emotion (other-accountability for anger; self-accountability for guilt; emotion-focused coping potential for fear/anxiety; and both problem-focused coping potential and future expectancy for sadness).

In addition, to assess accurately the effectiveness of the Stage 2 manipulation in *changing* appraisal and emotion, all analyses in this stage statistically controlled for all relevant Stage 1 variables (i.e. the emotion, the theme, and the relevant appraisal components) by entering them into the analyses prior to the variables of interest.

In constructing the theoretically derived path analyses the contrasts coding the manipulation effects were always assumed to be first in the causal sequence and to be followed, in order, by the appraisal components, the core relational themes, and the emotions. No attempt was made to assign causal priority among the appraisal components.

The ordering of the appraisal components and core relational themes was not intended to reflect a true causal process, because, as discussed above, the components and themes reflect alternative descriptions of the *same* relational meanings. Instead, the ordering of the appraisal variables reflects the emergent status of the core relational themes. Treating the components as "causally prior" to the themes allowed us to examine the degree to which the individual appraisal components contributed to the *definition* of the core relational themes, as hypothesised.

The direct effects on each variable were estimated by regressing the variable simultaneously on all causally prior variables. Thus, in Stage 1 the independent variables included any prior appraisal variables and the three scenario contrasts. In Stage 2 they included any causally prior variables from the second stage, all 15 constrasts, and all relevant Stage 1 variables.

Due to the complexity of the experimental design the results to be presented were simplified as follows: first, in presenting the findings for Stage 2, the effects of variables from the first stage are not depicted because they reveal little beyond significant stability across stages for all variables. In addition, all significant effects (at $P < 0.05$, two-tailed) directly relevant to the experimental hypotheses (e.g. main effects of the appraisal manipulations) are presented, but additional effects (e.g.

manipulation-by-scenario interactions) are discussed only if they in some way qualify the interpretation or generalisability of a theoretically relevant effect. Finally, in depicting the results of the second appraisal manipulation, simple change scores (from Stage 1 to Stage 2) are presented in lieu of the regression residuals upon which the statistical inferences are based, because the change scores preserve information about the absolute direction of change that is lost in the residuals, and the change scores were highly correlated with the residuals for each variable (average $r = 0.94$).

Predictions

Two sets of predictions corresponded to the two sets of appraisal manipulations. First, in Stage 1 the friend and TA scenarios were designed to evoke appraisals of other-blame, whereas the cancer and course scenarios were designed to evoke appraisals of loss/helplessness. Because both themes involve appraisals of high motivational relevance and high motivational incongruence, no systematic differences were anticipated for these appraisal components. However, the friend and TA scenarios, relative to the cancer and course ones, were expected to be high in both other-accountability and other-blame, whereas the cancer and course scenarios were expected to be relatively low in problem-focused coping potential and future expectancy and relatively high in loss/helplessness. These appraisal differences were expected to result in relatively high levels of anger in the friend and TA scenarios, and relatively high levels of sadness in the cancer and course scenarios. No systematic predictions were advanced for self-accountability, self-blame, and guilt, or for emotion-focused coping potential, threat, and fear-anxiety.

For the Stage 2 manipulation, motivational relevance and motivational incongruence were again not expected to vary across conditions. However, through appropriate changes in the relevant component(s) of secondary appraisal, each manipulation condition was expected to produce elevated levels of the targeted core relational theme, and it was expected that these themes would be associated with increases in the theoretically linked emotion. Thus, other-accountability, other-blame, and anger were expected to be elevated in the other-blame condition; self-accountability, self-blame, and guilt were expected to be elevated in the self-blame condition; emotion-focused coping potential was expected to be depressed, and both threat and fear/anxiety were expected to be elevated in the threat condition; and depressed levels of both problem-focused coping potential and future expectancy were expected to be accompanied by elevations in loss/helplessness and sadness in the loss/helplessness condition.

In all cases the path analyses were expected to provide support for the hypothesised sequence. The appraisal manipulation was expected to have direct effects on the relevant components of secondary appraisal, but, because these components help to define the core relational themes, the effects on the core relational themes were expected to be mediated through the appraisal components (as evidenced by direct effects of the components on the themes after controlling for the effects of the manipulation).

In addition, effects of the manipulation on emotion were expected to be mediated through the relational meanings (considered at both molecular and molar levels of analysis). However, because we consider the core relational themes to be more efficient summaries of the relational meanings than the individual appraisal components, we anticipated the themes would demonstrate direct effects on the emotions even after controlling for the contributions of the individual appraisal components. Conversely, to the extent that the core relational themes effectively captured the contributions of the individual appraisal components, the components of secondary appraisal (hypothesised to be responsible for differentiating one core relational theme from another) were not expected to exert direct effects on the emotions after controlling for the contributions of the themes.

RESULTS AND DISCUSSION

The results for both sets of manipulations are presented for each of the four emotions in turn, and the follow-up analyses are presented last. Table 3 presents the means depicting the main effects of the appraisal manipulations on all variables considered (i.e. appraisal components, core relational themes, and emotions).

Anger

Stage 1 Manipulation. Examination of Table 3 indicates that, as assumed, appraisals of motivational relevance (overall $M = 10.03$) and motivational incongruence (overall $M = 9.52$) were generally rated high. However, both appraisal components were higher in the loss/helplessness condition than in the other-blame one, and although small in absolute magnitude, these differences were statistically significant (motivational relevance: $\beta = -0.24$, $t(189) = -3.40$, $P < 0.001$; motivational incongruence: $\beta = -0.18$, $t(189) = -2.52$, $P < 0.05$).

More importantly, however, the appraisal manipulation produced the anticipated differences in other-accountability and other-blame, and these differences were accompanied by the predicted differences in anger. Other-accountability, $\beta = 0.28$, $t(189) = 5.07$, $P < 0.001$, other-blame, $\beta = 0.66$, $t(189) = 12.64$, $P < 0.001$, and anger, $\beta = 0.51$, $t(189) = 8.69$,

TABLE 3
Means for Main Effects of both Appraisal Manipulations

| | Manipulation Conditions | | | | | |
| | Stage 1 Manipulation | | Stage 2 Manipulation | | | |
Measure	Other-blame	Loss/Helplessness	Other-blame	Self-blame	Threat	Loss/Helplessness
Appraisal components						
Motivational relevance	9.72	10.34	−0.44	−0.25	0.10	−0.13
Motivational incongruence	9.18	9.87	−0.29	−0.48	0.22	0.08
Other-accountability	7.72	6.00	1.27	−2.42	−0.33	−0.02
Self-accountability	6.13	6.31	−1.38	1.88	−0.35	−0.81
Emot. foc. coping pot.	1.45	1.63	0.38	0.40	−0.51	−0.48
Prob. foc. coping pot.	0.22	−0.65	−0.19	0.38	−0.10	−0.27
Future expectancy	1.27	0.60	−0.65	−0.21	−0.96	−0.71
Core relational themes						
Other-blame	5.06	2.32	1.21	−1.05	0.53	−0.04
Self-blame	4.34	3.89	−0.97	1.60	0.10	−0.47
Threat	4.44	4.54	−0.47	−0.63	0.88	−0.08
Loss/Helplessness	3.96	4.63	0.37	−0.05	0.78	0.79
Emotions						
Anger	6.07	4.26	0.50	−0.93	0.11	−0.36
Guilt	4.29	5.11	−0.74	1.24	−0.05	−0.31
Fear/Anxiety	4.87	6.36	−0.92	−0.64	0.95	−0.30
Sadness	5.56	6.72	−0.40	−0.09	−0.07	0.22

Note. All means for Stage 1 reflect raw ratings for each scale. All means for Stage 2 reflect change scores from Stage 1 to Stage 2. Although change scores are reported here and in the text to preserve information about the absolute sign of change, all inferential statistics for Stage 2 data are based on residualised Stage 2 scores, obtained for each variable by partialling out the variance attributable to that variable in Stage 1.

$P < 0.001$, were each significantly higher in other-blame condition than in the loss/helplessness one.

The path analysis provided clear support for the proposed model. As predicted, controlling for the effects of the manipulation, other-accountability contributed directly to the core relational theme of other-blame, $\beta = 0.38$, $t(186) = 6.17$, $P < 0.001$, which in turn, had a strong direct effect on anger, even after controlling for the contributions of the individual appraisal components, $\beta = 0.51$, $t(185) = 6.84$, $P < 0.001$. After controlling for other-blame, however, other-accountability did not contribute directly to anger, $\beta = -0.01$, $t(185) < 1$, ns.

Contrary to expectations, comparison to the two different scenarios of loss/helplessness revealed a dissociation between other-accountability and other-blame in the cancer scenario. Comparison of the cancer and course scenarios indicated that other-accountability was elevated in the cancer scenario (cancer $M = 8.35$, course $M = 3.65$), $\beta = 0.56$, $t(189) = 9.96$, $P < 0.001$, but that this did not translate to either other-blame or anger. The cancer and course scenarios did not differ in the levels of other-blame they evoked (cancer $M = 2.33$, course $M = 2.32$), $\beta = 0.01$, $t(189) < 1$, ns, and anger was actually significantly lower in the cancer scenario ($M = 3.54$) than in the course scenario ($M = 4.97$), $\beta = -0.28$, $t(189) = -4.89$, $P < 0.001$.

Stage 2 Manipulation.   The results of the Stage 2 manipulation offer strong support for the predictions for anger. As reflected in the means shown in Table 3, relative to the other three conditions, the other-blame condition resulted in elevated levels of other-accountability, $\beta = 0.28$, $t(172) = 5.82$, $P < 0.001$, other-blame, $\beta = 0.26$, $t(172) = 6.55$, $P < 0.001$, and anger, $\beta = 0.18$, $t(172) = 3.60$, $P < 0.001$. Further, although not anticipated (but consistent with the model), relative to the combined threat and loss/helplessness conditions, the self-blame condition resulted in significantly reduced levels of other-accountability, $\beta = -0.22$, $t(172) = -4.54$, $P < 0.001$, other-blame, $\beta = -0.23$, $t(172) = -5.87$, $P < 0.001$, and anger, $\beta = -0.15$, $t(172) = -3.05$, $P < 0.01$.

The effects on anger of the other-blame manipulation did not interact with the first appraisal manipulation. However, the effectiveness of the self-blame manipulation in reducing anger did. This manipulation reduced other-accountability ($M = -3.08$), other-blame ($M = -1.91$), and anger ($M = -1.61$) more in the two scenarios in which they had previously been elevated (friend and TA), than in the scenarios originally associated with loss/helplessness (cancer and course; other-accountability: $M = -1.69$, $\beta = -0.18$, $t(172) = -3.68$, $P < 0.001$; other-blame: $M = -0.17$, $\beta = -0.23$, $t(172) = -5.96$, $P < 0.001$; anger: $M = -0.21$, $\beta = -0.18$, $t(172) = -3.68$, $P < 0.001$).

The path analysis indicated that, in accord with predictions, changes in other-accountability directly contributed to changes in other-blame, $\beta = 0.43$, $t(169) = 8.31$, $P < 0.001$, which, in turn, directly influenced the changes in anger, $\beta = 0.39$, $t(168) = 3.80$, $P < 0.001$. As in the first stage, after controlling for the changes in other-blame, changes in other-accountability did not contribute directly to the changes in anger, $\beta = 0.07$, $t(168) < 1$, ns.

Guilt

Stage 1 Manipulation.   The Stage 1 manipulation was not expected to influence appraisals of self-blame or feelings of guilt systematically, and consistent with this expectation, the first stage analyses of self-accountability, self-blame, and guilt primarily revealed effects specific to individual scenarios that will not be considered in detail. However, comparison of the cancer and course scenarios revealed a dissociation between emotion and appraisal in the cancer scenario somewhat analogous to the one observed for anger. Both self-accountability ($M = 4.13$) and self-blame ($M = 2.43$) were significantly lower in the cancer scenario than in the course scenario (self-accountability, $M = 8.50$, $\beta = -0.52$, $t(189) = -9.80$, $P < 0.001$; self-blame: $M = 5.35$, $\beta = -0.45$, $t(189) = -7.88$, $P < 0.001$). However, guilt was elevated equally in both scenarios (Cancer $M = 5.10$, Course $M = 5.11$), $\beta = 0.00$, $t(189) < 1$, ns. The net effect of this dissociation was that although the combined loss/helplessness scenarios did not reliably differ from the combined other-blame ones in terms of either self-accountability, $\beta = -0.03$, $t(189) < 1$, ns, or self-blame, $\beta = 0.10$, $t(189) = 1.73$, $P = 0.09$, guilt was significantly higher in the loss/helplessness scenarios ($M = 5.11$) than in the other-blame ones ($M = 4.29$), $\beta = -0.21$, $t(189) = -3.74$, $P < 0.001$.

This one anomaly aside, the results of the path analysis for guilt were largely consistent with predictions. Appraisals of self-accountability contributed directly to self-blame, $\beta = 0.71$, $t(186) = 12.91$, $P < 0.001$, which, in turn, directly influenced guilt, $\beta = 0.38$, $t(185) = 4.24$, $P < 0.001$, but self-accountability did not contribute directly to guilt, $\beta = 0.15$, $t(185) = 1.59$, $P = 0.11$.

Stage 2 Manipulation.   The results of the Stage 2 manipulation were straightforward. As can be seen in Table 3, relative to the other three conditions, the self-blame condition resulted in elevated levels of self-accountability, $\beta = 0.39$, $t(172) = 8.28$, $P < 0.001$, self-blame, $\beta = 0.37$, $t(172) = 7.90$, $P < 0.001$, and guilt, $\beta = 0.35$, $t(172) = 6.37$, $P < 0.001$. Further, the path analysis indicated that changes in self-accountability contributed directly to changes in self-blame, $\beta = 0.55$, $t(169) = 8.82$, $P <$

0.001, and changes in self-blame contributed directly to changes in guilt, $\beta = 0.32$, $t(168) = 3.24$, $P < 0.005$. In addition, the changes in self-accountability contributed directly to the changes in guilt, $\beta = 0.27$, $t(168) = 2.79$, $P < 0.01$.

Fear/Anxiety

Stage 1 Manipulation. The Stage 1 manipulation did not directly vary appraisals relevant to fear/anxiety. Nonetheless, as indicated in Table 3, fear/anxiety was significantly higher in the loss/helplessness scenarios than in those involving other-blame, $\beta = -0.31$, $t(189) = -4.68$, $P < 0.001$, but the corresponding effects were not observed for either emotion-focused coping potential or threat, both $ts < 1$, ns. Rather, examination of the individual scenarios indicated that fear/anxiety and its theoretically relevant appraisals (low emotion-focused coping potential and high threat) were elicited in the two loss/helplessness scenarios (which did not significantly differ) and, to a lesser degree, in the friend scenario. Relative to the TA scenario, emotion-focused coping potential tended to be depressed in the friend scenario (Friend $M = 0.98$; TA $M = 1.92$), $\beta = -0.13$, $t(189) = -1.87$, $P = 0.06$, and both threat (Friend $M = 5.02$; TA $M = 3.86$), $\beta = 0.23$, $t(189) = 3.23$, $P < 0.01$, and fear (Friend $M = 5.84$; TA $M = 3.90$), $\beta = 0.29$, $t(189) = 4.40$, $P < 0.001$, were elevated.

The path analysis indicated that the observed variation in fear/anxiety was largely mediated through appraisal: Low emotion-focused coping potential contributed to the theme of threat, $\beta = -0.53$, $t(186) = -8.88$, $P < 0.001$, which in turn, had a positive direct effect on fear-anxiety, $\beta = 0.40$, $t(185) = 5.70$, $P < 0.001$. Emotion-focused coping potential did not directly affect fear/anxiety, however, $\beta = -0.02$, $t(185) < 1$, ns.

Stage 2 Manipulation. The results of the Stage 2 manipulation provide further support for the predictions for fear/anxiety. As shown in Table 3, relative to the other three conditions, the threat condition resulted in reduced levels of emotion-focused coping potential, $\beta = -0.10$, $t(172) = -2.10$, $P < 0.05$, and elevated levels of both threat, $\beta = 0.15$, $t(172) = 2.82$, $P < 0.01$, and fear, $\beta = 0.18$, $t(172) = 4.40$, $P < 0.001$. Further, although not anticipated, relative to the combined self- and other-blame conditions, the loss/helplessness condition produced reduced levels of emotion-focused coping potential, $\beta = -0.13$, $t(172) = -2.72$, $P < 0.01$, and elevated levels of threat, $\beta = 0.25$, $t(172) = 4.84$, $P < 0.001$, and fear/anxiety, $\beta = 0.23$, $t(172) = 5.28$, $P < 0.001$. The path analysis indicated that reductions in emotion-focused coping potential contributed directly to increases in threat, $\beta = -0.44$, $t(169) = -5.61$, $P < 0.001$, which in turn directly influenced increases in fear/anxiety, $\beta = 0.31$, $t(168) = 4.96$, $P <$

0.001. In addition, reductions in emotion-focused coping potential contributed directly to increases in fear/anxiety, $\beta = -0.17$, $t(168) = -2.44$, $P < 0.05$.

Sadness

Stage 1 Manipulation.   As indicated in Table 3, the main effects of the Stage 1 manipulation for sadness were largely consistent with predictions. The loss/helplessness scenarios produced more pessimistic appraisals of problem-focused coping potential than did the other-blame ones, $\beta = 0.18$, $t(189) = 2.60$, $P < 0.05$, and tended to produce more pessimistic appraisals of future expectancy, $\beta = 0.12$, $t(189) = 1.80$, $P = 0.07$. These appraisals were accompanied by increased levels of loss/helplessness, $\beta = -0.19$, $t(189) = 2.69$, $P < 0.01$, and sadness, $\beta = -0.32$, $t(189) = 2.60$, $P < 0.05$.

However, inspection of the individual scenarios indicates that these anticipated differences primarily were due to the cancer scenario which, relative to the course scenario, produced particularly pessimistic appraisals of problem-focused coping potential (Cancer $M = -1.54$, Course $M = 0.25$), $\beta = -0.26$, $t(189) = -3.76$, $P < 0.001$, and future expectancy (Cancer $M = -0.52$, Course $M = 1.73$), $\beta = -0.30$, $t(189) = -4.33$, $P < 0.001$; and elevated levels of loss/helplessness (Cancer $M = 5.05$, Course $M = 4.23$), $\beta = 0.16$, $t(189) = 2.21$, $P < 0.01$, and sadness (Cancer $M = 7.07$, Course $M = 6.37$), $\beta = 0.13$, $t(189) = 2.06$, $P < 0.05$. Further, although there were no differences on any relevant appraisal variables (i.e. problem-focused coping potential, future expectancy, or loss/helplessness), the friend scenario resulted in significantly more sadness than the TA scenario (Friend $M = 6.35$; TA $M = 4.77$), $\beta = 0.32$, $t(189) = 4.90$, $P < 0.001$.

Although unable to account for this latter effect, the path analysis nonetheless indicated that the Stage 1 variations in sadness were generally consistent with the theoretical model. Controlling for scenario content, appraisals of both problem-focused coping potential, $\beta = -0.47$, $t(185) = -6.62$, $P < 0.001$, and future expectancy, $\beta = -0.19$, $t(185) = -2.66$, $P < 0.01$, contributed negatively to the core relational theme of loss/helplessness, which in turn directly influenced feelings of sadness, $\beta = 0.20$, $t(184) = 2.69$, $P < 0.01$. Neither future expectancy, $\beta = 0.01$, $t(184) < 1$, ns, nor problem-focused coping potential, $\beta = -0.12$, $t(184) = -1.50$, $P = 0.14$, contributed directly to sadness.

Stage 2 Manipulation.   The results of this manipulation provide, at best, tentative support for the model for sadness. Examination of Table 3 indicates that the loss/helplessness manipulation was largely ineffective in eliciting the intended appraisals. Problem-focused coping potential was only marginally more pessimistic in the loss/helplessness condition than the other three, $\beta = -0.10$, $t(171) = -1.66$, $P = 0.10$, and future expectancy did not significantly differ in this condition relative to the other three, $\beta = -0.03$, $t(171) < 1$, ns.

Although the core relational theme of loss/helplessness increased from the first to second stages in the loss/helplessness condition as intended, this increase was not reliably different from the changes in the other three conditions, $\beta = 0.09$, $t(171) = 1.55$, $P = 0.12$, largely because loss/helplessness also increased significantly in the threat condition relative to the combined self- and other-blame conditions, $\beta = 0.12$, $t(171) = 2.11$, $P < 0.05$. However, sadness was not significantly higher in the loss/helplessness condition relative to the other three, $\beta = 0.06$, $t(171) = 1.20$, ns, nor was it significantly elevated in the threat condition relative to the blame conditions, $\beta = 0.05$, $t(171) = 1.04$, ns. Thus sadness did not accompany these elevations in loss/helplessness.

Nonetheless, although not attributable to the appraisal manipulation, the path analysis indicated that the between-subject variation in sadness was consistent with the proposed model: Changes in both problem-focused coping potential, $\beta = -0.30$, $t(167) = -4.26$, $P < 0.001$, and future expectancy, $\beta = -0.26$, $t(167) = -3.17$, $P < 0.005$, contributed directly to changes in loss/helplessness, which, in turn, contributed directly to changes in sadness, $\beta = 0.28$, $t(166) = 3.52$, $P < 0.001$. Neither problem-focused coping potential, $\beta = 0.00$, $t(166) < 1$, ns, nor future expectancy, $\beta = 0.15$, $t(166) = 1.66$, $P < 0.10$, contributed directly to changes in sadness.

Follow-up Analyses of Discriminant and Predictive Validity

We believe the above analyses provide strong support for the predictions of the appraisal model for anger, guilt, and fear/anxiety, with the predictions for sadness receiving weaker support. By demonstrating that the various manipulations differentially produced the intended changes in appraisal components and core relational themes, and that these changes were associated with predicted changes in emotion, they suggest considerable discriminant validity for the model.

However, by considering each emotion separately, the above analyses do not preclude the possibility that, in addition to being associated with their theoretically relevant appraisals, the emotions are just as strongly associated with other appraisals theoretically associated with different emotions. For instance, it is possible that appraisals of threat are as closely associated with appraisals of future expectancy as they are with emotion-focused coping potential, or that fear/anxiety is as strongly associated with appraisals of loss/helplessness as with threat, and so on.

Further, the above analyses were designed to examine the relationships between appraisals and emotion considering both levels of relational meaning (i.e. appraisal components and core relational themes) simultaneously. However, the relative abilities of appraisal components and core relational themes to predict emotions are also of considerable interest.

In the path analyses the core relational themes consistently exerted strong direct effects on their associated emotions after controlling for the contributions of the appraisal components, but the secondary appraisal components did not consistently exert direct effects on the emotions after controlling for the contributions of the core relational themes. This lends support to our view of the themes as efficient molar summaries of the relational meanings associated with the various emotions.

Nevertheless, the presence of the themes in these analyses may have obscured the ability of the appraisal components to predict the emotions. One possibility is that the consistent effects of the themes were due to inadequate conceptualisation or measurement of the appraisal components. This possibility arises because our system of components is somewhat simpler than most previous dimensional systems (e.g. Ellsworth & Smith, 1988b; Frijda et al., 1989), and because the components were measured with single-item scales.

We performed two final sets of analyses to examine both of the above issues. The first set evaluated the discriminant and predictive validity of the overall appraisal model, and the second set directly compared the relative abilities of the appraisal components and core relational themes to predict their theoretically relevant emotions.

In the first set, the discriminant validity of the model was evaluated by examining the correlations between the components of secondary appraisal and the core relational themes, and between the core relational themes and the emotions, for both Stages 1 and 2. To the extent that there is solid discriminant validity, each individual component of secondary appraisal should be most highly correlated with the core relational theme it was expected to help define, and each core relational theme should be most highly correlated with its theoretically associated emotion. The results of these analyses are presented in Table 4.

The results for both of the experimental stages are very similar, and their implications parallel those of the earlier emotion-specific analyses. The model received strong support for anger, guilt, and fear/anxiety, but the evidence in support of sadness was weaker. For the first three emotions the theoretically linked components of secondary appraisal and core relational themes were always significantly more highly correlated with each other than with any other theme or component, and the theoretically linked core relational themes and emotions always displayed similar relations.

TABLE 4

Analyses of Discriminant Validity: Within-stage Correlations between Secondary Appraisal Components and Core Relational Themes, and between Core Relational Themes and Emotions

Secondary Appraisal Components	Stage 1 Core Relational Themes				Stage 2 Core Relational Themes			
	Other-blame	Self-blame	Threat	Loss/Helplessness	Other-blame	Self-blame	Threat	Loss/Helplessness
Other-accountability	0.44	−0.37	–	–	0.61	−0.34	–	–
Self-accountability	–	0.80	–	–	−0.28	0.79	–	–
Emot. foc. cop. pot.	–	–	−0.62	−0.39$_b$	–	–	0.59	−0.46$_b$
Prob. foc. cop. pot.	–	–	−0.25$_a$	−0.60	–	–	−0.28$_a$	−0.64$_c$
Future expectancy	–	–	−0.31$_a$	−0.46$_b$	–	–	−0.39$_a$	−0.58$_{b,c}$

Core Relational Themes	Stage 1 Emotions				Stage 2 Emotions			
	Anger	Guilt	Fear/Anxiety	Sadness	Anger	Guilt	Fear/Anxiety	Sadness
Other-blame	0.64	−0.26$_a$	−0.24$_a$	−0.26$_a$	0.65	−0.25	–	–
Self-blame	0.29$_b$	0.53	0.31$_b$	0.26$_b$	–	0.56	–	–
Threat	–	0.27$_b$	0.52	0.32$_b$	0.33$_a$	–	0.63	0.43$_a$
Loss/Helplessness	–	–	0.29$_b$	0.39$_b$	–	–	0.46$_a$	0.48$_a$

Note: For clarity of presentation only correlations significantly different from zero at $P < 0.001$ are presented. For each of the four analyses, all coefficients within each row or column not sharing a common subscript differ significantly at $P < 0.05$.

For example, consistent with the hypothesised role of emotion-focused coping potential in distinguishing threat from other core relational themes, emotion-focused coping potential was more highly correlated with threat than with any other theme, and threat was more highly correlated with emotion-focused coping potential than with any other appraisal component. In addition, threat was more highly correlated with fear/anxiety than with any other emotion; and fear/anxiety was more highly correlated with threat than with any other core relational theme.

Although analogous patterns were observed for the appraisals associated with anger and guilt, the differentiation was less evident for sadness. Some support was obtained for the hypothesised differentiation of loss/helplessness from threat; problem-focused coping potential was consistently more strongly correlated with loss/helplessness than it was with threat, and this correlation was significantly higher than the correlation between loss/helplessness and emotion-focused coping potential. However, the contribution of future-expectancy to the definition of loss-helplessness was less clear. Moreover, loss/helplessness did not show its predicted unique relationship with sadness. Despite being correlated with fear/anxiety significantly less than was threat, loss/helplessness was as highly correlated with fear/anxiety as it was with sadness, and in an analogous fashion, sadness was as highly correlated with threat as it was with loss/helplessness.

In the second set of analyses, the relative predictive abilities of the appraisal components and the core relational themes were examined by regressing each emotion first on just its hypothesised core relational theme, and second on just the set of three or four appraisal components hypothesised to define that theme (see Table 1). These regression analyses were repeated for both stages of the experimental task. Table 5 lists the proportion of emotion variance accounted for in each analysis (shrunken R^2, Cohen & Cohen, 1983, pp. 105–107).

As Table 5 indicates, with the exception of anger, for which the appraisal components were substantially less predictive than was the core relational theme, the appraisal components and core relational themes predicted the emotions to similar degrees. Moreover, these levels of prediction compare quite favourably to those obtained by Ellsworth and Smith (1988b). Using a somewhat more complicated dimensional model, these investigators were able to account for 25%, 23%, and 21% of the variance in guilt, fear/anxiety, and sadness, respectively.

The relative inability of the appraisal components to predict anger appears to be due to the already noted dissociation between other-accountability and other-blame within the cancer scenario. When this scenario was removed from consideration, and the analyses were repeated on the 146 subjects who imagined themselves in one of the other three scenarios, the three anger-relevant appraisal components accounted for

TABLE 5
Relative Predictive Validity of Appraisal Components and Core Relational Themes for
Each Emotion

	Proportion of Variance Accounted for By:			
	Appraisal Components		Core Relational Themes	
Emotion	Stage 1	Stage 2	Stage 1	Stage 2
Anger	0.03	0.16	0.40	0.42
Guilt	0.29	0.28	0.28	0.31
Fear/Anxiety	0.24	0.32	0.27	0.40
Sadness	0.22	0.28	0.15	0.23

Note. The coefficients in each column reflect the shrunken multiple squared correlations for each emotion within each stage obtained by regressing that emotion on either the three or four appraisal components or the single core relational theme hypothesised to be theoretically relevant to that emotion (See Table 1). With the exception of the coefficient obtained for anger in Stage 1 using the appraisal components, which is significantly different from 0 at $P < 0.05$, all listed coefficients are significantly different from 0 at $P < 0.001$.

28% and 38% of the variance in anger in the first and second stages, respectively (both $Ps < 0.001$). These levels compare favourably to the 31% and 43% of the variance in anger accounted for by other-blame in these same subjects, and to the 36% of the variance in anger accounted for by Ellsworth and Smith (1988b).

Thus, with the exception of anger within the cancer scenario, both the individual appraisal components and the core relational themes were found to be associated with their theoretically relevant emotions to similar degrees, and at levels comparable to previous findings. These results suggest that our conceptualisation and measurement of the appraisal components were adequate, and they support our view of the appraisal components and core relational themes as alternative descriptions of the relational meaning that underlies each emotion.

GENERAL DISCUSSION

The present data provide, we believe, strong experimental support for the predictive and discriminant validity of the specific appraisal model we proposed for anger, guilt, and fear/anxiety, but they provide weaker support for sadness. Not only were the first three emotions highly correlated with the theoretically appropriate appraisals, but they were more highly correlated with those appraisals than with any others.

That much of the emotion-related variation in appraisal was directly produced by the experimental manipulations provides particularly strong evidence for the strength and specificity of the observed relationships.

Manipulation of the appraisals theoretically relevant to anger in Stage 1 produced predicted differences in reported anger. In Stage 2, the appraisals theoretically associated with anger, guilt, and fear/anxiety were successfully manipulated within each of the four scenarios, and these manipulations resulted in the predicted changes in reported emotion. This model, therefore, provides a firm theoretical foundation upon which to base the further development and testing of a comprehensive theory of emotion.

We believe that an important contribution of this model is that it describes relational meaning, which we view as the core of an emotion, at two distinct levels of analysis, molar and molecular. The molar analysis synthesises the essence of the relational meaning into a single complex concept, and the molecular analysis identifies the individual appraisal components that, together in a particular configuration, imply that meaning. The simultaneous consideration of appraisal at both levels provides a theoretical bridge for relating dimensional appraisal models (e.g. Frijda et al., 1989; Scherer, 1984; Smith & Ellsworth, 1985), which have conceptualised appraisal in a manner akin to our appraisal components, to models of discrete emotions (e.g. Plutchik, 1980), which have treated appraisal more categorically in a manner akin to our core relational themes.

Even more importantly, the two levels of analysis are complementary, and, we believe, their respective properties lend them to different uses in the study of emotion. For example, the individual appraisal components, which reflect the issues that must be evaluated in a particular way for an emotion to be generated, should be especially useful for investigating the environmental and dispositional antecedents of emotion, as well as for predicting how these characteristics combine to produce the relational meanings for each emotion (see Lazarus, 1991a; Smith & Lazarus, 1990; and Smith & Pope, 1992, for theory and research along these lines).

In addition, given a particular emotional reaction, knowledge of the specific appraisal components that led to that reaction represents an important inferential tool for diagnosing the basis of the emotional reaction—for instance, why this particular individual responded to this particular set of circumstances in this particular way. This knowledge, in turn, could be quite useful clinically in designing interventions to alleviate troubled person-environment relationships (cf. Lazarus, 1989; Smith, in press; Smith & Lazarus, 1990).

The core relational themes, on the other hand, are more global, and reflect how the individual appraisal components combine into a central relational meaning for each emotion. These meanings are emergent in the sense that the relational harms and benefits they represent are holistic entities whose coherence is not easily captured by representing the relevant appraisals as a set of distinct judgements. We consider the core relational themes to be greater than the sum of the appraisal components that imply them, and to have properties and adaptational implications that cannot be easily derived from considering just the appraisal components taken individually.

Knowledge of the relevant core relational themes, because they efficiently represent the adaptational meanings around which emotions are organised (Smith & Lazarus, 1990), should be especially useful in investigating the effects of appraisal in shaping the physiological activities and the modes of action readiness associated with various emotions (e.g. Frijda, 1987; Frijda et al., 1989), as well as the influence of emotion on coping. The physiological activities and modes of action readiness are said to be organised around the adaptational requirements of the appraised encounter, and coping behaviours reflect the person's attempts to respond to those requirements. To us these adaptational requirements seem to be better expressed at the molar level than at the molecular level, and we would expect consideration of the core relational themes to be substantially more predictive of such things as action readiness and actual coping behaviour than consideration of the individual appraisal components.

In considering the utility of this model for future research, it is important to acknowledge that although most findings supported the model, there were unexpected results that raise important issues. Anger and guilt both demonstrated systematic dissociations from appraisal within the first stage of the cancer scenario, and the predictions for sadness generally received only weak support.

The failures of prediction for sadness can be partially attributed to ineffective manipulations or irrevocable loss/helplessness, the relational theme theoretically associated with that emotion. In the first manipulation, loss/helplessness was substantially elevated in only one of the two intended scenarios—the cancer scenario. It was no higher in the course scenario than in the two scenarios associated with other-blame (friend and TA). In the second manipulation, the loss/helplessness conditon did not differentially produce increases in appraised loss/helplessness relative to the other conditions. Because the path-analyses for both Stages 1 and 2 indicated that the appraisal model nonetheless accounted for a significant amount of the variance in sadness, the predictions for sadness may gain more support with better manipulations of loss/helplessness.

However, we suspect the weak findings may also reflect more fundamental puzzles about the nature of sadness. The model we employed was unable to differentiate sadness from fear in either experimental stage. In contrast, fear/anxiety and guilt were successfully differentiated from the other emotions in both stages even though their relevant appraisals were not directly manipulated in the first stage. In addition, several previous studies have also failed to find strong, discriminable relationships between specific cognitions and sadness (e.g. Ellsworth & Smith, 1988b; Smith & Ellsworth, 1987), and the special anomalies of sadness have been noted by Lazarus (1991a, c).

A major problem with sadness may be one of emotional *language*. Whereas the names of the other emotions examined—"anger", "fear/anxiety", and "guilt"—appear to denote fairly specific and acute emotional states, the meaning of "sadness", at least in the vocabulary of our subject population, appears to be considerably less specific. Perhaps many forms of sadness are really mood states rather than acute emotions. Also, as a counterpoint to "happy", which people use as a general-purpose adjective to describe a variety of emotional states associated with positive outcomes (cf. Ellsworth & Smith, 1988a; Weiner, 1985), we suspect, as Weiner (1985) has proposed, that people often use the term "sad" (and synonyms) nondifferentially to describe their emotional reactions to a variety of harmful circumstances. For example, the first stage of the friend scenario not only elicited fear/anxiety-relevant appraisals and fear-anxiety in a theory-consistent manner, but also elicited self-reported sadness in the relative absence of appraisals of loss/helplessness.

Nonetheless, our position differs from Weiner's (1985) in two important respects. First, the observed differentiation of sadness from both anger and guilt suggests that rather than a fully general-purpose adjective to describe responses to all kinds of harm, the term "sad" describes responses to harm in which the prospects of improvement are viewed as poor. Secondly, we do not consider the reactions subsumed by the term sadness to reflect a single undifferentiated state. Instead, we propose that the concept of sadness encompasses a number of distinct states, ranging from distress to resignation, that are associated with various stages of disengagement from a lost commitment (Lazarus, 1991a; Klinger, 1975; Smith & Lazarus, 1990). Each of these is hypothesised to be produced by distinct appraisals, and to have distinct motivational consequences.

We are also somewhat at a loss to explain the dissociations between appraisal and emotion within the cancer scenario, but we suspect they reflect subjects' attempts to cope with societal proscriptions against blaming helpless (and especially terminally ill and loved) victims. For instance, the dissociation of other-accountability and other-blame may have reflected subjects' attempts to deny being angry at their dying relative, even though they may have held that relative accountable for the disease, and perhaps the guilt they reported was in response to the very anger they were attempting to deny. Emotional states in these kinds of situations are likely to be complex and heavily laden with coping processes that address both the conditions producing these emotions and their social and intrapsychic implications.

Thus far, in conducting this study and in presenting and discussing the results, we have operated under the important, possibly controversial assumption that subjects were emotionally engaged while performing the imagery task. We assume that the subjects actively imagined themselves in the described scenarios, responded emotionally to the scenario contents, and then described their actual emotional reactions. Therefore, we would like to conclude by considering the implications of this assumption for interpreting our findings.

We made this assumption on the basis of previous imagery research which, using similar stimuli and instructions (e.g. Smith, 1989; Smith et al., 1986), has consistently demonstrated that subjects engaged in imagery produce (low-level) patterns of physiological activity consistent with the imagery-induced emotions they report experiencing. Although the physiological measures required to verify that our subjects were similarly engaged are not available in this study, we know of no compelling reason why subjects in the present study would have been systematically different from those in the previous ones.

Nonetheless, it is possible that our subjects might not have been emotionally engaged, but might have been performing a largely intellectual exercise in which they reported hypothetical emotions on the basis of their implicit emotional theories. If this were the case, we believe the conclusions to be drawn from the present experiment would change only a little. Instead of having directly demonstrated strong links between specific appraisals and actual emotional reactions, we would have demonstrated that these same strong appraisal-emotion linkages are present in our subjects' implicit theories of emotion.

In other words, at minimum we have demonstrated that our subjects' theories of emotion contain elaborate, specific, and shared hypotheses concerning the emotional consequences of specific appraisals. Because, as others have argued (e.g. Shaver et al., 1987), implicit theories are largely based on personal experience and tend to mirror that experience accurately, these hypotheses are likely to have considerable validity. In effect, we would then have indirectly demonstrated links between appraisal and emotion. Naturally, one would want to verify the validity of these links in subsequent research, but who would not want to do that in any event? Thus, whether one interprets our results as documenting the existence of actual appraisal-emotion relationships, or the presence of such relationships in our respondents' intuitive theories, we believe the present study provides a strong theoretical model upon which to base future research.

POSTSCRIPT: DIFFERENCES BETWEEN THE PRESENT MODEL AND THAT OF LAZARUS (1991a).

As previously noted, the model currently advanced by Lazarus (1991a, c) differs in a number of respects from the one examined in this article, which Smith (in press; Smith & Pope, 1992) continues to advance. In order to maintain clarity about our respective positions, we now briefly discuss the major differences between the models that are most relevant to the present article.

We both are seeking to identify the appraisal components and core relational themes that adequately capture the central relational meanings distinguishing the various emotions. Our aim is to generate the set of components and themes that best permits a parsimonious, deterministic analysis. We differ, in part, in how parsimonious to get without loss of essential meaning, and in the identity of some of the specific concepts needed to accomplish this.

One source of disagreement concerns whether primary appraisal should include a component capturing the specific contents of the goal(s) at stake in the encounter. Smith (e.g. Smith & Pope, 1992), although considering specific goal contents to be important antecedents of primary appraisal, does not consider them to be components of primary appraisal that differentiate directly among the emotions. Lazarus, in contrast, has long pursued the argument that specific goal contents distinguish among different emotions, such as anger, guilt, shame, and pride.

In developing his recent book, Lazarus (1991a) has come to believe that the concept of goal content is best subsumed under the concept of the strength of a number of different types of ego-involvement, for example, preservation and enhancement of self-esteem for anger and pride, wanting to sustain moral values for guilt, living up to an ego-ideal for shame, sustaining (existential) meanings and ideas in which we are invested for anxiety, such as commitment to other persons and their well-being and one's own life goals. Therefore, for Lazarus, goal content now becomes the appraisal component of type of ego-involvement, which in guilt is having transgressed a moral imperative, and in shame is having failed to live up to an ego-ideal, and so on. For example, consistent with the Smith formulation, both shame and guilt include the appraisal component of self-accountability, but it is the type of ego-involvement, which the Smith model does not include as an appraisal component, that, according to Lazarus, distinguishes between these two emotions.

A second point of disagreement concerns the necessity of maintaining problem- and emotion-focused coping potential as distinct components of appraisal. Smith (e.g. Smith & Pope, 1992) believes the distinction between these components to be important in differentiating between sadness and fear/anxiety and the action tendencies associated with these emotions. Lazarus no longer considers the distinction between these two appraisal components to be relevant for emotion generation, although the distinction between problem-focused and emotion-focused coping *strategies* remains important for the study of coping. His reasoning is that it does not matter for the emotion being shaped whether people believe they can cope by changing the situation or by intrapsychically changing the relational meaning. Instead, what matters is the degree to which they believe they can cope through any means. In addition, whereas Smith believes appraised coping potential is largely irrelevant to anger, Lazarus believes this component has a role in generating anger (proposed to be associated with relatively high coping potential) and in differentiating it from sadness and anxiety (proposed to be associated with low coping potential).

A further area of disagreement concerns the complexity of the core relational themes associated with the various emotions. Whereas Smith restricts the themes to combining outcomes along only three or four appraisal components, the Lazarus set is far more complex and elaborate in ways that go beyond the addition of the component of type of ego-involvement already discussed. For instance, Lazarus distinguishes between fright (fear) and anxiety, whereas Smith does not. For Lazarus, the core relational theme for anxiety is facing uncertain, existential threat, whereas for fright the threat is sudden and concrete, and the core relational theme is the imminent danger of physical harm. Clearly, these core relational themes overlap with the appraisal of danger or threat used in the present research for combined fear/anxiety, but they are more complex.

Similarly, drawing upon Aristotle's definition of anger, Lazarus (1991a, c) now defines the core relational theme for anger as a demeaning offence against me and mine. In addition to including the ego-involvement component of enhancing self-esteem, this theme captures the idea that the provocation for anger must be an action appraised as a personal slight that is judged to be arbitrary, intentional, or malicious, and that the provoking agent is capable of having acted otherwise. Thus, although both Smith and Lazarus agree that direction of accountability toward another is a key appraisal component in anger, Lazarus thinks the core relational theme for anger contains considerably more than this.

It should be noted that the theory building is a dynamic process— changing somewhat with time and what is observed—rather than a static arrangement, especially in a relatively new, emerging area of thought and investigation. In the area of emotion, where we are now trying to make sense of the cognitive processes underlying the emotions, we are still in an early stage of conceptualisation and evidence, and we must take a flexible and open approach in the struggle to understand and predict. The present research advances understanding by addressing many relevant appraisal components and core relational themes, even if, as Lazarus presumes, they are as yet problematical and imcomplete. The authors hope that the efforts and thinking underlying this research will stimulate speculation, discussion, and research by others, and that it moves us toward a better understanding of the relational meanings and appraisal components in emotion.

Manuscript received 30 October 1990
Revised manuscript received 10 November 1992

REFERENCES

Cohen, J. & Cohen, P. (1983). *Applied multiple regression/correlation analysis for the behavioral sciences* (2nd edn). Hillsdale, NJ: Lawrence Erlbaum Associates Inc.

Conway, M.A. & Bekerian, D.A. (1987). Situational knowledge and emotions. *Cognition and Emotion*, *1*, 145–191.

Ellsworth, P.C. & Smith, C.A. (1988a). Shades of joy: Patterns of appraisal differentiating pleasant emotions. *Cognition and Emotion*, *2*, 301–331.

Ellsworth, P.C. & Smith, C.A. (1988b). From appraisal to emotion: Differences among unpleasant feelings. *Motivation and Emotion*, *12*, 271–302.

Folkman, S. & Lazarus, R.S. (1988). The relationship between coping and emotion: Implications for theory and research. *Social Science in Medicine*, *26*, 309–317.

Frijda, N.H. (1986). *The emotions*. Cambridge University Press.

Frijda, N.H. (1987). Emotion, cognitive structure, and action tendency. *Cognition and Emotion*, *1*, 115–143.

Frijda, N.H., Kuipers, P., & ter Schure, E. (1989). Relations among emotion, appraisal, and emotional action readiness. *Journal of Personality and Social Psychology*, *57*, 212–228.

Horowitz, M.J. (1988). *Introduction to psychodynamics: A new synthesis*. New York: Basic Books.

Kimble, G.A. (1990). Mother nature's bag of tricks is small. *Psychological Science*, *1*, 36–41.

Klinger, E. (1975). Consequences of commitment to and disengagement from incentives. *Psychological Review*, *82*, 1–25.

Lang, P.J. (1979). A bio-informational theory of emotional imagery. *Psychophysiology*, *16*, 495–512.

Lazarus, R.S. (1966). *Psychological stress and the coping process*. New York: McGraw-Hill.

Lazarus, R.S. (1989). Constructs of the mind in mental health and psychotherapy. In A. Freeman, K.M. Simon, L.E. Beutler, & H. Arkowitz (Eds), *Comprehensive handbook of cognitive therapy*. New York: Plenum, pp. 99–121.

Lazarus, R.S. (1991a). *Emotion and adaptation*. Oxford University Press.

Lazarus, R.S. (1991b). Cognition and motivation in emotion. *American Psychologist*, *46*, 352–367.

Lazarus, R.S. (1991c). Progress on a cognitive-motivational-relational theory of emotion. *American Psychologist*, *46*, 819–834.

Lazarus, R.S. & Folkman, S. (1984). *Stress, appraisal, and coping*. New York: Springer.

Lazarus, R.S. & Smith, C.A. (1988). Knowledge and appraisal in the cognition-emotion relationship. *Cognition and Emotion*, *2*, 281–300.

Leventhal, H. (1984). A perceptual motor theory of emotion. In K.R. Scherer & P. Ekman (Eds), *Approaches to emotion*. Hillsdale, NJ: Lawrence Erlbaum Associates Inc, pp. 271–291.

Luborsky, L. (1977). Measuring pervasive psychic structures in psychotherapy: The core conflictual relationship. In N. Freedman & S. Grand (Eds), *Communicative structures and psychic structures: A psychoanalytic interpretation of communication*. New York: Plenum.

Luborsky, L. (1984). *Principles of psychoanalytic psychotherapy*. New York: Basic Books.

Plutchik, R. (1980). *Emotion: A psychoevolutionary synthesis*. New York: Harper & Row.

Roseman, I.J. (1984). Cognitive determinants of emotion: A structural theory. In P. Shaver (Ed.), *Review of personality and social psychology*, Vol. 5. *Emotions, relationships, and health*. Beverly Hills, CA: Sage, pp. 11–36.

Roseman, I.J. (1991). Appraisal determinants of discrete emotions. *Cognition and Emotion*, 5, 161–200.

Roseman, I.J., Spindel, M.S., & Jose, P.E. (1990). Appraisals of emotion-eliciting events: Testing a theory of discrete emotions. *Journal of Personality and Social Psychology*, 59, 899–915.

Rosenthal, R. & Rosnow, R.L. (1985). *Contrast analysis: Focused comparisons in the analysis of variance*. Cambridge University Press.

Scherer, K.R. (1984). On the nature and function of emotion: A component process approach. In K.R. Scherer & P. Ekman (Eds), *Approaches to emotion*. Hillsdale, NJ: Lawrence Erlbaum Associates Inc, pp. 293–317.

Scherer, K.R. (1988). Cognitive antecendents of emotion. In V. Hamilton, G.H. Bower, & N.H. Frijda, (Eds), *Cognitive perspectives on emotion and motivation*. Dordecht, The Netherlands: Kluwer, pp. 89–126.

Shaver, P., Schwartz, J., Kirson, D., & O'Connor, C. (1987). Emotion knowledge: Further exploration of a prototype approach. *Journal of Personality and Social Psychology*, 52, 1061–1086.

Smith, C.A. (1989). Dimensions of appraisal and physiological response in emotion. *Journal of Personality and Social Psychology*, 56, 339–353.

Smith, C.A. (1991). The self, appraisal, and coping. In C.R. Snyder & D. R. Forsyth (Eds), *Handbook of social and clinical psychology: The health perspective*. New York: Pergamon, pp. 116–137.

Smith, C.A. (In press). Evaluations of what's at stake and what I can do. In B.C. Long & S.E. Kahn (Eds), *Women, work, and coping: A multidisciplinary approach to workplace stress*. Montreal: McGill-Queen's University Press.

Smith, C.A. & Ellsworth, P.C. (1985). Patterns of cognitive appraisal in emotion. *Journal of Personality and Social Psychology*, 48, 813–838.

Smith, C.A. & Ellsworth, P.C. (1987). Patterns of appraisal and emotion related to taking an exam. *Journal of Personality and Social Psychology*, 52, 475–488.

Smith, C.A., Ellsworth, P.C., & Pope, L.K. (1990, Abstract). Contributions of ability and task difficulty to appraisal, emotion, and autonomic activity. *Psychophysiology*, 27, S64.

Smith, C.A. & Lazarus, R.S. (1990). Emotion and adaptation. In L.A. Pervin (Ed.), *Handbook of personality: Theory and research*. New York: Guilford, pp. 609–637.

Smith, C.A., Haynes, K.N., Lazarus, R.S., & Pope, L.K. (Submitted). *In search of the "hot" cognitions: Attributions, appraisals, and their relationship to emotion*. Vanderbilt University.

Smith, C.A., McHugo, G.J., & Lanzetta, J.T. (1986). The facial muscle patterning of posed and imagery-induced expressions of emotion by expressive and nonexpressive posers. *Motivation and Emotion*, 10, 133–157.

Smith, C.A. & Pope, L.K. (1992). Appraisal and emotion: The interactional contributions of dispositional and situational factors. In M.S. Clark (Ed.), *Review of personality and social psychology*, Vol. 14. *Emotion and social behavior*. Newbury Park, CA: Sage, pp. 32–62.

Weiner, B. (1985). An attributional theory of achievement motivation and emotion. *Psychological Review*, 92, 548–573.

APPENDIX

COMPLETE TEXT OF THE TA, CANCER, AND COURSE SCENARIOS

TA

Stage 1

You are enrolled in a course that is a prerequisite for your intended major. In general you are finding the course quite interesting and enjoyable, and you believe that you've chosen the right major. However, you don't get along with your TA. In your discussion section you often disagree with what he (she) says, and he (she) is highly critical of your comments. Recently you wrote a big paper for the class that your TA graded. You were really interested in the topic of the paper, and you wanted to show that you knew what you were talking about. So, you researched the topic very carefully, and put a lot of effort into writing what you believe is one of the best papers you'd ever written.

Today at the end of your discussion section the TA hands the papers back, and you see that you've been given a "C−".

Stage 2

All Versions.   After section the TA refused your request to regrade your paper, and said that you received the grade you did because the research was shoddy, and the paper was poorly written. In fact, he (she) said that the paper was one of the worst he (she) ever read, and that you should feel lucky to be getting a C−.

Other-blame.   You can't believe that the TA is doing this to you. You know that the paper is nowhere near as bad as the TA says, and believe that he (she) had no right to persecute you like this.

Self-blame.   Thinking back, you realise that you've been obnoxious and are at least partially to blame for this situation. You've given this person a very hard time. You've constantly argued with him (her), and because of you he's (she's) never been able to cover all the material he (she) planned to during section. Thinking about it, you realise that you've behaved badly, and really can't blame this person all that much for being hostile.

Threat.   You don't know how you're going to get by in this course. The TA obviously can't stand you and isn't going to give you the benefit of the doubt, putting you in danger of serious academic trouble. You don't know whether there's anything you can do to straighten out things so that your work will be evaluated objectively and you'll receive the grade you deserve in this course.

Loss/Helplessness.   You realise there's nothing you can do to please this person. You put out your very best effort and it was torn to shreds. This incident has ruined the whole course for you. Even though you had been enjoying the class, and had found the material and professor to be very interesting, you're certain that there's no way you'll be able to do well or enjoy the class as long as you have this TA. This is a great personal loss.

CANCER

Stage 1

You have a relative (e.g. aunt, uncle, or grandparent) who was always your favourite when you were growing up. You love this relative dearly. He (she) always took you places and told you amusing stories. Even though he (she) is older, you've always been able to talk about your problems with him (her), and on several occasions he (she) has gotten you out of trouble with your parents. The only thing that bothers you about this relative is that he (she) is a heavy smoker. In the past you've tried to get him (her) to quit, but to no avail.

You've just been told that your relative is in the hospital with lung cancer, which you know is often fatal within a short time.

Stage 2

All Versions. A couple of weeks have passed, and several days ago your relative had surgery. The news is bad. The cancer has spread so much that it's inoperable. Although the doctors will continue to do everything they can, they give your relative less than two months to live.

Other-blame. You can't understand why your relative let this happen to him(her)self. You don't understand why he (she) kept on smoking, even though he (she) knew it was dangerous, and even though you'd begged him (her) to quit. You also can't understand why he (she) waited so long before seeing a doctor. His (her) behaviour seems irresponsible and thoughtless of others.

Self-blame. You blame yourself for what has happened. You believe that you've let your relative down—that you weren't insistent enough in trying to get him (her) to stop smoking. If only you had made your relative realise how much you cared about him (her) and how important it was to you that he (she) quit smoking, then maybe this whole situation could have been avoided.

Threat. There is great danger he (she) will die, but no one can be sure. You don't know whether to believe the doctors or not. What if they're right and your relative dies? If that happens you don't know what you'll do without him (her) to turn to in times of trouble, or whether you'll ever again be able to enjoy the things you used to do together.

Loss/Helplessness. For the first time you're totally sure that your relative is going to die, and that there's nothing you or the doctors can do about it. You realise that you'll never again be able to go to this person with your problems, or share the enjoyable times you used to have with this relative. This is a great personal loss.

COURSE

Stage 1

This semester you've been taking a course that is required for your intended major. You selected this major because you've always been interested in the field, and you believe that it's ideal preparation for your career aspirations, which you've held for a long time. You've found this course to be much more difficult than you expected, and you scored well below the median on the midterm. Realising that it was very important for you to do well on the final, you redoubled your efforts, studied as hard as you could, and frequently sought out the TAs for help. You thought that the final was difficult, but left thinking that you had done fairly well.

268

The grades have just been posted, and you discover that you again scored well below the median, and have received a "C−" in the course.

Stage 2

All Versions. When you talked to your professor about the grade, he (she) explained that your performance was really in the low "D" range, but because you were obviously trying so hard, he (she) already raised your grade to a "C−", and couldn't in good conscience raise it any further.

Other-blame. Thinking back over the semester, you realise that the TAs were not very helpful. They always seemed to be in a rush to get rid of you when you went to see them, and they didn't know how to explain things clearly so that you could understand them. You believe that if the TAs had been competent and had done their jobs properly, you would have done much better in the course.

Self-blame. Thinking back over the semester, you blame yourself for doing so poorly in the class. You realise that although you worked very hard you made a lot of mistakes. You almost always waited until the last minute before completing your assignments or going to the TAs for help. Because of this the TAs were always very busy when you went to see them, and they couldn't devote much time to your problems. You believe that if only you had been more organised you would have done much better in the course.

Threat. You don't know what to do. You worked as hard as you could, and still you nearly flunked the course. You believe that if you stay with this major, no matter how hard you try you're in great danger of doing poorly in your classes and winding up with a rotten academic record. At the same time, however, because you've held your career aspirations for so long, and because they are so important to you, you really don't want to quit the major and abandon your dreams and plans.

Loss/Helplessness. You believe that you're not cut out for this major. You worked as hard as you could, and still you nearly flunked the course. You're certain that you should change your major and career plans. Right now, you're thinking about how long you've dreamed of achieving your career aspirations, how long you've been interested in this particular major, and how now you have to abandon these dreams and plans. This is a great personal loss.

COGNITION AND EMOTION, 1993, 7 (3/4), 271–293

Discriminating Emotions from Appraisal-relevant Situational Information: Baseline Data for Structural Models of Cognitive Appraisals

Rainer Reisenzein

Free University, Berlin, Germany

Thomas Hofmann

University of Technology, Berlin, Germany

Cognitive emotion theorists assume that the quality of emotions is determined by the appraisal of the eliciting states of affairs. Accordingly, a central criterion for the evaluation of structural models of cognitive appraisal is their capacity to discriminate between emotions on the basis of the proposed appraisal dimensions. It is suggested that a good model should approximate subjects' "natural" ability to distinguish emotions on the basis of appraisal-relevant situational information. Corresponding data for 23 common emotions, which can serve as a baseline for the evaluation of cognitive appraisal theories, are reported, and various factors that may have deflated the discrimination rates obtained so far in empirical studies are discussed.

INTRODUCTION

A major concern of recent cognitively oriented research on emotions consists of the enumeration of the basic dimensions of cognitive appraisal and their associations with different emotions. Several structural models of cognitive appraisal have been proposed during recent years (e.g. Dalkvist & Rollenhagen, 1989; Frijda, 1986; Ortony, Clore, & Collins, 1988; Roseman, 1984; Scherer, 1984; Smith & Ellsworth, 1985; Solomon, 1976; Weiner, 1986). These models differ with regard to the number and identity

---

Requests for reprints should be sent to Rainer Reisenzein, Department of Psychology, (WE 7), Free University Berlin, 1000 Berlin 33, Habelschwerdter Allee 45, Germany.

This research was supported by a grant from the Deutsche Forschungsgemeinschaft (DFG) awarded to the first author. We wish to thank Elizabeth Dunne, Wolfgang Debler, Hubert Feger, and Ellen Skinner as well as three anonymous reviewers for their helpful comments on earlier versions of the manuscript.

---

of the dimensions of appraisal that are proposed, the assumptions (if such are spelled out) concerning the association between particular emotions and patterns of appraisal, and with regard to the range of emotions that each theory seeks to cover (see e.g. Roseman, Spindel, & Jose, 1990).

Attempts to test these models presume criteria of empirical adequacy by which they can be evaluated. These criteria concern both the aptness of a model when considered separately, and when compared with other theories.

Recent empirical research has particularly emphasised one criterion of adequacy, namely the degree to which an appraisal model permits the discrimination among different emotions (e.g. Ellsworth & Smith, 1988; Frijda, 1987; Frijda, Kuipers, & ter Schure, 1989; Gehm & Scherer, 1988; Manstead & Tetlock, 1989; Smith & Ellsworth, 1985, 1987; Smolenaars & Schutzelaars, 1986/87; Tesser, 1990). Judged by this criterion, most of the theories tested so far can be said to have received some degree of empirical support, inasmuch as appreciable associations between emotions and the postulated dimensions of cognitive appraisal were obtained. To illustrate, Smith and Ellsworth (1985) found that knowledge of subjects' ratings of emotional episodes for 15 common affects on six appraisal dimensions permitted the correct statistical classification of 42% of these situations (37% if corrected for chance; Cohen's [1960] kappa × 100). Similarly, in the most extensive investigation to date, Frijda et al. (1989), using as predictors ratings on 19 (study 1) and 23 (study 2) appraisal scales designed to tap several further appraisal dimensions in addition to those proposed by Smith and Ellsworth, obtained statistical classification rates of 36% (chance-corrected 34%; study 1) and 43% (chance-corrected 41%; study 2) for the 32 emotions that were included.

It is more difficult to say: (1) how strong this support can be considered to be in an *absolute* sense (i.e. does a discrimination rate of 30–40% mean that the model is good, moderate, or poor?); and (2) what the discrimination data tell about the *relative* merits of the different theories. Considering first the last-mentioned issue, a direct comparison of most of the existing studies is difficult because they differed, apart from the appraisal dimensions included, with regard to several other factors. These include the number and kind of emotions that were investigated, the "reality mode" of the emotion-eliciting situations that were judged (e.g. real, remembered or hypothetical situations), the measurement of appraisals and emotions, and the statistical methods used to determine the predictive capacity of the proposed dimensions (e.g. discriminant analysis vs. multiple regression). A way out of this problem are comparative model-testing studies in which these potentially confounding factors are controlled and the discriminatory capacity of different appraisal dimensions, and combinations of such dimensions, is systematically examined (e.g. Roseman et al., 1990).

As to the first-mentioned issue, whether one judges the empirically obtained association between appraisals and emotions as high or low depends on how strong one expects this relation to be on theoretical, methodological, and empirical grounds. Concerning theory, most authors seem to assume that each distinct emotion is "associated", in some way or other, with a distinct pattern of appraisal. If this assumption is correct, perfect discrimination between emotions on the basis of appraisals should theoretically be possible, and the comparatively low empirical discrimination scores obtained so far could be interpreted as indicating that important dimensions of appraisals are missing in current models. But some cognitive emotion theorists (e.g. Frijda, 1986; Smolenaars & Schutzelaars, 1986/87) have suggested that part of the everyday distinctions between emotions reflect differences in aspects of emotions other than appraisals (such as action tendencies or bodily feedback).[1] If so, the association between appraisals and emotions obtained in empirical studies can a priori be expected to be less than perfect, perhaps substantially so (cf. Smolenaars & Schutzelaars, 1986/87). Furthermore, discrimination between emotions should be improved if information about the further relevant aspects of emotions is also taken into account. In line with this prediction, Frijda et al. (1989) found that the additional inclusion of action tendencies ("action readiness modes") as predictors increased the percentage of correctly classified emotions to up to 59% (Frijda et al., 1989, study 2).

However, even if a one-to-one association between emotions and patterns of appraisal is assumed to exist, empirical associations substantially stronger than those obtained so far need not necessarily be expected. First, some of the (presumably) different emotions included in the studies may, in fact, not be very sharply distinguished by people. It has frequently been suggested that the demarcations drawn by the average person between many of the mental states denoted by different emotion terms are fuzzy or even nonexistent and that emotion language is therefore full of "quasi-synonyms" (e.g. Marx, 1982; Osgood, 1966; Russell, 1980; Tomkins & McCarter, 1964). Related to this point, there may be substantial inter-individual differences in the use of some emotion words. Secondly, methodological factors could have deflated the truly existing associations between emotions and appraisal. Emotion-eliciting events frequently evoke multiple emotions (cf. Smith & Ellsworth, 1987); because the appraisal ratings typically referred to the total situation, the resulting

---

[1] This assumption presupposes that bodily feelings, action tendencies, etc. are not themselves completely determined by cognitive appraisals. Frijda et al. (1989, p. 225) suggest, for example, that emotion-related action tendencies may in part also depend on the individual's emotional response propensities, such as his or her proneness to fear, anger, or joy.

"mixtures" of appraisals may have blurred the association between emotions and appraisals (Frijda et al., 1989; see also Reisenzein & Hofmann, 1990; Roseman et al., 1990). In addition, the scales used to assess the appraisal dimensions may have partly suffered from low reliability or validity (e.g. Roseman et al., 1990; Tesser, 1990); and the statistical prediction models used may not have been fully adequate for the task (Frijda et al., 1989; Tesser, 1990).

Hence, the implications of the obtained discrimination scores for the aptness of the tested appraisal models remain ambiguous. They could indicate that important appraisal dimensions have been omitted, that some of the distinctions between emotions depend crucially on nonappraisal elements, that some of the examined emotions were not clearly distinguished by people or that there were substantial inter-individual differences in the use of some emotion words, that methodological problems were responsible, or that a combination of these factors was at work.

Ideally, one would like to compare the statistical discrimination scores with empirically obtained baseline data on people's ability to discriminate between emotions on the basis of information about cognitive appraisals, analogous to the strategy used in research on the components of facial expression that people use to infer emotional states (e.g. Ekman, 1982). There, the aptness of a proposed "component model" can be evaluated by comparing the predictive success of that model with data on the recognition of emotions from facial expressions by naïve judges. However, in contrast to facial expressions of emotions which can simply be photographed and then presented to judges, cognitive appraisals, being mental states, are not directly accessible to observation. In fact, it could be argued that one has to first know the dimensions of appraisal to be able to determine people's ability to discriminate emotions on their basis, implying that this ability cannot be determined in a theory-independent way at all.

However, although it may not be possible to determine people's ability to distinguish between emotions on the basis of appraisals in a way that does not already presuppose a structural theory of appraisals, there is a related issue that *can* be examined in a theory-independent manner and that provides information which is nearly as useful. This is the question of how well people can distinguish between emotions on the basis of *appraisal-relevant situational information*.[2] Provided that this information is sufficiently detailed to permit reliable inference of the appraisals of the emotion experiencer, data on people's ability to distinguish emotions on the basis of such information can be used as a baseline for the evaluation of

---

[2]The term "appraisal-relevant situational information" was suggested to us by one of the reviewers. As explained later, this information consists, more precisely, of a mixture of (selective) information about appraisals and about situational features from which appraisals can potentially be inferred.

appraisal models. The reason is that cognitive appraisal theorists assume that, whatever effects situations have on emotions, these effects are mediated (at least for more complex emotions, such as those considered here) by cognitive appraisals (e.g. Lazarus, 1982). If this mediational assumption is correct, "situations should add little or . . . nothing to prediction when the effect of dimensions is controlled" (Tesser, 1990, p. 218). Hence—unless this basic assumption is abandoned—it follows that whatever discrimination between emotions is possible on the basis of appraisal-relevant situational information must in some way be "picked up" or explained by appraisal models.

The aim of the studies reported later is to provide such discrimination data for 23 common emotions. Our approach was based on the assumption that salient perceived features of emotion-eliciting events—including those features that would be regarded as (contents of) appraisals by the theorists mentioned earlier (e.g. the valence of an event, its causal locus, or its probability)—are usually accessible to introspection and can therefore be reported. Indeed, when people in everyday life communicate to one another about their emotions, they seem frequently to refer either to their appraisals or to appraisal-relevant situational information to help the other person understand why they felt in a particular way in that situation (see Fiehler, 1990; Laucken, 1989). Our method may be regarded as a laboratory version of this procedure. Subjects were interviewed for reports of emotion-eliciting events for 23 common emotions. Special instructions were used to maximise the chances that their subjective appraisals of the eliciting situations, or at least appraisal-antecedent situational information from which the appraisals could be reliably inferred, rather than mere "objective" reports of what had happened, were elicited. Subsequently, different subjects were presented with condensed descriptons of these accounts, in which all information other than about eliciting conditions and appraisals was eliminated, and were asked to infer the emotion likely to be experienced by the story protagonists. In study 1, they had to do this by selecting the emotion terms deemed appropriate from the list of 23 terms, whereas in studies 2 and 3, they had to classify a subset of the emotion scenarios either into 23 standard categories which served as markers (study 2), or to sort them freely according to perceived similarity of the feelings elicited by these situations (study 3).

STUDY 1

Method

Subjects

Altogether, 78 subjects participated in study 1, 27 of them in the initial interview designed to obtain exemplars of emotion-eliticing situation descriptions, and the remaining 51 in the subsequent emotion discrimination experiment (main study). All subjects were students at the Free University Berlin who responded to posted advertisements in which paid volunteers for an unspecified "psychological experiment" were sought. The subjects were paid DM 10 (interview) and DM 40 (discrimination study) respectively for participation. Three subjects did not return their questionnaires, reducing the final sample size of the main study to 47 (including 1 subject who completed only two-thirds of the questionnaire). Of the 27 subjects of the interview study, 12 were male and 15 female (age $M = 24.2$, sd = 4.3); of the 47 subjects from the main experiment whose data were used, 25 were male and 22 female (age $M = 23.8$, sd = 3.2).

Selection of Emotion Types

A total of 23 emotions were included for study. Their selection was guided by both theoretical and empirical criteria. That is, on the one hand we wanted to include affects which have been accorded central importance by contemporary emotion theorists of both cognitive (e.g. Roseman, 1984; Weiner, 1986) and other (e.g. Izard, 1977; Plutchik, 1980) provenance; on the other hand, states which are regarded by lay subjects as typical examples of the category "emotion" as determined through empirical studies (e.g. Averill, 1975; Davitz, 1969; Fehr & Russell, 1984; Marx, 1982; Schmidt-Atzert, 1981) were to be included. The resulting list (cf. Table 1), which is a compromise between these two criteria, seems to be a fairly representative sample of the emotional spectrum (cf. Shaver, Schwartz, Kirson, & O'Connor, 1987).

Procedure

Interview.   The 27 subjects were interviewed individually by one of the two authors; about half by each. The subjects were asked to recount, for each of the 23 emotions, an episode (preferably one that had recently happened) where they had experienced the respective affect as the dominant emotion. In order to elicit, as much as possible, the subjects' cognitive appraisals of the emotional events, or at least appraisal-relevant antecedent information from which the appraisals could be inferred, the subjects were instructed to describe the events from their personal perspective, that is, as they had viewed them at the time when they occurred, and to provide enough detail to enable the experimenter—a person unfamiliar with their general life circumstances, attitudes, preferences, goals, etc.—to understand why they had felt the particular emotion in the respective situation. If necessary, this instruction was reiterated during the interview until the experimenter had the impression that he understood why the subject had felt the emotion in the situation reported (however, no report was ever rejected). In addition, the experimenter attempted to determine at which moment during an unfolding situation the affect first occurred and, if the situation was a complex one involving several emotions, which aspect of the situation, in the subject's opinion, was responsible for the affect. The interview was tape-recorded with the subjects' permission (no one declined) and later transcribed.

Questionnaire Construction. A total of 544 descriptions of emotional situations were obtained from the 27 subjects ($M = 20.2$, sd = 2.5). From this material we intended to construct, for each emotion, 20 non-redundant descriptions of eliciting events for use in the subsequent discrimination experiment. In a first step, the transcribed reports were condensed into short first-person stories according to the following rules. (1) First, background information concerning the subject's study area, sex, general life circumstances, preferences and attitudes toward specific issues, etc. was provided, if such information had been indicated by the subject to be relevant for an understanding of the emotional reactions. Examples are: "I am a passionate chess player"; "my relationship with my boyfriend has been going badly during the past few months". (2) This information was followed by the description of the event immediately responsible for the subject's emotion. The unfolding event (as appraised by the subject) was described up to and including the moment at which the emotion first occurred, ending with the standard phrase "At this moment, I experienced the following emotion: _____", or a semantically equivalent sentence. (3) All emotion terms as well as metaphors referring to emotions, if such had been mentioned by the subjects, were eliminated from the descriptions; similarly, if a subject had reported physiological symptoms, expressive or instrumental reactions, or responses of social partners, these kinds of information were also discarded. This elimination procedure precludes the possibility that subjects in the main study could have inferred emotions from information other than about appraisals and situational cues.

In a second step, we eliminated from each emotion category those situations that seemed redundant. If an affect category still contained more than 20 stories after this elimination procedure, as many as necessary were randomly removed to reduce their number to 20. For six of the emotion categories, fewer than 20 situations remained after elimination of redundant stories. Therefore, several additional subjects were interviewed specifically for these affects until 20 non-redundant situation descriptions had been obtained.

Finally, the 23 (affects) × 20 (number of situations per affect) = 460 stories were randomised and typed as a questionnaire. The length of the stories varied from a minimum of 12 words to a maximum of 120 words, with most of the stories being from 40 to 70 words long. To illustrate what the stories looked like, here is an example of a better recognised story from the embarrassment category:

> I am not accustomed to being the focus of other people's attention.—When I finished school, a big celebration was organised. I was the second best of my class. Although I did not regard this as a particularly noteworthy achievement (standards in our class were low), everybody made a big thing of it. During the celebration, I was asked to step out in front where everybody told me how great I was. When I was standing there, being the focus of everybody's attention, and heard everybody tell me how great it was, I experienced the following emotion: _____.

(This story was judged as an example of embarrassment by 78% of the subjects in the subsequent discrimination experiment.)

Discrimination Study.   Based on the results of pretesting, the questionnaire was divided into three parts which were to be completed during three separate 2 hour sessions, distributed over a period of 4 weeks. At each session, one-third of the questionnaire was handed out to the 51 subjects together with a list of the 23 emotion names arranged in alphabetical order. The subjects' task was to infer which emotions the person from whom the stories had been obtained might have experienced in each scenario, by selecting the emotion name which seemed to be the most appropriate label (*first answer*). In addition, the subjects were allowed to select a further emotion name (*second answer*) as a second-best guess. For each subject, the order in which the stories appeared in the questionnaire was additionally randomised through random arrangement of the 121 pages of the questionnaire.

Results[3]

A total of 21,323 first and 5927 second answers were obtained from the 47 subjects included in the data analysis. Missing first responses were uniformly due to subjects who overlooked a page or two of the questionnaire. The relatively low percentage of second responses (on average, for 28% of the stories) may have been due to the subjects' relatively great certainty regarding their first choices, but other factors, such as the desire to shorten the laborious task, were probably also influential.

To answer the question of how well the subjects discriminated among the 23 emotions on the basis of appraisal-relevant situational information,

---

[3]A more detailed description of the results, including additional data, is available from the first author on request.

we computed the chance-corrected proportion of agreement (Cohen's [1960] kappa) between their responses and the emotion labellings of the scenarios by the encoders (i.e. the persons from whom the scenarios had been obtained). In addition to an overall agreement coefficient, kappa coefficients were also computed separately for the 23 emotion categories (conditional kappa; see Fleiss, 1971; Hubert, 1977). Furthermore, all agreement statistics were calculated once considering only the subjects' first answers, and again when taking both their first and second answers into account. In the latter case, an agreement was defined to be present if at least one of the two answers corresponded to the comparison standard, and the chance correction factor involved in the computation of kappa was appropriately adjusted to reflect the increased probability of chance agreement.

The conditional kappa values for the 23 emotion categories, their ranks, and the corresponding raw proportions are shown in Table 1 in columns [1] to [6]. As is to be expected, given the large number of categories and the equal distribution of stories across the categories, the kappa values are only slightly lower than the corresponding raw proportions.

Considering first the agreements of the subjects' first responses with the encoders' (reported) emotional state, it can be seen from column [2] of Table 1 that the conditional kappa values ranged from a minimum of 0.30 (remorse/regret) to a maximum of 0.88 (disgust/revulsion) with a mean of 0.64 (sd = 0.15), which coincided with the overall agreement coefficient calculated for the pooled data. Three emotion categories had kappas $\geq$ 0.80, 9 $\geq$ 0.70, 14 $\geq$ 0.60, and 20 $\geq$ 0.50. Even for the three emotions which had agreement scores < 0.50 (contempt, shame, and remorse/regret), the conditional kappas were far beyond the chance level. Furthermore, the correct response category was always the most frequently chosen one and, for all emotions except remorse/regret, it was significantly ($P <$ 0.05; binomial z-test) more likely to be selected than any other category. On average, five times as many answers fell within the correct response category than within the most frequently chosen incorrect one (i.e. the latter contained, on average, only 13% of the responses). Hence, it is evident that the subjects discriminated rather well between the emotions.

Examination of columns [4] and [5] of Table 1 reveals that the agreement coefficients uniformly increased when both first and second answers were taken into account, whereas the rank order of the coefficients remained nearly constant (Spearman rho = 0.99). The maximum kappa value is now raised to 0.91 (disgust/revulsion) and the minimal value (remorse/regret) to 0.36, with a mean of 0.70 (sd = 0.13). One affect now had a kappa value $\geq$ 0.90; eight had kappas $\geq$ 0.80; 12 $\geq$ 0.70; 18 $\geq$ 0.60, and 21 $\geq$ 0.50. Hence, even if the subjects missed the correct emotion category at their first guess, they often had it ready as their second-best answer.

TABLE 1

Study 1: Overall Agreement of Subjects' Responses with the Criterion and Significant Disagreements

Emotion Category	Agreement with Criterion						Categories where Significant Disagreements Occurred[a]
	1st Answer			1st or 2nd Answer			
	Rank	Kappa	Prop	Rank	Kappa	Prop	
	[1]	[2]	[3]	[4]	[5]	[6]	[7]
Anger/Rage	9	0.72	0.74	9	0.79	0.81	disappointment (0.10); contempt (0.08)
Anxiety/Fear	6	0.76	0.77	7.5	0.80	0.81	
Contempt	21	0.49	0.51	20	0.58	0.61	disgust (0.14); anger (0.13); disappointment (0.09); pity (0.07)
Disappointment	10	0.69	0.71	10	0.78	0.80	anger (0.09)
Discontentment/ Dissatisfaction with self	14	0.60	0.62	13	0.69	0.72	hopelessness (0.11); anger (0.08)
Disgust/Revulsion	1	0.88	0.88	1	0.91	0.92	
Embarrassment	17.5	0.53	0.55	18	0.60	0.63	shame (0.11); discontentment (0.06)
Envy	11	0.67	0.68	12	0.71	0.73	jealousy (0.06); discontentment (0.06)
Gratitude	6	0.76	0.77	5.5	0.82	0.83	joy (0.10); relief (0.07)

Guilt	17.5	0.53	0.55	17	0.62	0.64	remorse (0.20); shame (0.09)
Hope	2	0.84	0.85	2	0.88	0.89	joy (0.08)
Hopelessness/Resignation	15	0.57	0.59	16	0.63	0.65	disappointment (0.17); sadness (0.07)
Jealousy	13	0.61	0.62	14	0.67	0.68	envy (0.11); disappointment (0.07)
Joy/Happiness	12	0.66	0.69	11	0.76	0.79	pride (0.09); surprise (0.06)
Loneliness	8	0.75	0.76	7.5	0.80	0.81	
Love	19.5	0.50	0.52	19	0.59	0.61	joy (0.26); hope (0.06)
Pity/Sympathy	4	0.78	0.79	3.5	0.82	0.83	sadness (0.06)
Pride	6	0.76	0.77	5	0.82	0.83	joy (0.16)
Relief	3	0.80	0.81	3.5	0.83	0.84	joy (0.06)
Remorse/Regret	23	0.30	0.32	23	0.36	0.39	discontentment (0.29); anger (0.12); disappointment (0.09); guilt (0.06)
Sadness/Sorrow	16	0.56	0.58	15	0.65	0.67	disappointment (0.17); loneliness (0.08)
Shame	22	0.38	0.40	22	0.47	0.50	embarrassment (0.23); discontentment (0.09); remorse (0.07); guilt (0.07)
Surprise	19.5	0.50	0.51	21	0.56	0.58	joy (0.24)
Mean		0.64	0.65		0.70	0.72	
sd		0.15	0.14		0.13	0.13	

[a]Numbers in parentheses are proportion disagreements.

An analysis of the observed *disagreements* is shown in column [7] of Table 1, which contains, for each of the emotions, those disagreements which occurred with conditional probabilities significantly different from the base probabilities of the respective response category in the total pool of observations (as determined by the binomial z-test with alpha set at 0.05; see e.g. Allison & Liker, 1982). As can be seen, systematic disagreements occurred for all emotions except anxiety/fear, disgust/revulsion, and loneliness, but these disagreements were in all cases restricted to a small subset of the possible 22 "incorrect" affects, mostly to those which intuitively appear to be related to the respective "correct" emotions (see also Shaver et al., 1987). The systematic disagreements accounted for 55% of all observed disagreements; therefore only 16% of the total first responses of the subjects remain as random answers. Within the 23 emotion categories, random disagreements ranged from 6% (contempt) to 28% (embarrassment). Furthermore, emotions with lower agreement scores tended to be confused with greater numbers of affects ($r = -0.55$).

To obtain more information about the sources of the differing overall agreement scores of the various emotions and the observed disagreements, analyses analogous to the ones just reported were performed separately for the 20 scenarios within each emotion category. The main results of these analyses were as follows. (1) *All* emotion categories contained at least some well-discriminated scenarios. If only well-discriminated scenarios were considered, high accuracy scores were obtained for nearly all emotions. For example, if only the best-discriminated situation from each category was considered, agreement ranged from 1.0 (anxiety/fear, disgust/revulsion, gratitude, hope, and loneliness) to 0.70 (remorse/regret) with $M = 0.91$ and sd $= 0.09$; and 14 emotions had proportion agreement values ≥ 0.90, 21 ≥ 0.80, and all 23 ≥ 0.70. (Data for the 10 best-discriminated scenarios are presented later in Table 2.) (2) Every single one of the 460 situations had at least one mode (meaning, in the present context, a significant elevation from baseline), implying that no situation was responded to completely randomly. (3) Of the 460 situations, 229 (49.8%) were unimodal, 179 (38.9%) were bimodal, 47 (10.2%) had three, and 5 (1.1%) had four modes. Hence, about half of the scenarios suggested more than a single emotion as the dominant one to the decoders. (4) Finally, for 73 (or 16%) of the scenarios, the most frequently used response category was different from the emotion intended by the encoder. These scenarios had uniformly low agreement scores (≤ 0.40). Thus, a substantial number of cases were observed which suggested a different emotion to the decoders than the one intended by the encoder. However, all but three of these scenarios were also multimodal, and in only 11 of these cases did the intended emotion not appear as an additional significant mode. If the *modal* response to these scenarios is regarded as the correct response category, the overall agreement kappa increased to 0.67 (first response only) and 0.74 (first or second response correct).

Discussion

Considering the potential methodological limitations of the procedure, which could have negatively affected the results (in particular, that not all of the appraisal-relevant situational information was elicited in the interview), the findings suggest that subjects can rather well discriminate between emotions, at least those considered, on the basis of appraisal-relevant situational information. The overall discrimination performance of our naïve subjects was, for example, not much below the reliability generally considered sufficient in observational or judgement studies using trained observers (e.g. Rosenthal, 1982), and for many of the emotion categories, it was entirely adequate. In addition, it appears that nearly perfect discrimination ($M = 0.91$) can be obtained if complex or ambiguous scenarios are excluded.

Nevertheless, the finding that rather low average agreement scores were obtained for some emotions raises the possibility that recognition of these affects may crucially depend on information other than about cognitive appraisals (e.g. Frijda et al., 1989; Smolenaars & Schutzelaars, 1986/87). However, the fact that even these emotion categories contained at least a few well-discriminated scenarios speaks against this possibility and suggests that other factors may have been responsible. First, the lower accuracy rates may have been due, in part, to linguistic factors; that is, there may be relatively great inter-individual inconsistencies concerning the meanings of the corresponding emotion labels. This possibility was further examined in study 2. Secondly, the less well-discriminated scenarios of these emotion categories may have been primarily situations which, rather than being ambiguous (i.e. situations which left it unclear which of two or more emotions occurred) were complex, that is, unambiguously suggested the simultaneous presence of several emotions (cf. Smith & Ellsworth, 1987). In the latter case, the subjects' uncertainty and possible errors (in the present study) would have been due only to the fact that they could not clearly decide which emotion was the *dominant* one. To check this latter possibility, we presented the 231 multimodal situations to two additional subjects together with the modal responses and asked them to indicate for each of these situations how likely it was, in their opinion, that the respective emotions had been experienced by the story protagonist (on a scale from 1 = very unlikely to 7 = practically certain). For nearly all of the scenarios, the raters were relatively certain (score > 5) that *all* modal affects had occurred. Thus, complexity of the eliciting situations may indeed have been a major factor responsible for lower agreement on particular emotions.

STUDIES 2 AND 3

To validate the results of study 1, two further studies were conducted. Both were partial replications of study 1, using different methods designed to overcome some of the potential limitations of the first investigation. In particular, we attempted to control for the possibility that the moderate agreement scores for some emotions observed in study 1 were due to the fact that the subjects disagreed to some extent on the meanings of the corresponding emotion words. To assess the importance of this factor, a fixed and free sorting method was used in studies 2 and 3, respectively. Linguistic differences concerning the emotion terms should be controlled by this method to some degree, because scenarios should be grouped into the same target category if they are seen as eliciting the same emotion(s) as the target situation, regardless of how the subjects choose to call them. Due to space reasons, and because the results of these studies were very similar to those of study 1, they will be described only briefly (see footnote 3).

Subjects and Procedure

Subjects were 21 (study 2) and 24 (study 3) students from the same subject pool as those of study 1. In study 2, the subjects were presented with 23 "standard scenarios" consisting of the best-discriminated scenario from each of the 23 emotion categories (according to the results of study 1) and were asked to sort the better-discriminated half of the remaining scenarios, which had been typed on index cards, into the 23 categories according to perceived similarity to the emotion(s) experienced in the standard situations. After the subjects had completed the sorting, they were asked to name the emotion(s) believed to be experienced in the 23 categories of situations, using from one to three emotion terms of their choice. Subsequently, they were presented with the list of the 23 emotion names used in study 1 and were again asked to label the categories, this time using only the names appearing on the list.

Because of the high cognitive demands of the free-sorting procedure, in study 3 only 46 scenarios, 2 out of each of the 23 emotion categories (deck A), had to be sorted. However, this task was replicated for a second set of 46 scenarios (deck B). Following standard instructions for free-sorting tasks (e.g. Fillenbaum & Rapoport, 1971; Miller, 1969), the subjects were asked to sort the scenarios into piles on the basis of perceived similarity of emotions. They were allowed to use as many piles as they wanted and to put as many scenarios in a pile as they wished. Subsequently, they were asked to suggest one or more labels for the emotions experienced in each cluster of scenarios.

Results and Discussion

Study 2

The major results of study 2 are presented in Table 2. Agreement with the standard, averaged across emotion categories, was kappa = 0.73 (sd = 0.17). This is slightly lower than the corresponding statistic obtained in study 1 for the same scenarios ($M = 0.77$, sd = 0.14). Five emotions (envy, guilt, jealousy, regret/remorse, and shame) were discriminated significantly better in study 2 than in study 1 (as determined by t-tests on the means of the individual kappa scores; alpha = 0.05, df = 66), whereas the reverse was true for six different emotions (anger, anxiety, disappointment, embarrassment, joy, and surprise); the remaining 12 did not differ. The increases in classification accuracy observed in study 2 (which included regret/remorse and guilt, the two affects which had the lowest accuracy scores in study 1) would be consistent with the hypothesis that the moderate to low scores obtained for these emotions in study 1 were in part due to inter-individual differences concerning the meanings of the emotion labels. In contrast, the observed decrements in accuracy were unexpected, but closer examination suggested that they were either due to the fact that the single scenarios, which served as markers, suggested as a salient emotion one that was not available as a response in study 1 (e.g. the surprise scenario also suggested admiration and fascination), or that idiosyncratic features of the criterion scenarios, which are not generally characteristic of the situations associated with the target emotion, were also attended to in classification. This explanation was confirmed by additional analyses (cf. footnote 3).

Columns [6] and [7] of Table 2 show that on average 79% (sd = 21) of the self-produced emotion labels per category were literally correct, (column [6]), ranging from 38% (surprise) to 100% (anxiety/fear). Of those labels that were not literally correct, about one-third may be considered to be sufficiently similar to the preassigned labels to be taken, in the present context, as semantic equivalents of them (these labels are italicised in column [7]). If these labels are included among the correct ones, on average 86% of the labels are correct (sd = 16). The results of the additional category labelling, where the emotion names had to be selected from the list of labels used in study 1, were even more impressive: For all but three emotions (embarrassment, hopelessness, and surprise) this labelling was 100% correct. In sum, the results of study 1 were largely

TABLE 2

Study 2: Agreement Indices, Significant Disagreements and Labelling of the Categories

Emotion Category	Agreement with Criterion				Categories where Significant Disagreements occurred[b]	Self-produced Emotion Labels	
	Study 2		Study 1[a]			Literally correct	Other
	Rank	Kappa	Rank	Kappa			
	[1]	[2]	[3]	[4]	[5]	[6]	[7]
Anger/Rage	15	0.70	10	0.84		0.95 (20)	*sore* (1)
Anxiety/Fear	10.5	0.80	4	0.89		1.00 (21)	
Contempt	16	0.65	21	0.58	Anger (0.08); Disgust (0.07)	0.48 (10)	*superiority* (7); lack of understanding for other (3); hate (1)
Disappointment	19.5	0.56	11	0.81	Hopeless (0.11); Anger (0.09); Sad (0.06)	0.95 (20)	lack of solidarity (1)
Discontentment/ Dissatisfaction with self	17.5	0.63	15.5	0.72	Hopeless (0.10)	0.48 (10)	*own insufficiency* (5); *feeling useless* (1); frustration about self (2); disappointed about self (2); tired (1)
Disgust/Revulsion	2	0.94	1	0.96		0.95 (20)	lack of understanding for other (1)
Embarrassment	21	0.54	19.5	0.65	Shame (0.26)	0.33 (7)	*perplexed* (3); *insecure* (9); incompetent (1); forsaken (1)
Envy	3	0.92	12	0.80		0.90 (19)	*jealous of other's possessions* (1); jealous (1)
Gratitude	8	0.84	4	0.89		0.86 (18)	*loyalty* (1); liking (1); needy (1)
Guilt	10.5	0.80	17	0.68	Remorse (0.15)	0.90 (19)	*self-reproachful* (1); remorse (1)

Hope	4.5	0.90	2	0.93		0.86 (18)	*optimism* (1); new beginning (2)
Hopelessness/Resignation	13	0.75	13	0.78	Dissatisfied (0.14)	0.57 (12)	*despairing* (2); *discouraged* (1); lack of control (1); depressed (1); stressed (1); frustrated (3)
Jealousy	6.5	0.86	15.5	0.72		0.95 (20)	feeling ignored (1)
Joy/Happiness	22	0.53	9	0.85	Love (0.26); Surprise (0.07)	0.95 (20)	*joyful surprise* (1)
Loneliness	4.5	0.90	7.5	0.87		0.95 (20)	loss (1)
Love	12	0.76	18	0.67	Joy (0.07); Gratitude (0.06); Surprise (0.06)	0.57 (12)	*liking* (1); elated (2); happiness (6)
Pity/Sympathy	6.5	0.86	7.5	0.87		0.90 (19)	*empathy* (1); disgust (1)
Pride	1	0.95	4	0.89		0.81 (17)	*self-enhancement* (2); joy at one's success (1); happy (1)
Relief	9	0.82	6	0.88		0.95 (20)	liking for other (1)
Remorse/Regret	17.5	0.63	22.5	0.46	Guilt (0.11); Dissatisfied (0.09)	0.71 (15)	*self-reproachful* (1); guilty (2); unfairness (1); angry at self (2)
Sadness/Sorrow	14	0.71	14	0.77	Disappointment (0.22)	0.76 (16)	*feeling of loss* (5)
Shame	19.5	0.56	22.5	0.46		0.86 (18)	embarrassment (3)
Surprise	23	0.21	19.5	0.65	Joy (0.46)	0.38 (8)	*struck* (1); funny (1); fascinated (3); admiration (5); authority (1); autonomous (1); unclassifiable (1)
Mean		0.73		0.77		0.79 (16.5)	
sd		0.17		0.14		0.21 (4.4)	

aFor the 230 scenarios used in study 2.
bNumbers in parentheses are proportion disagreements significant at alpha = 0.05.

replicated, and some indication was obtained that linguistic factors (disagreement on the meanings of emotion terms) contributed to the lower accuracy scores obtained in study 1 for some of the emotions.

Study 3

On average, 15.4 (sd = 4.1) clusters were constructed for deck A, and 16.2 (sd = 3.9) for deck B. For decks A and B separately, individual incidence matrices were first formed, which were then summed across subjects. These matrices were correlated with a theoretically derived "perfect" discrimination matrix, which would have been obtained if all subjects had formed 23 clusters containing exactly the two scenarios belonging to the same emotion category. The obtained correlation coefficients were 0.68 for deck A and 0.70 for deck B. In addition, we compared the average probability that a card was sorted together with the second one from the same emotion category, with the average probability that the two cards were sorted together with a card from a different category. The average within-category probabilities were 0.61 (sd = 0.20) for deck A, and 0.71 (sd = 0.17) for deck B, whereas the average between-category probabilities were only 0.05 (sd = 0.01) and 0.04 (sd = 0.02) for decks A and B respectively. Hence, a card was on average 11.5 (deck A) or 17.8 (deck B) times more likely grouped together with its partner from the same emotion category than with a card belonging to a different one. These results are comparable to the corresponding average within- and between-category similarities calculated for the data from study 2 (0.62 and 0.04, respectively, resulting in a same/different ratio of 15.5). Finally, the percentage of correct emotion labels (using all codable ones) was lower than that found in study 2 ($M = 0.54$ for deck A and 0.59 for deck B), but the modal label used to name the two scenarios from each emotion category was correct for all (deck B) or all but one (deck A) of the emotions.

It may therefore be concluded that subjects' spontaneous discriminations between emotions on the basis of appraisal-relevant situational information were comparable to, or at least not substantially worse than those found in the first two studies.

GENERAL DISCUSSION

The aim of the studies reported in this article was to provide baseline data on people's ability to discriminate emotions from appraisal-relevant situational information. Taken together, the results of the studies suggest that subjects can discriminate rather well between emotions, at least those considered, on the basis of such information. Although the average obtained discrimination accuracy of about 65 to 70% is still considerably below perfect, the data suggest that this may be due to factors such as complexity of the eliciting situation (study 1) and disagreements on the meanings of emotion terms (study 2). This is supported by the finding that there were at least a few scenarios for nearly all emotions on which nearly perfect agreement was obtained (study 1).

As explained in the Introduction, these baseline data can serve as a standard of comparison for the results obtained in empirical studies of structural models of appraisals. It is evident that, even if one uses the average discrimination scores as the baseline, the empirical results obtained so far are still fairly below that baseline. How can this discrepancy be explained? In the Introduction, several possible reasons were mentioned: (1) some of the examined emotions may not be clearly distinguished by people or there may be substantial inter-individual differences in the use of emotion labels; (2) the distinctions drawn by people between different emotions may in part be based on nonappraisal elements; (3) important dimensions of appraisal may be missing in current appraisal models; and (4) methodological problems could have deflated the associations between emotions and appraisals. As mentioned, some support for (1) was obtained in study 2, but in general, the role of this factor, as well as that of (2) seem to have been minor for the emotions considered here. However, these factors do remain a possibility for other emotions, particularly emotions that appear to be highly similar (e.g. Smolenaars & Schutzelaars, 1986/87). In the remainder of this discussion, however, we concentrate on factors (3) and (4), by briefly reviewing the evidence that exists to date on the potential relevance of these factors.

Additional Dimensions of Appraisal

Suggestive evidence that current appraisal models may omit important dimensions of appraisal (with different models omitting different ones) comes from several studies. Tesser (1990), in a replication of Smith and Ellsworth's (1985) study, found that the inclusion of additional potential appraisal dimensions (that are, however, regarded as "situational features" by Tesser), namely personal relevance, interpersonal distance (close vs. distant other), and social comparison (self outperforms other vs. other outperforms self; a dimension that could be reconstructed as a form of self-evaluation) improved the accuracy of prediction for several of the emotions studied. Frijda et al. (1989) also included several further appraisal dimensions in addition to those proposed by Smith and Ellsworth. Although direct comparisons with the Smith–Ellsworth dimensions are not reported, the fact that predictive accuracy (chance-corrected) was about as high as that obtained by Smith and Ellsworth, even though twice as many emotions were included, suggests that the additional dimensions significantly contributed to emotion prediction. Reisenzein and Hofmann (1990), using a modified version of Kelly's (1955) repertory grid technique, obtained evidence for the relevance of further potential appraisal dimensions not explicitly considered so far in most empirical studies, in particular focus (event affects primarily the self vs. other) and evaluation of other/quality of social relationship. They also found that the inclusion of these dimensions enhanced prediction of emotions as compared with a subset of dimensions also used by Frijda et al. (1989). In fact, the statistical classification accuracy obtained in this study (in which the same 23 emotions were included as in the present investigations) was 62% (chance-corrected) and hence approximated the average accuracy obtained in the present study 1. However, Reisenzein and Hofmann's study differed from others also in further respects (the events *typically* conducive to the emotions had to be judged, and an attempt was made to specify more precisely the objects of appraisals). In a recent investigation, Reisenzein and Spielhofer (submitted) had subjects rate remembered emotion-eliciting events for 30 emotions on 22 scales designed to tap potential appraisal dimensions; for the 22 emotions also included in the present studies, 56% (chance-corrected) correct classifications were obtained.

An interpretative problem that arises in this context is that several of the further potential dimensions of appraisal included in these studies, although improving emotion discrimination, may not really be dimensions of *appraisal* at all (cf. Lazarus & Smith, 1988; Reisenzein & Hofmann, 1990; Tesser, 1990). A decision on this issue presupposes that clear criteria existed for considering a proposed dimension, a dimension of appraisal (as opposed to, particularly, a dimension denoting "situational features"), in addition to discriminatory potential. Several suggestions for such criteria have been made (e.g. Lazarus & Smith, 1988; Reisenzein & Hofmann, 1990; Reisenzein & Spielhofer, submitted), but this issue is not yet settled. However, even if several of the further dimensions measured in these studies were ultimately excluded from the category of appraisal dimensions, their results do support the point of the present studies that an appreciable amount of variance in emotions due to situations is not accounted for by current appraisal models.

Methodological Factors

In the Introduction, three kinds of methodological factors were mentioned that could have deflated the relations between emotions and appraisals: (1) in most existing studies of emotional appraisals, subjects were asked to judge the total "emotional situation" on the appraisal scales; this could have blurred the associations obtained between appraisals and emotions;

(2) the scales used to measure appraisals may have suffered from low reliability or validity; and (3) the statistical prediction models used may have been partly inadequate.

Some suggestive evidence does exist for the relevance of all of these factors. Concerning (1), Reisenzein and Hofmann (1990) obtained higher prediction rates in a study in which it was attempted to specifying more precisely the objects of appraisals (see also, Roseman et al., 1990). However, because no control group receiving standard appraisal instructions was included, the importance of this factor could not be clearly determined. Concerning (2), several studies found that some of the scales used to measure appraisal dimensions had low internal consistencies (Roseman et al., 1990; Tesser, 1990) and reliability (Reisenzein & Spielhofer, submitted). Also, they may not always have been used as intended by the researchers. Reisenzein and Spielhofer (submitted) found, for example, that an "expert" coding of the 460 scenarios used in the present study pointed to a number of significant differences in scale use as compared with that of naïve subjects (who judged remembered emotion-eliciting scenarios) and that statistical discrimination accuracy was substantially higher (chance-corrected 71%) for the expert coded situations. Finally, concerning (3), the appraisal dimensions may not combine additively in affecting emotion judgements (Tesser, 1990), or the scales may not be linearly related to emotions (e.g. Price, Barrell, & Barrell, 1985). The existence of nonlinear relations between appraisals and emotions could have additionally contributed to the higher discrimination scores obtained by Reisenzein and Hofmann (1990) and Reisenzein and Spielhofer (submitted), as these authors used binary variables as predictors (cf. Neter & Wasserman, 1974). However, the current data are only suggestive. Future research in this area should explore these possibilities in greater detail.

Manuscript received 14 August 1989
Revised manuscript received 18 January 1992

REFERENCES

Allison, P.D. & Liker, J.K. (1982). Analyzing sequential categorical data on dyadic interaction: A comment on Gottman. *Psychological Bulletin*, *91*, 393–403.

Averill, J.R. (1975). A semantic atlas of emotional concepts. *JSAS catalog of selected documents in psychology*, *5*, 330 (MS No. 421).

Cohen, J. (1960). A coefficient of agreement for nominal scales. *Educational and Psychological Measurement*, *20*, 37–46.

Dalkvist, J. & Rollenhagen, C. (1989). *On the cognitive aspects of emotions: A review and a model*. Report No. 703 from the Department of Psychology, University of Stockholm.

Davitz, J. (1969). *The language of emotion*. New York: Academic Press.

Ekman, P. (Ed.) (1982). *Emotion in the human face*. Cambridge University Press.

Ellsworth, P.C. & Smith, C.A. (1988). From appraisal to emotion: Differences among unpleasant feelings. *Motivation and Emotion*, *12*, 271–302.

Fehr, B. & Russell, J.A. (1984). Concept of emotion viewed from a prototype perspective. *Journal of Experimental Psychology: General*, *113*, 464–486.

Fiehler, R. (1990). *Emotion und Kommunikation* [Emotion and Communication]. Berlin: de Gruyter.

Fillenbaum, S. & Rapoport, A. (1971). *Structures in the subjective lexicon*. New York: Academic Press.

Fleiss, J.L. (1971). Measuring nominal scale agreement among many raters. *Psychological Bulletin*, *76*, 378–382.

Frijda, N.H. (1986). *The emotions*. Cambridge University Press.

Frijda, N.H. (1987). Emotion, cognitive structure, and action tendency. *Cognition and Emotion*, *1*, 115–143.

Frijda, N.H., Kuipers, P., & ter Schure, E. (1989). Relations among emotion, appraisal, and emotional action readiness. *Journal of Personality and Social Psychology*, *57*, 212–228.

Gehm, T.L. & Scherer, K.R. (1988). Relating situation evaluation to emotion differentiation: Nonmetric analysis of cross-cultural questionnaire data. In K. Scherer (Ed.), *Facets of emotion: Recent research*. Hillsdale, NJ: Lawrence Erlbaum Associates Inc, pp. 61–77.

Hubert, L. (1977). Kappa revisited. *Psychological Bulletin*, *84*, 289–297.

Izard, C.E. (1977). *Human emotions*. New York: Plenum.

Kelly, G. (1955). *The psychology of interpersonal constructs*. New York: Norton.

Laucken, U. (1989). *Denkformen der Psychologie* [Types of psychological thinking]. Bern: Huber.

Lazarus, R.S. (1982). Thoughts on the relations between emotion and cognition. *American Psychologist*, *37*, 1019–1024.

Lazarus, R.S. & Smith, C.A. (1988). Knowledge and appraisal in the cognition-emotion relationship. *Cognition and Emotion*, *2*, 281–300.

Manstead, A.S.R. & Tetlock, P.E. (1989). Cognitive appraisals and emotional experience: Further evidence. *Cognition and Emotion*, *3*, 225–240.

Marx, W. (1982). Das Wortfeld der Gefühlsbegriffe [The semantic field of emotion concepts]. *Zeitschrift für experimentelle und angewandte Psychologie*, *29*, 137–146.

Miller, G.A. (1969). A psychological method to investigate verbal concepts. *Journal of Mathematical Psychology*, *6*, 169–191.

Neter, J. & Wasserman, W. (1974). *Applied linear statistical models*. Homewood, IL: Irwin.

Ortony, A., Clore, G.L., & Collins, A. (1988). *The cognitive structure of emotions*. Cambridge University Press.

Osgood, C.E. (1966). Dimensionality of the semantic space for communication via facial expressions. *Scandinavian Journal of Psychology*, *7*, 1–30.

Plutchik, R. (1980). A general psychoevolutionary theory of emotion. In R. Plutchik & H. Kellerman (Eds), *Emotion: Theory, research, and experience*, Vol. 1. New York: Academic Press, pp. 3–33.

Price, D., Barrell, J.E., & Barrell, J.J. (1985). A quantitative-experiential analysis of human emotions. *Motivation and Emotion*, *9*, 19–38.

Reisenzein, R. & Hofmann, T. (1990). An investigation of dimensions of cognitive appraisal in emotion using the repertory grid technique. *Motivation and Emotion*, *14*, 1–26.

Reisenzein, R. & Spielhofer, C. (Submitted). Subjectively salient dimensions of emotional appraisal.

Roseman, I.J. (1984). Cognitive determinants of emotion: A structural theory. In Shaver, P. (Ed.), *Review of personality and social psychology*, Vol. 5. Beverly Hills: Sage, pp. 11–36.

Roseman, I.J., Spindel, M.S., & Jose, P.E. (1990). Appraisals of emotion-eliciting events:

Testing a theory of discrete emotions. *Journal of Personality and Social Psychology*, *59*, 899–915.

Rosenthal, R. (1982). Conducting judgment studies. In K.R. Scherer & P. Ekman (Eds), *Handbook of methods in nonverbal behavior research*. Cambridge University Press, pp. 287–361.

Russell, J.A. (1980). A circumplex model of affect. *Journal of Personality and Social Psychology*, *39*, 1161–1178.

Scherer, K.R. (1984). On the nature and function of emotion: A component process approach. In Scherer, K.R. & Ekman, P. (Eds), *Approaches to emotion*. Hillsdale, NJ: Lawrence Erlbaum Associates Inc, pp. 293–317.

Schmidt-Atzert, L. (1981). *Emotionspsychologie* [The psychology of emotion]. Stuttgart: Kohlhammer.

Shaver, P., Schwartz, J., Kirson, D., & O'Connor, C. (1987). Emotion Knowledge: Further exploration of a prototype approach. *Journal of Personality and Social Psychology*, *52*, 1061–1086.

Smith, C.A. & Ellsworth, P.C. (1985). Patterns of cognitive appraisal in emotion. *Journal of Personality and Social Psychology*, *48*, 813–838.

Smith, C.A. & Ellsworth, P.C. (1987). Patterns of appraisal and emotion related to taking an exam. *Journal of Personality and Social Psychology*, *52*, 475–488.

Smolenaars, A.J. & Schutzelaars, A.J.H. (1986/87). On 'cognitive' semantics of emotion words: Solomon quasi-ecologically tested. *Journal of Semantics*, *5*, 207–231.

Solomon, R.C. (1976). *The passions*. Garden City, NY: Anchor Press/Doubleday.

Tesser, A. (1990). Smith and Ellsworth's appraisal model of emotion: A replication, extension, and test. *Personality and Social Psychology Bulletin*, *16*, 210–223.

Tomkins, S.S. & McCarter, R. (1964). What and where are the primary affects? Some evidence for a theory. *Perceptual and Motor Skills*, *18*, 119–158.

Weiner, B. (1986). *An attributional theory of motivation and emotion*. New York: Springer.

COGNITION AND EMOTION, 1993, 7 (3/4), 295–323

Making Sense of Emotion in Stories and Social Life

Brian Parkinson

Psychology Department, University of Leicester, UK

A.S.R. Manstead

Department of Social Psychology, University of Amsterdam, The Netherlands

This paper is concerned with some limitations of the vignette methodology used in contemporary appraisal research and their implications for appraisal theory. We focus on two recent studies in which emotional manipulations were achieved using textual materials, and criticise the investigators' apparent implicit assumption that participation in everyday social reality is somehow comparable to reading a story. We take issue with three related aspects of this cognitive analogy between life and its narrative representation, by arguing that emotional reactions in real life are not necessarily mediated by symbolic processes, that people are involved participants of real life rather than neutral observers, and that in real life people's evaluations and emotions are typically part of an ongoing dialogue rather than the expression of a soliloquy. Results from these studies of emotional vignettes therefore tend to overestimate the importance of constructive, abstract, and individualistic processes in the everyday causation of social emotions. In real life, people do not necessarily have to calculate, transform, or internally represent the meaning of the dynamic situation in order to make emotional sense of what is happening to them in the social world.

INTRODUCTION

Imagine yourself in the following situation: A favourite relative is dying of lung cancer. There is little hope of recovery, and nothing you can do will help. Now how do you feel? How do you think you would feel if the situation was genuinely happening, if the consequences were real and you couldn't stop thinking about them however hard you tried? Is there a

---

Requests for reprints should be sent to Brian Parkinson, Psychology Department, University of Leicester, University Road, Leicester LE1 7RH, UK.

The authors would like to thank Nico Frijda, Batja Mesquita, Pierre Philippot, and Rainer Reisenzein for their comments on an earlier version of this article.

difference between the emotion conjured up by imagining the situation and that which you would feel if you were actually there, caught up in the real-life drama of it all?

The present paper is concerned with the question of how good an analogue of real-life emotional experience is provided by appraisal studies of emotion which work from representations of emotional episodes instead of the emotional events themselves. Obviously some kinds of representation might be considered better or more accurate than others, but are any of them capable of matching up perfectly with all the important factors influencing emotional phenomena in the real world?

We think that the answers to these questions are fairly straightforward and obvious and we doubt that anybody would disagree that there is a difference at least of degree between emotions generated by reading about a potentially emotional episode and those that arise in the natural course of events. But the precise basis for this difference is contestable and well worth considering from the standpoint of appraisal theory.

In the present paper, we will evaluate the "vignette" methodology of manipulating appraisal and emotion (e.g. Roseman, 1991; Smith & Lazarus, this issue). Our argument suggests that it is only by presupposing the validity of a particular cognitive constructivist standpoint that narrative representations of emotional events can be treated as functionally comparable to the corresponding real-life encounters. We will move on from this specific methodological critique to a more general discussion of the presuppositions of the appraisal approach, paying particular attention to the phenomena that it tends to exclude from the theoretical account of emotion.

What is interesting about the vignette methodology, from our point of view, is that it brings to the surface some of the implicit and hidden assumptions of certain versions of appraisal theory, and of the traditional cognitive approach in general; assumptions that we feel do not stand up to closer scrutiny. These assumptions can be summarised under the following theme: Involvement in real life is somehow comparable to the process of making sense of a story. According to many versions of appraisal theory, for example, a person becomes emotional only after having interpreted the situation and evaluated its personal significance (e.g. Lazarus, 1991). The emotion is constructed by the application of the individual's comprehension processes to the raw material provided by a partially independent world. In other words, real life provides a text which the individual gives a personal reading. Similarly, most traditional cognitive approaches to nonemotional phenomena also assume that reality is understood on the basis of internal semantic representations, and that meaning has to be constructed out of inchoate sensory data as a function of information-processing.

In this paper, we will concentrate on three aspects of the implicit cognitive analogy between life and story. First, that our reactions to events are necessarily mediated by representations of these events. Secondly, that people should be theorised primarily as observers of ongoing real-life episodes, rather than involved participants. Finally, that the central focus of our accounts of action and emotion should be on the single accountable individual rather than the always developing relationship between actors and their unfolding social context; that monologue rather than dialogue is the correct model for the structure of experience.

Although we do not deny that cognitive explanations have their place in the attempt to provide a comprehensive analysis of emotion, we think it is a mistake to presuppose their centrality, thereby marginalising perceptual, interpersonal, and dynamic factors. We will conclude our paper with a few preliminary suggestions for a research strategy for emotion that accepts the individualistic cognitive story as just a single strand of the interwoven theoretical narrative of emotion.

ECOLOGY OF COGNITION

An obvious place to start an investigation of emotional phenomena would be to observe the relevant processes in real time and in real life. For example, Coyne and Lazarus (1980, p. 148) argued as follows:

> A transactional perspective requires that ecological validity be demonstrated, not simply assumed. It calls for alternative methodologies appropriate to describing the continuous flow of person-environment relationships as they occur in stress and coping in the natural setting. Such flow needs to be examined in purely descriptive terms before one asks the more analytic, deterministic questions in controlled experimental studies.

The problem with this kind of ecological research is that it is very onerous and time consuming, especially in the case of the emotions, where the relevant observations are difficult to identify and select.

No surprise then that researchers have generally taken relatively early principled decisions about which parts of emotional reality are important, and investigated these specific aspects in a more controlled and systematic setting than the everyday social world can provide. Zooming in from the wide angle of exploratory observation, these investigators have chosen to focus on particular theoretically specified areas of the broadly defined field of emotion. Although this is clearly a sensible and pragmatic strategy, it can become problematic when the limited definition of the phenomena adopted in service of empirical advance then gets substituted for the real-world processes themselves, so that anything outside the constrained perspective of the chosen operational definition is rendered invisible. There comes a time when it becomes necessary to test the limits of the simplifying assumptions. We think that this time has now arrived (cf. Russell, 1987).

The prevalent interpretation of emotion among contemporary researchers is a cognitive constructivist one (e.g. Lazarus, 1991; Leventhal, 1984; Ortony, Clore, & Collins, 1988; Schachter, 1971; Scherer, 1984; Smith & Ellsworth, 1985). In this view, the important facts about emotion concern the processes of information transformation that are associated with the phenomenon. Typically, sensory data are thought to be processed by a series of internal structures which ultimately output emotional experience and behaviour, and the task of the emotion theorist is to characterise the operation of these various mediating structures.

In one version of contemporary appraisal theory, for example (Lazarus & Smith, 1988), emotion is seen as a product of two kinds of cognitive representations: the first set are based on *knowledge* and depend on our internal representation and categorisation of the prevailing situation; whereas the second set link these knowledge-based representations to the personal experience of emotion, and are based on *appraisal* of the situational information. These appraisal representations determine the implications of the current encounter for personal well-being and directly produce the emotion itself. In other words, emotion is a product of representations of the situation and representations of how the situation impacts on the self. Of course, it may be that judgements about the personal significance of the situation are themselves based on knowledge, and correspondingly that our categorisation of situations may often depend on their evaluated impact on our concerns, so that the two aspects of the representational process overlap and shade into one another. In any case, what is important from our point of view is that this version of appraisal theory sees emotion as a product of representational processes, wherever these processes might be directed. Later in this paper, we will consider an alternative view of the role of representational factors in emotional experience, but for now let us examine the implications of the cognitive constructivist account for the empirical study of emotional experience, using narrative "vignettes".

THE VIGNETTE APPROACH

According to the traditional cognitive approach, meaning and emotion are the output of a series of stages of internal information-processing: sense data are registered, categorised, transformed, and so on, to produce an internal representation that will then guide intention and action. In this model, what comes out of the system is not crucially dependent on what goes in because any input that triggers the same internal processes will have equivalent effects. In effect, one can take a short-cut to the mechanisms of interest by *simulating* the output of the earlier processing stages. Hence the provision of emotional information given in a written story, for example, can in some sense be seen as equivalent to on-line provision of emotional information in the "real world" (together with its real-time appraisal by the protagonist). As long as the narrative's symbolic content corresponds to what would have been produced in the early stages of information-processing anyway, then the same internal representation will be activated, and the output will be equivalent. In other words, if structure is added to experience intrapsychically, then the process of adding meaning is what is important rather than the bits of information to which meaning is added. The relevant pieces of cognitive machinery might equally well be set into motion by sensory stimuli or by precoded narrative material.

Thus the cognitive constructivist approach legitimises the vignette methodology where a fixed written text is substituted for dynamic social reality in the process of emotion production (e.g. Roseman, 1991; but see also Weiner, Russell, & Lerman, 1978). The advantage of this substitution for appraisal researchers is that it allows a simple and systematic manipulation of the kinds of information that are presented to experimental participants, so that the appraisal dimensions underlying emotional experience can be uncovered.

In the standard vignette procedure, participants are asked to make judgements about emotions experienced by the fictional protagonists of short written narrative passages or "vignettes". The typical findings of this kind of study show that emotional judgements are made in line with the protagonist's appraisal of the situation as it is described in the stories. In the next two sections of this paper we will take a close look at two studies which have employed this vignette technique. The reason for our attention to detail is that we think the methodology highlights some of the central and problematic assumptions of certain versions of the appraisal approach to emotion, and by extension, traditional cognitive perspectives on many other psychological phenomena. Our basic argument is that the findings of these studies have limited applicability to life outside the laboratory.

Roseman's Simulation Study

Roseman (1991, p. 168) acknowledged the obvious difficulties of investigating real-time emotional experience experimentally: "There are major problems with using an experimental procedure to study subjects' emotions directly. One is the practical difficulty involved in manipulating appraisals to produce genuine emotional response in the laboratory." The alternative, as Roseman saw it, was to *simulate* emotional experience rather than examine the real phenomenon itself.

In Roseman's experimental procedure, the content of the presented vignettes was manipulated so that the situation as interpreted by the central character implied a range of different appraisals. The prediction was that the various combinations of appraisal dimensions depicted in the stories would lead the reader to make differential judgements about the protagonist's emotional state. This prediction was substantially confirmed.

For example, if the protagonist of the story was described as getting something she wanted deservedly as a result of her own actions, she was likely to be rated by the reader as experiencing the emotion of pride. If, on the other hand, the vignette portrayed a situation where the central character failed to get something she wanted and deserved, and someone else was to blame, she was judged to be experiencing anger more intensely than any other emotion. Thus, the description of different outcomes and different evaluations of these outcomes was interpreted by participants as implying different emotional reactions.

What do these results tell us? On the surface, they show that people think that different emotions are related to different appraisals of environmental contingencies, or, in other words, that there is a consensual implicit theory linking emotions with the ways situations are evaluated. This in itself would be an uncontroversial and quite useful finding. It would suggest, for example, that Roseman's theory of the dimensions of appraisal and their relationship to emotional experience corresponds quite well to some of our everyday understandings about how emotion works (or at least how it works in this kind of narrative vignette).

But Roseman goes somewhat further than this in his discussion of the results. Rather than limiting his conclusions to emotional representations (cf. Russell, 1987), he suggests that the study provides data directly relevant to the issue of how ongoing emotions are actually determined by different appraisal patterns. Although Roseman admits that the experiment provides a simulation of emotion rather than manipulating emotion directly, he interprets the obtained connections between linguistic representations of situations and linguistic representations of emotional reactions as evidence of a causal relationship between the corresponding real-world, real-time phenomena.

Roseman is perfectly explicit about this. He claims that (1991, pp. 196–197):

> Although it is possible, there is no particular reason to believe that subjects would in fact respond differently from what is indicated by these data if they were actually in the vignette situations. For example, is there any reason to believe that subjects would not respond with joy if they got the grade they wanted in an exam, with sadness if they did not, or with anger if they blamed the teacher for low grades?

Well, perhaps not. However, real life does not usually come precoded into neatly packaged verbal formulas such as getting the grade you want in an exam. By starting from a specific representation of the emotional situation and the protagonist's evaluation of the personal significance of this situation, Roseman evades the issue of how real-time situations are dynamically encoded in ongoing emotional experience. Moreover, his implication that subjects could actually be "in the vignette situations" reflects an unsupported assumption that the version of social reality presented in a conventional narrative can serve as a workable representation of all the factors that are functionally relevant to the real-time causation of emotion.

Smith and Lazarus' "Directed Imagery" Procedure

The assumed equivalence between linquistic representations of emotional events and the real-time processes themselves is taken one stage further in another recent study by Smith and Lazarus (this issue). This study followed a similar procedure to Roseman's except that the presented stories were written in the second rather than the third person, and participants were asked to project themselves into the described situation then rate their own emotional reactions, rather than those of the story's fictional protagonist. Thus, Smith and Lazarus changed the kind of simulation procedure used by Roseman into a "directed imagery task", where participants were supposed to make their own appraisals in accordance with the information contained in the story, and experience genuine emotional reactions as a consequence.

Like Roseman, Smith and Lazarus found that emotion ratings (in this case, self-reports) were related to the appraisal structure of the vignettes. In addition, Smith and Lazarus conducted regression analyses to determine the impact of the depicted situation on appraisal, and of rated appraisal on reported emotion. In general, the different stories differentially affected appraisal ratings, and appraisal ratings correlated with emotion scores in accordance with the authors' predictions.

There are two possible ways of interpreting Smith and Lazarus's results. First, it may be that participants genuinely immersed themselves in the story and experienced the described situation first-hand, this experience in turn leading to the appropriate emotional reactions. We think that this is unlikely given the brevity of the stories and the fact that participants' reading of the passages was interrupted half-way through by the task of completing 83 rating scales, but it is still conceivable. In this case, the study proves that you can manipulate emotions using different verbally defined situations together with different verbally defined evaluations of these situations. It does not tell us, of course, that this is how emotional meanings are constructed from the flow of information in real life, because we have no evidence that ongoing episodes ever get formulated into the kind of language used in these narratives. Even if we accept that actual emotion is produced as a function of the text, the study cannot prove that this emotion is mediated by the manipulated appraisals. The story content may have had a more direct influence on emotion which in turn mediated the effect on appraisal ratings. We still have the familiar problem of untangling the direction of causality, path analyses notwithstanding.

A final limitation of these results, according to this first interpretation, is that we do not know how far they can be generalised. Even if the manipulation of appraisal via presentation of vignettes mediated the actual experience of differential emotions in Smith and Lazarus' experiment, this in itself does not establish that this is the *only* way the particular emotions are caused in real life. However seriously we take the findings, they do not rule out other possible causal pathways leading to these particular emotions.

The second way of interpeting Smith and Lazarus' results is to assume that participants performed the experimental task without getting emotionally involved in the stories and completed the rating task by making inferences about the kind of emotions that they thought the authors of the passages intended to convey. In this case, Smith and Lazarus' procedure provides a close parallel of Roseman's study and their results may similarly reflect the content of participants' implicit theories rather than the structure of ongoing emotional experience.

Smith and Lazarus argue that even if this second more limited interpretation is the correct one, their findings would still provide indirect evidence about the causal relations between actual appraisals and emotions, as long as the additional assumption is made that participants' ideas about emotion in fact correspond with reality: "At minimum we have demonstrated that our subjects' theories of emotion contain elaborate, specific, and shared hypotheses concerning the emotional consequences of specific appraisals. Because . . . implicit theories are largely based on personal experience and tend to mirror that experience accurately, these hypotheses are likely to have considerable validity."

One point to be made about this argument is that there is no good or direct empirical evidence that implicit theories of emotion actually are accurate. Indeed, if this assumption of accuracy is a safe one, it seems odd that researchers should go to such lengths to create sophisticated methodologies for studying emotions, when they could obtain an equally good answer to the empirical questions simply by asking people what they think are the causes of different emotions!

But what would this accuracy mean in practice, anyway? Participants in Smith and Lazarus' study were presented with descriptions of people in certain situations and asked to make judgements about their evaluative and emotional experience. The only kind of accuracy that could be directly relevant to the interpretation of the results would reflect the connection between the predescribed situational and appraisal information on the one hand, and the representations of emotion and appraisal as made by respondents on presupplied rating scales, on the other. Even if we were willing to admit that participants possessed accurate knowledge about this kind of relationship, this would not imply that the situation as described in the vignettes corresponded to what goes on in everyday real life, nor that participants' characterisations of appraisals and emotions on the rating scales veridically represented the way emotion would be produced if the situation were in real time.

In other words, if we decide that Smith and Lazarus' results reflect implicit theories rather than ongoing emotions, then three basic assumptions are needed before the findings can be generalised to real-world appraisal-emotion linkages. These assumptions all relate to the way appraisal and emotion are represented, both in stories and in the heads of experimental participants. First, we need to assume that the structure of ongoing life is adequately represented in the vignettes, or, in other words, that the representations contained in the texts of the situation and the evaluation of the situation correspond to ongoing situations and ongoing evaluations. Secondly, we must suppose that participants have fairly accurate knowledge about how these represented situations typically lead to conventionally described emotional reactions. Finally, we have to make the assumption that the various rating scales presupplied by the experimenters validly capture the essence of real-life ongoing appraisals and emotions (Parkinson & Manstead, 1992).

If any of these assumptions turns out to be false or incomplete, then the conclusions that can be drawn from Smith and Lazarus' findings must be correspondingly limited. For example, even if we know from the results that when the appraisal representation is present it will lead to an emotion representation, we still cannot be sure that such appraisal representations ever characterise our real-life emotional experiences. The laboratory situation might have no counterpart in our lives outside the laboratory. In short, the issue of how a real-life situation leads to an actual lived experience of emotion is not directly addressed by the vignette approach. The putative representations may play no role whatsoever in this real-world process.

Of course, it is entirely possible that there are situations when life is interpreted in an analogous way to that represented in the vignettes, but it also seems highly likely that there are other occasions when these representations provide incomplete, inaccurate, and distorted versions of what really goes on when someone gets emotional.

The Experimental Participant's View of the Vignette Procedure

To get a better idea of how participants might react to the vignette methodology, it is worth examining more closely the details of Smith and Lazarus' procedure, and imagining yourself in the position of the subject.

Take a single vignette: The "Cancer" scenario referred to at the beginning of the present paper. In one version of this narrative, Smith and Lazarus try to produce the pattern of appraisal theoretically associated with sadness. In the first part of the story, you are asked as a participant to imagine that a favourite relative is in hospital with lung cancer. This is a situation that is supposed to conflict with your desires as the protagonist of the story (reflecting your primary appraisal of "motivational incongruence"), and this conflict is also intended to be personally significant to you ("motivational relevance"). Such a situation should predictably lead to a negative emotional reaction.

The final part of the vignette contains the manipulation of appraisals relevant to "loss/helplessness", the "core relational theme" that is supposed to be the direct and most proximal cause of the emotion of sadness. Imagine yourself in the following situation:

> For the first time, you're really sure that your relative is going to die, and that there's nothing you or the doctors can do about it. You realise that you'll never again be able to go to this person with your problems, or share the enjoyable times you used to have with this relative. This is a great personal loss.

Now your appraisal components are assessed. You are asked to answer the following questions "as you think you would if you were actually experiencing the situation"; "How much do you care about what is happening in this situation?"; "Think about what you didn't want in this situation. To what extent were these undesirable elements present in the situation?"; "How certain were you that you would, or would not, be able to deal emotionally with what was happening in the situation however it turned out?" Next come some items related to the "core relational themes" or molar combinations of appraisal components. To what extent do the following statements describe the way you are thinking about the situation?: "I feel a sense of loss"; "Something I cared about is gone"; "Something important to me has been destroyed"; "I feel helpless"; "This situation is hopeless"; and so on.

Finally, you are asked to indicate how you feel. To what extent do the following adjectives describe your emotional experience: Sad? Sorrowful? Downhearted?

To the extent that you endorse items suggesting that you construe this situation as one of irrevocable loss, and that you are sad, your ratings are interpreted by the investigators as providing direct support for the causal role of specific appraisals in the generation of this emotion. Even if you did not completely immerse yourself in the narrative, the authors argue that the correlation of appraisal and emotion ratings demonstrates that your "theories of emotion contain elaborate, specific . . . hypotheses concerning the emotional consequences of specific appraisals".

Of course, in this description of the Smith and Lazarus procedure, we have selected a single version of one of four stories and selected some of the more obviously relevant items out of a much larger battery of rating scales, but nonetheless we think the central point is clear. Smith and Lazarus' "directed imagery" task seems to us to assess participants' ability to make sense of stylised depictions of emotional episodes, and the relationships between their appraisal and emotion ratings may be almost completely determined by the semantic similarity between the various items. For example, we can see little substantive difference in meaning between agreeing with the statement "I feel a sense of loss" (appraisal or "core relational theme") and endorsement of the adjective "down-hearted" (emotion). Furthermore, when the story has ended with the sentence "this is a great personal loss", it is not difficult to predict how the reader will respond to both of these rating scales.

If you are asked to imagine yourself in a story where someone close to you is dying, it does not require much emotional sophistication to reach the assumption that you are intended to feel sad. Similarly, you are also likely to realise that you are not supposed to like what is happening in the story, that it is meant to be important to you, and that you are going to have trouble dealing with the emotional consequences. These effects will be further reinforced when the story uses exactly this kind of language to describe the episode in the first place. A straightforward explanation of all these effects, however complicated the pattern of correlations might seem, is that you know what the conventional depiction of sadness in a narrative is like: You have seen enough movies and read enough stories, you have heard enough people talking, to be sufficiently socially competent to recognise an emotion stereotype when you are presented with one.

But the fact that you use certain implicit theories about emotion when making sense of stories does not necessarily imply that the theories correspond to what actually happens when you or other people get emotional in the real world. Nor do the connections established between reported appraisals and reported emotions mean that your real-time appraisals always precede your experience of the related emotion in an ongoing transaction.

Of course, it is perfectly possible that part of our understanding of the way stories work derives from our experience with real-life situations, and no one would want to argue that reactions to narratives can tell us nothing about everyday psychological function. However, we do want to suggest that the version of reality provided in stories is always a particular formulation which concentrates on certain elements at the expense of others. The aspects that are emphasised in stories do not always necessarily correspond to the factors that are most causally relevant in real life.

In this section, we have tried to demonstrate the limits on the inferences that can be drawn from vignette studies of appraisal and emotion. Most of the interpretational difficulties of these experiments relate to their procedure of substituting a linguistic text for a real-time encounter between the person and the environment. The fact that appraisal researchers routinely substitute stories for real life suggests that they may consider the two to be in some sense functionally equivalent in the emotion generation process, or at least that they believe there is sufficient correspondence between narrative representations and real-life emotional episodes for the former to provide a scientifically useful analogue of the latter.

Rather than emphasising the similarities between stories and real life, it might be worthwhile first to consider the differences between them. If these differences turn out to be at all important with respect to emotional phenomena, it would seem reasonable to temper our assumptions about the mediation of emotion by cognitive appraisal and about the accuracy of emotional representations. In the next section, we focus on three central differences between stories and real life that we think have important implications for the interpretation of vignette studies of appraisal, and for the development of appraisal theory.

DIFFERENCES BETWEEN STORIES AND REAL LIFE

There are several obvious differences between written narratives and real-time experience of the world. Here are just a few of them.

A text provides limited information and details must be filled in or left out whereas life has all the current details readily available. Stories are expressed in words; life only partly so. The specific choice of category implied by the linguistic formulation of a story pushes interpretation in a certain direction, but you feel your own way through life. You can turn away from and stop reading a story, get more or less involved in it; not so with life which you are stuck in the thick of, and which does not stop happening if you pause for a moment. Stories can be taken at their own pace; life sets a pace of its own. A story has a beginning and an end as does life, but the time-scale is certainly different.

Life is directly involving whereas a story requires some cognitive participation from the reader: Limited information has to be fleshed out by imaginative construction, which is nevertheless constrained by the pre-interpreted structure of the text. There are occasions when this kind of cognitive participation is necessary in life but they are rarer than might be imagined, and may be over-represented in memory because they are registered more saliently than more "mindless" (Langer, 1978) or socially co-ordinated episodes.

Many of these differences between stories and real life are relevant to our interpretation of vignette studies of appraisal. However, in this paper, we will draw attention to just three apsects of the life-story analogy, because we believe that these have wider implications for the assessment of appraisal theory and of the traditional cognitive approach to experience. The first of these concerns the fact that stories provide a particular representation of reality.

Are Emotions always Mediated by Representations?

As argued earlier, certain basic assumptions are necessary before accepting that the appraisal-emotion relationships reported in Roseman's and Smith and Lazarus' studies adequately represent actual processes that might occur in our ongoing transactions with the real world. The most central of these presuppositions is that the structure provided by the particular kind of narrative representation contained in the experimental vignettes maps on to the actual structure of real-time emotional episodes in a meaningful way. If the informational and symbolic structure of these stories bore no relation to real life, then the processes that link story content to emotional judgement would have little relevance to real-time emotional processes. If, on the other hand, story structure provided a completely faithful representation of the texture of social reality as filtered through the individual's ongoing appraisal processes, then reactions to these emotional narratives would provide direct evidence about the actual phenomena of appraisal and emotion. Of course, the truth lies somewhere between these two extremes.

One reason why some appraisal researchers are willing to use a story as a proxy for real life is that they believe that emotional reactions to the world are typically mediated by representational processes anyway (specifically representations based on knowledge, and representations relating to appraisal) and they may assume that stories can conjure up these representations in a similar way to ongoing transactions with the world. For example, Smith and Lazarus (this issue) argue as follows: "We consider a well-developed mental representation of one's circumstances to be a necessary . . . condition of emotion". This might be regarded as a reasonable assumption but it is worth considering more closely.

Representations are thought to be necessary mediators of emotion mainly because life situations are considered to be inherently ambiguous to the actors caught up inside them, who must therefore perform some cognitive analysis in order to make sense of things. For example, Lazarus and Folkman (1984, p. 258) argue that "to understand the way the distal social environment, which is without personal significance for the individual, affects the person requires understanding its proximal psychological meaning, which is determined through cognitive appraisal". Indeed, it is hard to argue with the fact that in many circumstances the way people interpret their surroundings shapes their response to them. For example, the emotional sense that can be made out of a silent film depicting an unfamiliar tribal ritual may depend upon the kind of interpretative framework that is used by the viewer (Lazarus & Alfert, 1964). This level of ambiguity is probably rather unusual in real life, however, and the role of sense-making activity lessens with the increasing specificity of the information directly provided by the dynamic structure of the social and physical environment (Baron, 1988; Gibson, 1979; Parkinson & Manstead, 1992). To the extent that the meaningful real-time organisation of experience can be directly apprehended by the perceiver, there is little necessity for supplementary disambiguating representational processes. In short, although representations may sometimes play a part in the causation of emotion, there is no reason to suppose that they *always* do so.

Of course, it may be that even if there is adequate structure in the dynamic stimulus array to specify the emotional meaning of the situation, this information still needs to activate an internal representation (or some other mental process) before any intrapsychic emotion can be produced. In this case, the role of the cognitive mechanism in the generation of the emotion is fairly trivial but still necessary. In any case, our point is not that cognitive mediation is not relevant, only that its importance is often overemphasised.

The theoretical emphasis on cognitive mediational processes has consequences both for methodological decisions about how to investigate emotion, and for practical applications for emotion theory. In terms of methodology, the cognitive emphasis has reinforced the strategy of investigating emotion in terms of an individual's reaction to impoverished emotional stimuli, such as still pictures, verbal texts, or video clips, rather than looking at how emotion arises in the participative multi-media presentation that makes up everyday social life. As far as practical applications go, the emphasis on cognitive mediation of emotion has sometimes encouraged those who wish to modify "maladaptive" emotional reactions to intervene at the level of information-processing rather than directly dealing with the emotional situation. For example, in cognitive therapy for depression (Beck, Rush, Shaw, & Emery, 1979), the focus is on changing the client's "faulty thinking", instead of confronting real problems in the depressive's social relationships (Coyne, 1982, and see later). Changing the emphasis of appraisal theory from intrapsychic to interactional processes might facilitate the development of alternative therapeutic strategies for emotional problems.

In this section so far we have raised the question of whether emotion is always mediated by representational processes. An additional relevant issue concerns the specific form that any mediational representational process is supposed to take, and the particular nature of representation that it might draw upon. Vignette research apparently rests on the assumption that certain textual representations that follow a traditional narrative formula correspond to, or are compatible with, the kinds of personal representations constructed by people in their everyday lives. Although we are prepared to agree that emotion is at least sometimes dependent on repesentations, we do not believe that the mediating representations are always of this nature. Below, we will have more to say about the restricted model of the person implicit in the conventional individualistic narrative tradition. For now, it should suffice to observe that although people might often rely on conventional cultural representations to make sense of their experience, in those times, for example, when life seems most like soap opera, we cannot assume that these are the only forms of representations that are relevant.

Even if we accept that representations mediate emotional experience and that the vignettes used by appraisal researchers accurately reflect people's real-time representations of real-life episodes, there still remains the question of how the original information gets structured into the internally represented narrative, a question sidestepped in vignette studies where participants are provided with precoded representations. Given the considerable overlap in semantic content between the items used to rate emotion and appraisal in these experiments (see earlier), we might be tempted to say that once we have got as far as explaining the "core relational theme", or "proximal cause" of emotion (Lazarus, 1991), there is little more explaining to be done. If people have reached the point when they could say accurately to themselves things like "this is a great personal loss" with the necessary degree of conviction, it would be difficult to argue that they are not already experiencing the emotion of sadness.

In the internal representation view, then, the models derived from vignette research may be accurate but incomplete because they still need to specify how incoming information gets organised into appraisal dimensions. To the extent that structure is already provided by the unfolding patterns of information directly available from the social and physical environment, the role of cognitive mediation in the apprehension of emotional meaning is correspondingly reduced.

The Emotional Subject: Detached Observer or Involved Participant?

A second important difference between stories and real life from the point of view of the theory of emotion concerns the relative distance imposed between the position of the individual and the place where the action is. People can get involved in a story they are reading, but this can never approach their level of direct involvement with an ongoing emotional episode. This is not simply a question of emotional intensity. Some people, for example, are far more inclined to weep when they are reading a novel or watching a movie than as a result of everday life experiences. The difference is that people are right "in the thick of things" in real life, whereas they are always detached or detachable from stories they read. You can always put a book down, or skip a few pages. No directly comparable strategies are available for dealing with real-time emotional experience.

Part of this difference in involvement relates to the fact that life is not a fixed text apart from the actors who play out their roles within it. One of the attractions of stories for some people is that they are nonreactive. Whatever your attitude to them, the words, sentences, and paragraphs printed on the pages stay the same. In social life, people are continually responding to your actions and reactions, and your interactions and transactions, by definition, can never carry on independently of other people. Not only social reality itself, but also the various representations of it that arise in our ongoing relationships with other people, are continually negotiated and renegotiated achievements. There is no way of stopping the process of real life, of stepping aside as a neutral observer. There may be social occasions in which you might wish to be invisible, but this is never a realistic option, and even your disappearance would attract comment, approval or censure.

Now this intersubjective nature of real-time social experience may be seen as a complicating problem for the cognitive methodologist. It might be seen as a necessary move to make the simplifying assumption that individuals can be abstracted in some meaningful way from their social context. This abstraction is precisely what is achieved by casting research participants as readers of stories rather than actors in the improvised drama that is real life.

What difference does this kind of detachment make? The kind of involvement implied in reading a story is an imaginative involvement based on mental activity, which is always guided by the fixed structure of the story. Involvement in life often reflects physical as well as mental participation, and the immediate consequences of each of the individual's acts feed back to influence the next stage of the ongoing interpersonal process. Readers of stories follow a preset course of action and reaction: The protagonist discovers that a relative is seriously ill, for example, and knows there is nothing that can be done about it. The scenario and the protagonist's movements within it are purely abstract, not part of the embodied and unfolding experience of the reader. It is not an option for readers to give physical expression to emotional responses which might elicit real sympathy from people who are close to them and share the same emotional concerns, for example. After all, it is only a story, there is no point in trying to change things, and it does not *really* matter anyway. There is nothing the reader can do cognitively, emotionally, or physically that could possibly have any impact on the structure of the interpersonal situation.

So the vignette methodology tends to exclude from consideration two sets of factors relating to the actor's participation in real-time episodes. The first is the interactive role of the physical body in emotion (e.g. Nieuwenhuyse, Offenberg, & Frijda, 1987), and the second is the dynamic presentation of environmental and social feedback. With respect to the first factor, it is clear that many of our attitudes to the world are directly expressed via the medium of the body (Radley, 1988). These physical expressions of attitudes may be picked up by others (and by ourselves) in emotional interactions and contribute to the developing mutual definition of the situation in emotional terms. To the extent that these bodily expressions are not direct reflections of cognitive appraisals, they may have some independent impact on emotion (e.g. Zillmann, 1978). With respect to the second factor, it is clear that by abstracting the individual from the environment, vignette studies give a static rather than dynamic account of the emotion process.

By excluding bodily and dynamic factors, vignette studies correspondingly overestimate the necessity for internal representational processes in mediating emotion. The information normally available from bodily feedback and from the situation as it unfolds in real time instead has to be contained in the vignettes, the participant's head, or both. Ratings of appraisal and emotion made in these experiments may either depend on the fact that participants' involvement in the stories is based on an act of imagination, or alternatively may derive more directly from the informational content of the text. In either case, the relations obtained between appraisal and emotion ratings reflect the reader's cognitive participation in the structure of the text. There is no reason to suppose that this kind or this level of cognitive participation always accompanies emotion in real life.

To what extent are the implicit assumptions of the vignette methodology also held by appraisal theorists? Lazarus (1991) explicitly acknowledges that appraisals are based on ongoing and embodied transactions between the person and situation, and that they adjust moment by moment to the unfolding encounter. Clearly, the theoretically implied detachment of subject and object in the emotions process is less than that suggested by vignette methodology. Nevertheless, we think that in principle the same problem still applies in theory as it does in practice. According to Lazarus' appraisal theory, the emotional impact of an event is completely dependent on how it is appraised by the individual. Personal significance is always ultimately mediated by a relatively intricate intrapsychic process which translates the external situation into an internal reaction. In such a theory, then, the actor is conceptualised as being always at least one critical step away from the social world, and never close to direct contact with social reality. This assumption might be seen as making little difference in theory, but the fact that it supports certain empirical and therapeutic practices itself makes it worthy of our reconsideration.

Emotion Accounts in Monologue or Dialogue?

Our final criticism of the presuppositions of vignette methodology and their implicit life-story analogy concerns the specific form of narrative used in these studies. The stories read by participants in these studies all relate the experiences of a single narrator whose account of events is addressed to an unacknowledged reader. This is a conventional form of narrative, but it is important to realise that it presents a specific view of reality, and that there are alternative modes of story-telling which place the reader in a very different set of relations to the text (e.g. Hermans, Kempen, & van Loon, 1992; Shotter & Gergen, 1989). We have already argued that the vignette methodology casts the participant as a more or less detached observer of the depicted events. Our final point is that the narratives of appraisal present an account from a single voice in monologue, rather than putting this voice into contact with the related and contrasting dialogical positions that give it meaning and purpose.

Let us attempt to clarify this point: Every statement we make, whether it is spoken or written, is made in a certain context and from the point of view of a specific set of concerns which only make sense in relation to other positions. Our utterances always carry performative implications; they are produced for specific socially defined and conversationally determined purposes (Austin, 1962; Wittgenstein, 1953). This fact even applies to our supposedly objective descriptions of reality, or our denials that such descriptions are possible. The presentation of a "neutral" and "detached" account is always a move in an ongoing dialogue with actual or imagined other people (Billig, 1987).

Authors of fiction have attempted to convey this idea of messages as part of a wider social communicative context, by incorporating into their narratives alternative voices, surrogates of the reader, explicit admissions of unreliability by the narrator, and so on (e.g. Lodge, 1971). Emotional reactions to these less conventional texts would be harder to specify and determine, but at least they open up the possibility that the version of reality depicted in the conventional first-person narrative is hardly the whole story.

The representation of life offered by the appraisal narratives gives authority to a single voice providing what is intended to be a faithful portrayal of personal reality. Judgements of the emotion attached to this voice are bound to reflect its intact individuality and independence from the dialogue of real social life. The form of supposedly neutral representation that is contained in the appraisal narratives does not in fact reflect the kinds of dialogic representations that people make us of in their everyday interactions with other people. If our real-life emotional reactions are sometimes mediated by representations, they are surely quite different from those supplied by the "realistic" narrator of the stories presented in the vignette studies. They are representations with particular social functions that are mapped out in the dynamic structure of our interpersonal concerns.

To take an example from Roseman's (1991) study, let us consider the only section of a vignette that is presented verbatim by the author, namely "version 41 of the examination story" (p. 170) which relates how a female student fails a sociology test. Her evaluation of this event is implied in the description of her visit to the course instructor's office to collect the grade for the examination. Presumably a conversation of some kind has taken place in this office, but this assumed interpersonal episode is reported only in abstract and indirect terms (p. 170):

> When finals week was over, she went to Ms. Evans' office to pick up her exam. As it turned out she had gotten an F. Apparently the students' grasp of basic concepts had been relatively good. But Ms. Evans was being uncommonly strict about her grading. In fact, it seemed she had given all the members of her class low grades.

Note that this narrative is supposed to be an accurate simulation of what happens in real-life emotional episodes (see Roseman, 1991, pp. 196–197, quoted above), but if the subjects were actually in this vignette situation, they would have made their interpretations of the reasons for failing the exam partly as a function of their conversation and pre-existing relationship with Ms. Evans. The conclusion that Ms. Evans had "apparently been uncommonly strict with her grading" is not a straightforward descriptive representation of an internal monologue, but a particular kind of claim made in reaction to the position of a conversational opponent. The role played by this representation in the production of emotion might, for example, reflect the student's internal rehearsal of the things she would say and do to Ms. Evans, given the chance, and the way she planned to recount the episode to her friends in the bar that evening.

This is not a simple process of an internal categorisation and personal evaluation mediating emotion, but the continuing development of a whole interacting set of social relations. Rather than describing an individual cognitive appraisal that someone else was the causal agent for an illegitimate negative outcome, the statement quoted above functions pragmatically as a complaint about unfairness addressed towards a sympathetic audience, and already implies the way anger can be expressed rhetorically in conversation (even the angry intonation is suggested by the specific choice of words in the vignette). A student who is ready to describe the situation in such a way is more likely to be preparing a social justification for her angry attitude than characterising her cognitive appraisal processes that are about to lead to the emotion of anger.

Our general point here is that the real and imagined audience for the representation of any particular evaluation quite clearly makes a vital difference to our everyday emotional expression, both verbal and non-verbal (Fridlund, 1991). Vignette studies miss out on these interpersonal factors by placing appraisal squarely in the realm of internal soliloquised representations. This move of decontextualisation inevitably unbalances the theoretical model of emotion. In the vignettes, a univocal narrative representation is interposed between fictional situational causes of emotion and the reader's rating of the protagonist's reaction. In real life, the sense we make of things is a socially motivated sense which always already carries its own developing emotional content.

Again, in contrast to vignette research, appraisal theory often specifically acknowledges the transactional basis of emotional experience (e.g. Lazarus, 1991). However, the emotion itself is still always thought to be based finally on an individual appraisal of the transactional context. This focus has encouraged research into emotion that tends to treat individual and cognitive factors as central and primary, and social and relational factors as marginal and secondary. The only allowable role of dialogical factors in the causation of emotion, according to most versions of appraisal theory, depends on their being represented within an individual's cognitive system, and this process of representation could be activated just as easily in other non-social ways. Our argument (as developed below) is that social and dialogic factors are right at the heart of many emotional phenomena, and their exclusion implies an over-restricted view of what constitutes an emotional experience.

So far we have discussed the role of representation in emotion implied by vignette studies and, to a greater or lesser extent, appraisal theory itself. In the next sections, we will develop our alternative view of how representations of the situation and of emotion might function in everyday social life.

PRAGMATICS OF REPRESENTATION

According to most traditional views, one of the basic functions of representation (whether internal or external, cognitive or narrative) is to provide an accurate description, or at least a workable model, of reality. Adequacy of a representation is thought to depend on its degree of structural or practical correspondence with reality. Much of what we have said above has suggested that in many important ways, traditional narratives do not adequately correspond to the nature of everyday emotional episodes in real social life. In the present section, we want to move on from our consideration of the match between representation and reality to an examination of the way real representations actually function in ongoing social processes. In our view, representations, like emotions, in reality are always intimately embedded in an ongoing social context, and their function is rarely simply to describe the situation. They play a decisive pragmatic role in our ongoing social lives rather than existing in some separate abstract realm of mentation.

Considering first the external representations provided in vignette studies of appraisal: Rather than offering a neutral portrayal of an emotional event, these stories are formulated in a particular way based on a conventional narrative style, and give emphasis to certain aspects of the episode thought by the investigators to be relevant to appraisal and emotion. Correspondingly, participants' readings of these stories during the experiments probably depended on their assumed communicative context, and not only on their superficial descriptive content. For example, participants were fully aware that the stories were materials provided by the experimenters and constructed with a specific purpose, namely to manipulate particular emotions, or to help develop a scientific understanding of how emotion works. It would be naïve to assume that the pragmatic force of these narrative communications had no impact on the semantic meaning that was derived from them.

In addition, participants' ratings of their appraisals and emotions were themselves communicative acts with the experimenter as intended recipient. It seems likely that in a very real sense participants did not simply tell the investigator what they knew or what they felt, but rather reported what they thought was required of them, presenting their experience in a way that they believed was appropriate to this particular social situation. If this conclusion is correct, then it may well be that the kinds of representations used by participants when making their ratings of emotion in these vignette studies were quite different to those they might employ in their everyday formulations of emotional scenarios. The former representations might derive, for example, from participants' conventionalised accounting repertoires for explaining emotions in retrospect, from their cognitive strategies for completing comprehension exercises on emotional narratives, or even from their well-practised routines for providing socially relevant replies in conversations with strangers.

Turning finally to the ways people make representations of their own experience in their everyday encounters with social and physical reality, we believe that here too the processes of categorisation, interpretation, and evaluation are critically shaped by the interpersonal context. In our view, the cognitive representations implicated in everyday emotional experiences can also be analysed in socially pragmatic terms, and often serve functions other than simple description. To be more specific, we do not think that real-life emotional appraisals typically draw upon abstract descriptive categories of person-environment transactions based on dimensions relating to agency, unexpectedness, future expectancy, and the like, but rather that they derive from rhetorical characterisation of the current situations which are specifically formulated with regard to particular real or imagined audiences.

For example, when you say that you blame yourself for something bad that has happened, you are not usually describing a cognitive appraisal that took place and caused you to feel guilty. Rather you are making a plea that you would like someone to excuse you for your actions. This plea is symptomatic of the emotion of guilt rather than being its determinant: It expresses an aspect of the social relationship that produced the emotion. Interestingly, you do not even need to believe that you are actually responsible for the bad event to feel guilty about it (see Frijda, this issue). All that is necessary is that you should be involved in a relationship with a person from whom you desire some kind of absolution.

Although we certainly do make statements in everyday conversation that seem to refer to appraisals, the representations underlying these statements are not necessarily descriptive but may serve other pragmatic and rhetorical functions. Furthermore, the relation of these representations to our emotions is not a simple causal one. In many cases, the characterisations of ourselves and the situation implied by appraisal statements are part of the content of an already developed emotional position.

According to the appraisal account suggested by vignette studies, emotion is a function of the way the person-environment transaction is represented by the individual to him- or herself. In our alternative view, emotion often depends upon the way the ongoing interpersonal situation is characterised by interactants to each other in mutual negotiation. In conventional understanding, the prototypical emotional phenomenon is an internal passive reaction to an appraised momentary event. However, we do not think this is the only kind of emotional episode worthy of our psychological attention. Other possible kinds of emotions emerge more gradually over time as a function of our developing relationships with other people. On these occasions, changes in emotion may reflect evolving rhetorical positions in an ongoing dialogue, and may be largely, if not completely definable in relation to the contrasting or corresponding positions of relevant others. Sometimes, we even get emotional deliberately in order to achieve our interpersonal aims. Most current versions of appraisal theory would have problems accounting for this kind of strategic use of emotion in social interaction.

In our view, the kinds of representations implicated in ongoing emotional episodes are not abstract intrapsychic entities but support conversational moves: Representations made by someone to someone else. The representations of emotion employed by participants in vignette studies, according to this argument, are unlikely to be equivalent to all the alternative representations that might sometimes underlie emotions in everday life.

COGNITIVE APPRAISAL IN SOCIAL CONTEXT

Appraisal theory suggests that the way individuals interpret and categorise events determines the strength and nature of their emotional reactions. In this account, social factors are allowed to enter into the causal process at a number of stages, but only have an influence on emotion to the extent that they shape personal appraisals. For example, the precipitating event might be something someone else is doing, someone else's opinions might influence the way one interprets an event, someone may be available to help deal with the situation and so on, but the only effects of these social factors on emotion depend on their consequences for appraisal.

This conventional narrative of emotion seems sensible and complete because it fits perfectly with prevailing Anglo-American cultural presuppositions about personal responsibility and the primacy of the individual (Sampson, 1977) which are also reflected in the conventional form of first-person narrative stories. Because people in Western society can be called to account for their actions (and emotions), conventional discourse tends to emphasise personal explanations. This is exactly the reason why it is more difficult to make sense of alternative accounts. In this section, we want to raise the question whether such an individualistic narrative of emotion can ever tell the whole story.

As an illustration of how social factors can enter into the determination of emotional episodes, we will discuss Coyne's (1976) model of depression. Our presentation of this theory is not intended to provide an *alternative* to the appraisal account, but instead to show how appraisal processes derive their function and meaning from the evolving social situation.

Coyne argued that a single-minded focus on cognitive factors in the causation of depression has led to a de-emphasis of the processes of social feedback which maintain and exacerbate the negative reactions over the course of a depressive episode (Coyne, 1982). Implicit in his sophisticated analysis is the view that depression is not simply an affective reaction but a mode of communication about the sufferer's present life-situation, and a call for help. We think that this kind of performative content of emotional behaviour is similarly characteristic of many other examples of the class of phenomena we usually refer to as emotions. Emotions can be communicative acts that have a meaning in the wider social context rather than simply reactions that come over individuals (cf. Averill, 1983).

Coyne's analysis interprets depressive symptoms as messages sent out to other people, asking for reassurance about the person's continuing importance to these people. Unfortunately, the fact that any reassurance is produced only on demand undermines its value to the person who has requested it.

The starting point for depression, in Coyne's account, is some kind of threat to the person's social standing. The victim at first responds to this threat with withdrawal and expressions of helplessness, communicative acts which serve the function of getting others to take control of any interaction with the depressed person. Help is requested by the depressed person and may be supplied by significant others.

The depressed person is now faced with two conflicting ways of characterising the support offered by other people. This support might reflect their continuing concern for the depressive, or it could be a direct response to the received request for help. Given that a threat to identity is what has precipitated the response in the first place, and reassurance is exactly what is required, it is vital for the depressive to determine which of these alternative interpretations is the more appropriate one. Unfortunately, the only way of obtaining clarification of the apparent messages of support is to renew the call for help by producing more depressive symptoms.

For the people close to the depressive who have been offering support, this continued exhibiting of symptoms by the depressive is hard to understand. They begin to suffer a kind of compassion fatigue and although they will tend to respond with sympathy because of a sense of duty and guilt, this sympathy and support will be given with increasing reluctance, which will be manifest in certain aspects of communication such as their nonverbal behaviour. In other words, their supportive messages will arrive mixed with other qualifying messages. Of course, this means that the message received is now even more ambiguous than before. Thus an exacerbating spiral of rejection and loss of support leading to more complaints and more rejection is established.

In Coyne's view, the interactive social behaviour of depressives leads to increasing rejection from others which those others will themselves explicitly deny. If this is true, the supposedly distorted thought processes of the depressive focused on by cognitive therapists (e.g. Abramson, Seligman, & Teasdale, 1978; Beck et al., 1979) may actually reflect relatively realistic doubts about relationships with others. These other people may say they care about the depressive, but the way they express this care is bound to arouse legitimate suspicions.

If Coyne's analysis is correct, cognitive accounts of depression can never give a complete picture of how the emotional syndrome is caused, nor how best to deal with it. Many of the crucial variables only become apparent when looking at the interactions between people in the developing social situation. It may be that part of the impact of these developing interactions on the depressive's emotional reaction depends on the way they are appraised, but this is only a small part of the story, and not one that necessarily makes an important difference to how emotional sense is created in this situation.

The advantage of Coyne's model of depression from the present point of view is that it allows us to examine emotions (and appraisals) as part of a *dialogue* between the individual and relevant others, rather than as private, internal states which may or may not be expressed by the individual. We think that this is a productive approach to the study of emotion, and one that is implicitly discouraged by many versions of appraisal theory.

A RESEARCH STRATEGY FOR EMOTION

In this paper we have criticised one research strategy adopted by appraisal theorists in their attempt to provide an account of how emotion is caused. We believe that many of our criticisms of the vignette approach also apply to a greater or lesser extent to the other methodologies that have been used to investigate the role of appraisal in emotion (see Parkinson & Manstead, 1992, for a related critique for retrospective and rating-scale studies). Their common limitation, in our view, is that they focus primarily on individual representational processes rather than on how emotion emerges in real-time social interactions.

So what are our alternatives to appraisal research as it is presently conducted? One of the reasons why it is more difficult in this case to offer constructive suggestions than it is to criticise is that appraisal research works from an established tradition, whereas alternative methodologies are less developed, untried, and untested. Despite this limitation, we would still like to make a few preliminary recommendations about future research directions.

Our first suggestion is that representations of emotion should be studied in their own right rather than being used as a means of getting at real-time emotional experience. There is no substitute, in this regard, for collecting naturally occurring instances of emotional talk which may then be analysed with respect to content and function (e.g. Potter & Wetherell, 1987). It is necessary to investigate representations made for a range of purposes in a variety of contexts before we can make proper sense of the performative use of emotional language. There is little point in trying to elicit neutral and decontextualised implicit theories of emotion from respondents. Some social stake is always involved in the version of reality that is presented. It is best, therefore, to take it for granted that emotional talk serves communicative functions other than simple description (Bedford, 1957). Consideration of the different uses to which the relevant language is put will provide us with valuable information about how emotional concepts are used in everyday conversation (e.g. Parkinson, 1991). Secondly, it will allow us to consider how well these particular functions map on to the requirements of theory construction. Until we understand how emotional language functions in everyday social life, we will have little hope of making sense of the way people make their self- and other-ratings of emotion and appraisal in psychological experiments.

The second methodological proposal is an obvious one given much of what we have said earlier: It is that we need to study emotions in their real-life social context. One possible step in this direction would be to conduct research on people who are already in established emotional relationships and investigate how they behave together and describe their emotions interpersonally. We are thinking, for example, of studies of interaction during relationship counselling, where verbal and nonverbal actions are recorded and subsequently provide the basis for further in-depth interviews, in which the interviewees aid in the experimenter's interpretation of the encounter. Given our distrust of the single-minded narrative account of emotion, it would be of obvious interest to compare the formulations of the encounter produced by each of the interactants independently and that produced consensually as a function of negotiation of emotional meaning. Of course, the discussion of emotional episodes is likely to lead to emotion itself. Thus it may be possible to investigate emotional representation and emotional experience in the same interpersonal situation. If the sense of emotion derives from the unfolding social context as we have suggested, then this is the place to look for it. The strategic role of emotional talk and expression might be investigated in terms of how it functions in an ongoing dialogue. Again, people's interpretations of these functions and their reports of intentions are also clearly of relevance here.

Our final research suggestion is that we should pay attention to the dynamic structure of emotional episodes over time (e.g. Frijda, Mesquita, Sonnemans, & Van Goozen, 1991). Rather than measuring emotion and appraisal in one shot, it would be interesting to examine how the relationship between these variables develops over the course of a particular encounter, collecting data before, during, and after a specific emotional incident, for example. The use of often-repeated measures in short-term longitudinal research may be one way of getting closer to the real-time micro-structure of ongoing emotional experience (e.g. Epstein, 1983; Williams et al., 1991). Rather than focusing on the instant at which an appraisal triggers an emotion, it would be useful to look at how the complete emotional episode unfolds over time, looking at as many aspects of the interpersonal actions and reactions as possible.

None of these options is easy, and all require the careful development of appropriate methodologies, but we believe that the necessary effort would be worthwhile.

SUMMARY AND CONCLUSION

Most appraisal research does not directly address real-life emotional phenomena but instead focuses on the way people describe and represent their emotions. Even if emotions themselves are not always cognitively determined, it is likely that these representations and formulations of emotion often are. The question that remains is how much these representations bear on real-life emotion rather than being a specific consequence of the cognitive mode of exploration and analysis. The vignette approach translates the real-time multileveled emotional episode into a verbal text to be decoded and assumes that individuals carry out this same translation whenever they get emotional.

In this paper we have argued that the limitations of vignette methodology reflect more general conceptual problems with certain cognitive appraisal theories of emotion (and by implication, many cognitive approaches to other psychological phenomena). The central assumption of traditional cognitivism that personal meanings are mediated by internal representational processes legitimises the use of representations of emotions rather than emotions themselves in research, and the results of this research are in turn seen as providing further support for a cognitive account of emotion. The theory and the methodology are mutually reinforcing in a closed circle of reasoning. What we have tried to do in the present paper is to break this circle.

Manuscript received 1 March 1992
Revised manuscript received 26 July 1993

REFERENCES

Abramson, L.Y., Seligman, M.E.P., & Teasdale, J.D. (1978). Learned helplessness in humans: Critique and reformulation. *Journal of Abnormal Psychology*, *87*, 49–74.

Austin, J.L. (1962). *How to do things with words*. Oxford University Press.

Averill, J.R. (1983). *Anger and aggression*. New York: Springer.

Baron, R.M. (1988). An ecological framework for establishing a dual-mode theory of social knowing. In D. Bar-Tal & A.W. Kruglanski (Eds), *The social psychology of knowledge*. Cambridge University Press, pp. 48–82.

Beck, A.T., Rush, A.J., Shaw, B.F., & Emery, G. (1979). *Cognitive therapy of depression*. New York: Guilford Press.

Bedford, E. (1957). Emotions. *Proceedings of the Aristotelian Society*, *57*, 281–304.

Billig, M. (1987). *Arguing and thinking: A rhetorical approach to social psychology*. Cambridge University Press.

Coyne, J.C. (1976). Toward an interactional description of depression. *Psychiatry*, *39*, 28–40.

Coyne, J.C. (1982). A critique of cognitions as causal entities with particular reference to depression. *Cognitive Therapy and Research*, *6*, 3–13.

Coyne, J.C. & Lazarus, R.S. (1980). Cognitive style, stress perception, and coping. In I.L. Kutash & L.B. Schlesinger (Eds), *Handbook on stress and anxiety*. San Francisco: Jossey-Bass, pp. 144–158.

Epstein, S. (1983). A research paradigm for the study of personality and emotions. In M.M. Page (Ed.), *Nebraska Symposium on Motivation 1982: Personality—Current theory and research*. Lincoln: University of Nebraska Press, pp. 91–154.

Fridlund, A.J. (1991). Sociality of solitary smiling: Potentiation by an implicit audience. *Journal of Personality and Social Psychology*, *60*, 229–240.

Frijda, N.H. (this issue). The place of appraisal in emotion. *Cognition and Emotion*.

Frijda, N.H., Mesquita, B., Sonnemans, J., & Van Goozen, S. (1991). The duration of affective phenomena or emotions, sentiments, and passions. In K.T. Strongman (Ed.), *International review of studies on emotion*, Vol. 1. Chichester: Wiley, pp. 187–225.

Gibson, J.J. (1979). *The ecological approach to visual perception*. Boston, MA: Houghton Mifflin.

Hermans, H.J.M., Kempen, H.J.G., & van Loon, R.J.P. (1992). The dialogical self: Beyond individualism and rationalism. *American Psychologist*, *47*, 23–33.

Langer, E. (1978). Rethinking the role of thought in social interaction. In J.H. Harvey, W.J. Ickes, & R.F. Kidd (Eds), *New directions in attribution research*, Vol. 2. Hillsdale, NJ: Lawrence Erlbaum Associates Inc, pp. 35–58.

Lazarus, R.S. (1991). *Emotion and adaptation*. Oxford University Press.

Lazarus, R.S. & Alfert, E. (1964). Short circuiting of threat by experimentally altering cognitive appraisal. *Journal of Abnormal and Social Psychology*, *69*, 195–205.

Lazarus, R.S. & Folkman, S. (1984). *Stress, appraisal, and coping*. New York: Springer.

Lazarus, R.S. & Smith, C.A. (1988). Knowledge and appraisal in the cognition-emotion relationship. *Cognition and Emotion*, *2*, 281–300.

Leventhal, H. (1984). A perceptual-motor theory of emotion. *Advances in Experimental Social Psychology*, *17*, 117–182.

Lodge, D. (1971). *The novelist at the crossroads and other essays on fiction and criticism*. London: Routledge.

Nieuwenhuyse, B., Offenberg, L., & Frijda, N.H. (1987). Subjective emotion and reported body experience. *Motivation and Emotion*, *11*, 169–182.

Ortony, A., Clore, G.L., & Collins, A. (1988). *The cognitive structure of emotions*. Cambridge University Press.

Parkinson, B. (1991). Emotional stylists: Strategies of expressive management among trainee hairdressers. *Cognition and Emotion*, *5*, 419–434.

Parkinson, B. & Manstead, A.S.R. (1992). Appraisal as a cause of emotion. In M.S. Clark (Ed.), *Review of personality and social pscyhology*, Vol. 13. New York: Sage, pp. 122–149.

Potter, J. & Wetherell, M. (1987). *Discourse and social psychology*. London: Sage.

Radley, A. (1988). The social form of feeling. *British Journal of Social Psychology*, 27, 5–18.

Roseman, I.J. (1991). Appraisal determinants of discrete emotions. *Cognition and Emotion*, 5, 161–200.

Russell, J.A. (1987). Comments on articles by Frijda and by Conway and Bekerian. *Cognition and Emotion*, 1, 193–197.

Sampson, E.E. (1977). Psychology and the American ideal. *Journal of Personality and Social Psychology*, 35, 767–782.

Schachter, S. (1971). *Emotion, obesity, and crime*. New York: Academic Press.

Scherer, K.R. (1984). Emotion as a multicomponent process: A model and some cross-cultural data. In P. Shaver (Ed.), *Review of personality and social pscyhology*, Vol. 5. Beverley Hills: Sage, pp. 37–63.

Shotter, J. & Gergen, K.J. (Eds) (1989). *Texts of identity*. New York: Sage.

Smith, C.A. & Ellsworth, P.C. (1987). Patterns of appraisal and emotion related to taking an exam. *Journal of Personality and Social Psychology*, 52, 475–488.

Smith, C.A. & Lazarus, R.S. (this issue). Appraisal components, relational themes, and emotion. *Cognition and Emotion*.

Weiner, B. Russell, D., & Lerman, D. (1978). Affective consequences of causal ascriptions. In J.H. Harvey, W.J. Ickes, & R.F. Kidd (Eds), *New directions in attribution research*, Vol 2. Hillsdale, NJ: Lawrence Erlbaum Associates Inc, pp. 59–88.

Williams, K.J., Suls, J., Alliger, G.M., Learner, S.M., & Wan, C.K. (1991). Multiple role juggling and daily mood states in working mothers: An experience sampling study. *Journal of Applied Psychology*, 76, 664–674.

Wittgenstein, L. (1953). *Philosophical investigations*. Oxford: Blackwell.

Zillmann, D. (1978). Attribution and misattribution of excitatory reactions. In J.H. Harvey, W.J. Ickes, & R.F. Kidd (Eds), *New directions in attribution theory*, Vol. 2. Hillsdale, NJ: Lawrence Erlbaum Associates Inc, pp. 335–368.

COGNITION AND EMOTION, 1993, 7 (3/4), 325–355

Studying the Emotion-Antecedent Appraisal Process: An Expert System Approach

Klaus R. Scherer

University of Geneva, Switzerland

The surprising convergence between independently developed appraisal theories of emotion elicitation and differentiation is briefly reviewed. It is argued that three problems are responsible for the lack of more widespread acceptance of such theories: (1) the criticism of excessive cognitivism raised by psychologists working on affective phenomena; (2) the lack of process orientation in linking appraisal to the complex unfolding of emotion episodes over time; and (3) the lack of consensus on the number and types of appraisal criteria between theorists in this domain. Although readers are referred to recent theoretical discussions and evidence from the neurosciences with respect to the first two issues, an empirical study using computerised experimentation is reported with respect to the third issue. Data obtained with an expert system based on Scherer's (1984a) "stimulus evaluation check" predictions show the feasibility of this approach in determining the number and types of appraisal criteria needed to explain emotion differentiation. It is suggested to use computer modelling and experimentation as a powerful tool to further theoretical development and collect pertinent data on the emotion-antecedent appraisal process.

INTRODUCTION

The notion that emotions are elicited and differentiated via appraisal of situations or events as centrally important to a person has a venerable history. The idea can be traced from the writings of early philosophers such as Aristotle, Descartes, and Spinoza to theoretical suggestions by pioneering emotion psychologists such as Stumpf (see Reisenzein & Schönpflug, 1992). In the 1960s, Arnold (1960) and Lazarus (1968) had

---

Requests for reprints should be sent to Klaus R. Scherer, Department of Psychology, University of Geneva, 9, Rte de Drize, Carouge, CH-1227 Geneva, Switzerland.

This paper was specifically prepared for the special issue of *Cognition and Emotion* on Appraisal and Beyond. The author gratefully acknowledges important contributions and suggestions by George Chwelos, Nico Frijda, Keith Oatley, Ursula Scherer, and two anonymous reviewers.

---

explicitly formulated theories incorporating rudimentary appraisal criteria in an effort to explain the emotional consequences of being faced with a particular event. At the beginning of the 1980s a number of psychologists independently proposed detailed and comprehensive sets of appraisal criteria to explain the elicitation and differentiation of the emotions (De Rivera, 1977; Frijda, 1986; Johnson-Laird & Oatley, 1989; Mees, 1985; Ortony, Clore, & Collins, 1988; Roseman, 1984, 1991; Scherer, 1981, 1982, 1983, 1984a,b, 1986; Smith & Ellsworth, 1985, 1987; Solomon, 1976; Weiner, 1982) and engaged in empirical research to demonstrate the validity of these hypothetical suggestions (Ellsworth & Smith, 1988; Frijda, 1987; Frijda, Kuipers, & ter Schure, 1989; Gehm & Scherer, 1988; Manstead & Tetlock, 1989; Reisenzein & Hofmann, 1990; Roseman, 1984, 1991; Roseman, Spindel, & Jose, 1990; Smith & Ellsworth, 1985, 1987; Tesser, 1990; Weiner, 1986). In a comparative review of such "appraisal theories of emotion differentiation" Scherer (1988) attempted to show the extraordinary degree of convergence of the different theoretical suggestions, especially with respect to the central criteria postulated in the different approaches (see Table 1, reproduced from Scherer, 1988). This convergence is all the more surprising since the theorists concerned come from widely different traditions in psychology and philosophy. The impression that appraisal theories of emotion differentiation have generated a highly cumulative body of research has been confirmed in more recent reviews as well as in some comparative empirical studies (Lazarus & Smith, 1988; Manstead & Tetlock, 1989; Reisenzein & Hofmann, 1990; Roseman, et al. 1990; Scherer, 1988).

It seems reasonable to take such theoretical and empirical convergence as an indication of the plausibility and validity of appraisal theories, particularly in the light of the absence of rival theories that could reasonably claim to explain emotion differentiation by alternative conceptual frameworks. Yet, appraisal theories currently face three major challenges which seem to prevent more widespread acceptance of this explanatory framework: (1) the reproach of excessive cognitivism; (2) the lack of process orientation; and (3) the lack of consensus on the number and types of appraisal criteria.

1. The Reproach of Excessive Cognitivism

Appraisal theorists are often accused of excessive cognitivism by psychologists dealing with a wide variety of different affective phenomena. Critics question the likelihood that elaborate cognitive evaluations are performed during the few milliseconds that seem sufficient to bring about an emotion episode. It is further suggested that affective arousal can be triggered without any evaluative processing at all (Zajonc, 1980). The "cognition-emotion controversy" (Lazarus, 1984a,b; LeDoux, 1987, 1989; Leventhal

TABLE 1

Convergence of Sets of Appraisal Criteria as Suggested by Different Appraisal Theorists

Scherer	Frijda	Ortony/Clore	Roseman	Smith/Ellsworth	Solomon	Weiner
Novelty	Change			Attention		
Suddenness	Familiarity					
Familiarity						
Predictability		Unexpectedness				
Intrinsic pleasantness	Valence	Appealingness		Pleasantness		
Goal significance						
Concern relevance	Focality		App/Ave Motives		Scope/Focus	
Outcome probability	Certainty	Likelihood	Probability	Certainty		
Expectation	Presence	Prospect realisation				
Conduciveness	Open/Closed	Desirability	Motive consistency	Goal/Path obstacle	Evaluation	
Urgency	Urgency	Proximity		Anticipated effort		
Coping potential						
Cause: Agent	Intent/Self-Other	Agency	Agency	Agency	Responsibility	Locus of causality
Cause: Motive				Agency		Stability
Control	Modifiability					Controllability
Power	Controllability		Power		Power	Controllability
Adjustment						
Compatibility standards						
External	Value relevance	Blameworthiness		Legitimacy		
Internal						

App, Approach; Ave, avoidance. Reproduced from Scherer (1988, p. 92).

& Scherer, 1987; Zajonc, 1980, 1984; Zajonc & Markus, 1984) is centrally concerned with this issue. The crux of the matter, however, is the definition of *cognition*, a term which has not gained in precision by becoming increasingly fashionable. Although the formulations used by some theorists may suggest that appraisal is viewed as a conscious, and consequently exclusively cortically based process, other theorists in this tradition have insisted early on that the cognitivistic connotations of the terms "appraisal" or "evaluation" do *not* preclude that a substantial part of these processes occur in an unconscious fashion, mediated via sub-cortical, e.g. limbic system, structures (Scherer, 1984a,b). Leventhal and Scherer (1987) have pointed out that evaluation can occur at the sensori-motor, schematic, or conceptual levels, respectively, and that, rather than discussing the cognition issue on an abstract level, one should determine the precise nature of the information-processing involved.

LeDoux (1989), from a neuropsychological point of view, has likewise advocated to address the issue of the nature of emotion-antecedent information-processing and its underlying neural pathways rather than getting sidetracked by the issue of the definition of cognition: "The process involved in stimulus evaluation could, if one chose, be called cognitive processes. The meaning of the stimulus is not given in physical characteristics of the stimulus but instead is determined by computations performed by the brain. As computation is the benchmark of the cognitive, the computation of affective significance could be considered a cognitive process" (LeDoux, 1989, p. 271). LeDoux and his coworkers have in fact empirically demonstrated the existence of subcortical stimulus evaluation patterns for affect eliciting situations in rats (LeDoux, 1987, 1989; LeDoux, Farb, & Rugiero, 1990).

The empirical demonstration of such patterns in humans is hardly to be expected at present because most current research on emotion-antecedent appraisal in human subjects uses self-report of emotional experiences (necessarily involving higher centres of the brain). Subjects are generally asked to recall or infer the nature of their event or situation appraisal, often with the help of rating scales constructed on the basis of the theoretically assumed appraisal dimensions. Clearly, verbally reported appraisal patterns are mediated via conscious, almost exclusively cortically controlled information-processing, and are thus easy targets for charges of excessive cognitivism. They are also subject to the criticism that such recall or inference illustrates social representations of emotions rather than reflecting the actual emotion-eliciting process.

Given the difficulty of settling these issues empirically, Scherer (1993) has suggested to look toward potential contributions from the neurosciences to better understand the nature of the appraisal process. The author denotes a number of possibilities of empirically studying controversial questions related to the appraisal notion with the help of modern neuroscience technology, such as electroencephalographic signal analysis and imaging techniques, and adopting neuropsychologically oriented experimental designs as well as case studies of neurologically impaired patients. Such procedures might help to overcome one of the most serious limitations of current empirical research on emotion-antecedent appraisal: The reliance on respondents' verbal reports of recalled or inferred situation evaluations.

2. The Lack of Process Orientation

The second problem mentioned earlier, lack of a process orientation in many appraisal theories, is responsible for the frequently encountered opinion that appraisal theories basically provide a semantic grid for the comprehension of the use of emotion terms or labels, and are thus limited to structural analyses or explications of semantic fields of emotion terms. This impression is due partly to the explicit semantic orientation of some of the models that have been proposed (Ortony et al., 1988), and partly to the use of verbal labels in all theories to identify the emotional states that are seen to be elicited and differentiated by the appraisal process.

It is certainly one of the legitimate applications of appraisal theories to identify the nature of the emotion-antecedent appraisal process that determines which verbal label will be chosen to communicate the nature of the emotion episode. However, appraisal theories need to go beyond semantics and attempt to specify the true nature of the emotion-antecedent appraisal process. This process might result in an emotional state that the person concerned is unable or unwilling to label with one of the standard emotion terms that are currently used in emotion research. Scherer (1984a) has argued that the stimulus or event evaluation process can elicit as many different emotional states as there are distinguishable outcomes of the appraisal process. This suggestion clearly contradicts the notion that there are a very limited number of "basic" or "fundamental" discrete emotions (Ekman, 1984, 1992; Izard, 1977; Tomkins, 1984). In order to allow systematic discussion of this issue, it is necessary to agree on a consensual definition of emotion that helps to explicate the boundaries between different emotional states and their components (see Scherer, 1993).

A further requirement for advancing in the debate on this issue is the specification of the *micro-genetic process* of appraisal and reaction. Although many emotion theories give the impression that emotions are static states that can be conveniently labelled with a single term, there can be little doubt that we need to talk about *emotion episodes* that are characterised by continuously occurring changes in the underlying appraisal and reaction processes (see Folkman & Lazarus, 1985; Frijda,

1986; Scherer, 1984a,b). In consequence, it is not sufficient to specify a pattern of appraisal results that is supposed to explain a static emotion as indexed by a label. The nature of the appraisal *process* and the immediate effects of the evaluation results on the other components of emotion (such as subjective feeling, physiological responses, motor expression, and action tendencies) need to be explored. Unfortunately, most of the appraisal theorists have so far devoted only very limited attention to the process underlying the evaluation of situations, events, or actions.

An exception to this general pattern is the component process theory suggested by Scherer (1984a,b, 1986, 1988), which postulates that the appraisal criteria (stimulus evaluation checks, abbreviated as SECs) proposed occur in an invariant *sequence* (in the order shown in Table 2). The sequence notion, which is based on phylogenetic, ontogenetic, and microgenetic (logical) considerations, cannot be discussed in detail in the present context. Generally speaking, it is assumed that the appraisal process is *constantly operative* with evaluations being continuously performed to update the organism's information on an event or situation (including the current needs or goals of the organism and the possibility to act on these). In consequence, the sequential stimulus evaluation checks are expected to occur in very rapid succession (similar to a rotating radar antenna updating the reflection patterns on the screen). This continuous operation can explain the sudden changes that can occur during emotion episodes and which are often based on re-evaluations of the event or of one's coping potential (cf. Lazarus', 1968, "secondary appraisal"; see Scherer, 1984a,b, for further details on the hypothesised sequential processing).

Many different objections have been raised against this sequence notion. Quite a few of these can be refuted on logical grounds or on the basis of recent insights into the neural bases of information-processing, particularly with respect to neural networks (see Scherer, 1993, for a detailed discussion). However, empirical research is needed to demonstrate the feasibility of the sequence hypothesis and to encourage further work in this direction. Unfortunately, our dependence on verbal report of recalled or inferred appraisal processes does not lend itself to the study of the sequence hypothesis. It is likely that the different steps of the evaluation process occur extremely rapidly and are not generally represented in awareness. Any reconstruction of these processes is likely to miss the temporal dynamics of the process. In the future, neuroscience technology might allow us to monitor such rapidly occurring evaluation sequences directly. Also, it seems feasible to develop sophisticated research designs making use of latency time measures in carefully designed stimulus presentation modes to shed some light on these time-critical processes (see

Scherer, 1993, for concrete suggestions on adopting appropriate paradigms from the cognitive neurosciences). Unfortunately, such studies might well be slow in the making.

3. The Lack or Consensus on the Number and Types of Appraisal Criteria

The third problem concerns the issue of how many and precisely which evaluation or appraisal dimensions are necessary to account for the degree of emotion differentiation that can be empirically demonstrated. Although, as mentioned earlier, there is much convergence in this field, authors do differ with respect to the number and definition of appraisal dimensions that are proposed. A few recent studies have attempted to compare different appraisal theories and to empirically determine how many dimensions are needed and which dimensions seem to account for most of the variance (Manstead & Tetlock, 1989; Mauro, Sato, & Tucker, 1992; Reisenzein & Hofmann, 1990; Roseman et al., 1990). All of these studies are limited to *post hoc* evaluation of how well the dimensions studied explain differentiation between the emotions reported by the subjects. In other words, the same group of subjects provides both the emotion and the appraisal information and statistical analysis is limited to identifying the shared variance. Needless to say, the results cannot be generalised beyond the respective set of emotions and dimensions studied. Even though such information is eminently useful for the further development of appraisal theories, it seems desirable to develop a model that emphasises the *prediction* of emotional states on the basis of a minimal set of necessary and sufficient dimensions or criteria of appraisal.

The empirical study to be reported in this paper suggests such a predictive approach. Based on Scherer's component process model of emotion (1984a,b, 1986, 1988), an expert system on emotion differentiation that contains such a minimal set of evaluation criteria is presented and submitted to a first empirical test.

As shown earlier, the question of how many and which appraisal criteria are minimally needed to explain emotion differentiation is one of the central issues in research on emotion-antecedent appraisal. It is argued here that one can work towards settling the issue by constructing, and continuously refining, an expert system that attempts to diagnose the nature of an emotional experience based exclusively on information about the results of the stimulus or event evaluation processes that have elicited the emotion. The knowledge base of the expert system would contain a limited set of evaluation or appraisal criteria together with theoretically defined (and empirically updated) predictions about which pattern of evaluation results is likely to produce a particular emotion out of a limited

TABLE 2
Patterns of Stimulus Evaluation Checks (SEC) Predicted to Differentiate 14 Major Emotions

	ENJ/HAP	ELA/JOY	DISP/DISG	CON/SCO	SAD/DEJ	DESPAIR	ANX/WOR
Novelty							
Suddenness	low	hi/med	open	open	low	high	low
Familiarity	open	open	low	open	low	v low	open
Predictability	medium	low	low	open	open	low	open
Intrinsic pleasantness	high	open	v low	open	open	open	open
Goal significance							
Concern relevance	open	self/rela	body	rela/order	open	open	body/self
Outcome probability	v high	v high	v high	high	v high	v high	medium
Expectation	consonant	open	open	open	open	dissonant	open
Conduciveness	conducive	v conducive	open	open	obstruct	obstruct	obstruct
Urgency	v low	low	medium	low	low	high	medium
Coping potential							
Cause: Agent	open	open	open	other	open	oth/nat	oth/nat
Cause: Motive	intent	cha/int	open	intent	cha/neg	cha/neg	open
Control	open	open	open	high	v low	v low	open
Power	open	open	open	low	v low	v low	low
Adjustment	high	medium	open	high	medium	v low	medium
Compatibility standards							
External	open	open	open	v low	open	open	open
Internal	open	open	open	v low	open	open	open

332

	FEAR	IRR/COA	RAGE/HOA	BOR/IND	SHAME	GUILT	PRIDE
Novelty							
Suddenness	high	low	high	v low	low	open	open
Familiarity	open	open	low	high	open	open	open
Predictability	low	medium	low	v high	open	open	open
Intrinsic pleasantness	low	open	open	open	open	open	open
Goal significance							
Concern relevance	body	order	order	body	self	rela/order	self
Outcome probability	high	v high	v high	v high	v high	v high	v high
Expectation	dissonant	open	dissonant	consonant	open	open	open
Conduciveness	obstruct	obstruct	obstruct	open	open	high	high
Urgency	v high	medium	high	low	high	medium	low
Coping potential							
Cause: Agent	oth/nat	open	other	open	self	self	self
Cause: Motive	open	int/neg	intent	open	int/neg	intent	intent
Control	open	high	high	medium	open	open	open
Power	v low	medium	high	medium	open	open	open
Adjustment	low	high	high	high	medium	medium	high
Compatibility standards							
External	open	low	low	open	open	v low	high
Internal	open	low	low	open	v low	v low	v high

Abbreviations: ENJI/HAP, enjoyment/happiness; *ELA/JOY,* elation/joy; *SAD/DEJ,* sadness/dejection; *IRR/COA,* irritation/cold anger; *RAGE/HOA,* rage/hot anger; *BOR/IND,* boredom/indifference; *v,* very; *rela,* relationships; *nat,* nature; *cha,* chance; *neg,* negligence; *int* or *intent,* intention; *oth* or *other,* other person(s). Reproduced from Scherer (1988, p. 112).

set of possibilities. At present, this system is limited to predicting the verbal labels given to the emotions experienced and to obtain the required information about appraisal processes by requesting verbal report of recalled or inferred evaluation results. As shown earlier, this is a highly imperfect approach to study the dynamic appraisal and reaction processes involved in emotional episodes, many of which do not require involvement of consciousness or language—or may not even be accessible to them. However, even an approximative approach to a predictive model seems useful at our present state of knowledge.

METHOD

Designing the Expert System

The aim was to develop a computer program that would allow a user to enter information on a situation in which a strong emotion had been experienced and have the program predict or diagnose the nature of that emotional state (as represented by a verbal label).[1] Using TurboPascal 3.0, a program called GENESE (Geneva Expert System on Emotions) was developed.[2] In contrast to expert systems based on IF-THEN rules the present system is of the type that employs algorithms determining the relative similarity between input vectors and prototypical category vectors representing the knowledge base. In the present case the "knowledge base" consists of a set of vectors (one for each emotion) which contain quantified *predictions* relative to the typical stimulus evaluation check outcomes for specific emotions. These vectors have been derived from the prediction tables published by the author in earlier work (Scherer, 1984a,b, 1986, 1988). The most recent set of predictions is shown in Table 2 (reproduced from Scherer, 1988).

Concretely, then, for each of the specific emotions contained in the expert system, a vector of numbers (which represent the predicted results of selected stimulus evaluation checks for the respective emotions) constitutes the prototypical pattern which will be used to classify user-generated input vectors. The input vector for a target emotion to be classified (which is determined by the user's choice of a recalled emotional experience he or she wants to have diagnosed) is determined by the computer asking the 15 questions listed in Table 3 and requiring the user to answer with the help of predefined answer categories. Each of these

---

[1] A similar approach was independently developed by Frijda and Swagerman (1987).

[2] The prototype of the system was written in 1987 by Philippe Narbel and Roland Bapst based on specifications by the author who has continuously modified the program since.

questions corresponds to a particular stimulus evaluation check or sub-check. The numbers representing the predicted prototypical answer alternatives for each question constitute the entries for the stimulus evaluation checks into the prediction vector for the respective emotion. These prediction vectors are shown in the second row of the vector matrices for the 14 emotions in Table 5.

It should be noted that although the prediction vectors have been derived from earlier prediction tables, not all of the stimulus evaluation subchecks listed in Table 2 have been included in the quantified prediction vectors of the GENESE expert system. The need for a selection of what seemed to be the most important and differentiating checks was imposed by the necessity to curtail the number of questions posed to the user. Furthermore, for some subchecks, e.g. agent of causation, several questions had to be asked to obtain the required quantitative information. Table 3 shows the correspondence between the stimulus evaluation checks or subchecks and the specific questions. It should be noted further that the prediction vectors (as contained in the system and shown in Table 5) are based on but do not necessarily correspond exactly to the earlier prediction tables (e.g. Table 2). The author considers theory development a dynamic process. Consequently, predictions change and evolve over time. For example, the prediction vectors in Table 5 show some changes over earlier hypothesising. In particular, an attempt has been made to reduce the number of "open" or "not pertinent" predictions (see Table 2)—particularly in the case of shame and guilt—as these reduce the discriminative power of the vectors in the expert system.

The present version of GENESE contains prediction vectors for the 14 emotions listed in Table 2. The choice of these 14 emotions was determined by the arguments advanced in Scherer (1986) advocating to distinguish between more quiet and more aroused varieties of some of the major emotions, e.g. irritation/cold anger vs. rage/hot anger.

The input vector, as based on the user's answers to the 15 questions, is systematically compared to the 14 predicted emotion vectors, using Euclidian distance measures. The distance indices obtained in this fashion are then adjusted on the basis of theoretical considerations concerning the need to weight particular combinations of input values. The following adjustments of the distance indices are used in the present version of the expert system:

- − 0.3 for shame and guilt if the causal agent is "self"
- + 0.8 for all positive emotions if the event is evaluated as unpleasant and hindering goal attainment
- + 0.3 for contempt except in cases in which another person is the causal agent and the act is highly immoral (− 0.6)

- 0.5 for sadness and desperation if the event happened in the past and if power and adjustment are low
- 0.5 for irritation and anger if power and adjustment are high
- 0.3 for joy, desperation, fear, and anger if the intensity of the emotion is rated above 4 on a 6-point scale

The nature of the adjustments and the size of these increments or decrements of the distance value computed on the basis of the comparison of the input vector with the prediction vectors are based on rules of thumb and are subject to change in future versions of the system.

TABLE 3
Questions Posed by the Expert System and their Correspondence to
the Stimulus Evaluation Checks (SECs)

1. Did the situation that elicited your emotion happen very suddenly or abruptly? [SEC1–NOVELTY]

(0) not pertinent   (1) not at all   (2) a little   (3) moderately   (4) strongly   (5) extremely

2. Did the situation concern an event or an action that had happened in the past, that had just happened or that was to be expected for the future? [see text]

(0) not pertinent   (1) the event had happened a long time ago
(2) it happened in the recent past   (3) it had just happened at that moment
(4) it was to be expected for the near future   (5) it was to be expected in the long run

3. This type of event, independent of your personal evaluation, would it be generally considered as pleasant or unpleasant? [SEC2–INTRINSIC PLEASANTNESS]

(0) not pertinent   (1) very unpleasant   (2) rather unpleasant   (3) indifferent
(4) rather pleasant   (5) very pleasant

4. Was the event relevant for your general well-being, for urgent needs you felt, or for specific goals or plans you were pursuing at the time? [SEC3–RELEVANCE]

(0) not pertinent   (1) not at all   (2) a little   (3) moderately   (4) strongly   (5) extremely

5. Did you expect the event and its consequences before the situation actually happened? [SEC3–EXPECTATION]

(0) not pertinent   (1) never in my life   (2) not really   (3) I did not exclude it
(4) a little   (5) strongly

6. Did the event help or hinder you in satisfying your needs, in pursuing your plans or in attaining your goals? [SEC3–CONDUCIVENESS]

(0) not pertinent   (1) it hindered a lot   (2) it hindered a little   (3) it had no effect
(4) it helped a little   (5) it helped a lot

7. Did you feel that action on your part was urgently required to cope with the event and its consequences? [SEC3–URGENCY]

(0) not pertinent   (1) not at all   (2) a little   (3) moderately   (4) strongly   (5) extremely

(Continued)

TABLE 3
(Continued)

8. Was the event caused by your own actions—in other words, were you partially or fully responsible for what happened? [SEC4–CAUSATION]

(0) not pertinent (1) not at all (2) a little, but unintentionally
(3) somewhat, but I was unaware of the consequences
(4) quite responsible, I knew what I was doing
(5) fully responsible, I absolutely wanted to do what I did

9. Was the event caused by one or several other persons—in other words, were other people partially or fully responsible for what happened? [SEC4–CAUSATION]

(0) not pertinent (1) not at all (2) a little, but unintentionally
(3) somewhat, but he/she/they were unaware of the consequences
(4) quite responsible, he/she/they knew what they were doing
(5) fully responsible, he/she/they absolutely wanted to do what they did

10. Was the event mainly due to chance? [SEC4–CAUSATION]

(0) not pertinent (1) not at all (2) a little, but human action was the decisive factor
(3) somewhat, but human action contributed to it (4) strongly (5) exclusively

11. Can the occurrence and the consequences of this type of event generally be controlled or modified by human action? [SEC4–CONTROL]

(0) not pertinent (1) not at all (2) a little (3) moderately (4) strongly (5) extremely

12. Did you feel that you had enough power to cope with the event—i.e. being able to influence what was happening or to modify the consequences? [SEC4–POWER]

(0) not pertinent (1) not at all (2) a little (3) moderately (4) strongly (5) extremely

13. Did you feel that, after having used all your means of intervention, you could live with the situation and adapt to the consequences? [SEC4–ADJUSTMENT]

(0) not pertinent (1) not at all (2) with much difficulty (3) somewhat (4) quite easily
(5) without any problem at all

14. Would the large majority of people consider what happened to be quite in accordance with social norms and morally acceptable? [SEC5–NORM COMPATIBILITY]

(0) not pertinent (1) certainly not (2) not really (3) probably (4) most likely
(5) certainly

15. If you were personally responsible for what happened, did your action correspond to your self-image? [SEC5–SELF COMPATIBILITY]

(0) not pertinent (I was not responsible) (1) not at all (2) not really (3) somewhat
(4) strongly (5) extremely well

The emotion with the smallest overall distance measure is suggested to the user as diagnosis of the experienced emotional state. If the user does not accept the diagnosis as valid, the emotion with the vector that shows the second smallest distance is proposed as a second guess. If the user rejects this one also, he or she is prompted to provide the correct response in the list of the 14 emotions contained in the standard version of the system. If the user identifies one of these 14 emotions as correct, the respective prediction vector is changed in the direction of the empirical input vector (using an adaptable weighting function) to establish an empirically updated prediction matrix *for this particular user*. The user can indicate that none of the 14 emotion labels proposed corresponds to the real emotion that was felt. He or she then has the possibility to enter a freely chosen verbal label for that particular state. This label, together with the input vector, is then added to the personalised prediction matrix. In this manner, an unlimited number of new emotions can be added to the personalised knowledge base of a user. It should be noted that the personalised knowledge base for a particular user no longer represents pure theoretical predictions because the prediction vectors have been adapted to fit the empirical input. After prolonged usage by a particular user, the prediction matrix may actually represent a true empirical knowledge base—at least for that particular user.

The system stores all the information provided by the user in two separate data files, one which contains the complete protocol of the session and one that contains the personalised vector matrix.

Procedure

The system has been designed in such a fashion that it does not require any intervention by an experimenter. Users are expected to start the program and follow instructions on the screen which should be self-explanatory. In the following, a brief summary of the typical procedure is given.

Following a title page and the entry of a user code that permits repeated access and establishes a personalised data base, the user is requested to remember a situation that has produced a strong emotional response:

> Please recall a situation in which you experienced a strong emotional feeling. The emotion might have been elicited by an event that happened to you or by the consequences of your own behaviour. This might have happened recently or quite some time ago.
>
> I will ask you a certain number of questions concerning this situation and will then attempt to diagnose the emotion you felt at that time.
>
> Before continuing, please recall the situation as best as you can and try to reconstruct the details of what happened.

The program then pauses until the subject confirms to now recall a situation very vividly by pressing a key. He or she is then asked to type a brief description of the situation on the keyboard. To ensure anonymity and privacy, the text typed is not shown on the screen. Then, the 15 questions shown in Table 3 are presented consecutively. The questions are always presented in the order given in Table 3 because the underlying theory predicts that this is the natural micro-genetic appraisal sequence. It is hypothesised that following the original sequence of the appraisal in assessing the different checks may help the subject to recall the appraisal process faster and with fewer errors. The subject is then asked to enter the intensity with which the emotion was felt on a 6-point scale from very weak to extremely strong, as well as his/her age group and gender. Then, the subject is presented with the following message:

> I have now completed a first diagnosis of the affective state elicited by the situation you described and I am about to present you with a label that I consider to be a good description of the emotion you experienced. Please remember that, at the time, you may not have been conscious of all aspects of your emotional experience. Therefore, it is quite possible that the verbal label you normally use to describe your feelings in that situation does not exactly correspond to the term I will suggest in my diagnosis. If that is the case, please consider the possibility that the diagnosis which I suggest might reflect some part of what you felt in the situation—possibly without realising it.

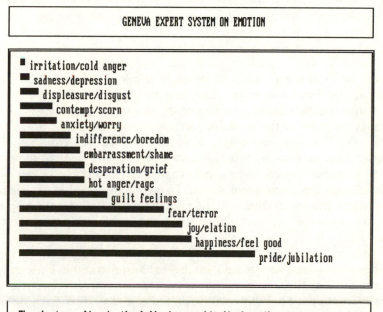

FIG. 1.   Feedback screen showing relative distances of input vector to predicted vectors for different emotion concepts.

The system then presents the first diagnosis or suggested hypothesis and asks the user to indicate whether it is correct or not. If the user enters "incorrect", a second diagnosis is presented. If that is again incorrect, the user is presented with the list of 14 emotions and asked to indicate the correct emotion. Following either of these three cases the user is presented with feedback on the diagnostic process in form of a graph showing the relative distances of the various emotion concepts to the situation described (see Fig. 1).

If the subject indicates that none of the 14 emotion labels in the list describes the felt affect accurately, he or she is given the opportunity to enter a new concept:

Aha, something new!?
Do you really want to teach me a new emotion? It will change your personal knowledge base!
Your decision—[y = yes/n = no followed by the new concept]

After each of the four possible options: (1) first diagnosis correct; (2) second diagnosis correct; (3) correct emotion identified in list; (4) new concept entered, the user is given the possibility to enter a new situation or to exit.

Administration

This expert system was used in a number of pilot studies, using English, German, and French versions. The French version was used for a first major study of the accuracy of the expert system in diagnosing emotional states on the basis of theoretically predicted appraisal patterns.

The program was inserted in a batch-file environment that allows automatic administration. After each user completes a session, the system returns to a title screen inviting potential users to test the power of the system to diagnose emotional states. To avoid the possibility that users would start a session and leave in the middle, a time limit for the responses to each screen was set. If the time limit is exceeded the system returns automatically to the title page.

A personal computer (Olivetti M240) on which this batch-file system had been installed, was placed in the exhibition of the University of Geneva at the 1990 Geneva book fair (Salon du Livre). This is a large international bookshow with exhibitors and visitors from different countries, mostly French speaking. Posters positioned around the PC invited passers by to test the GENESE emotion expert system. During three days of the exhibition, 201 persons used the system entering generally one, but sometimes two or three situations. In addition, 35 first year students in psychology at the University of Geneva (in their first 2 months of study) used the system as part of a course exercise (also in a completely automatised fashion). In all, 236 persons entered the data for a total of 282 emotional situations in this manner.

Data Analysis

A major concern for the analysis is the possibility that some users may have entered nonsensical information while just playing with or trying to mislead the system. However, there were very few cases where the text entered suggested that this was the case. In some cases no text was entered and it was difficult to decide whether the input vector constituted a serious trial or not. To avoid biasing the data by subjective judgement of the "seriousness" of the entry it was decided to retain all situations, assuming that nonsensical entries should work against finding accurate diagnoses and thus lead to a conservative estimate of the power of the system.

Data were excluded only in the following, clearly discernible cases: In some situations there was virtually no variability in the responses to the questions, e.g. a user responding with 1 to all questions. Fifteen situations in which 13 or more of the answers had the same numerical value were excluded. In 14 cases of the total of 282 situations entered, users neither judged any of the diagnoses as correct nor identified any of the 14 emotion labels suggested as the correct response. In these cases new concepts were entered. Because the number of such cases was small, and because in some cases strange concepts like "le spleen total" were entered, it was decided to exclude these cases from analysis.

After having excluded these cases, a total of 253 situations were analysed with respect to the number of hits and misses and the correlation between the predicted and the empirically obtained appraisal profiles for the 14 emotions studied.

RESULTS

Tables 4 and 5 show the major results of the analyses. In Table 4, the first column contains the total number of situations that were entered for each of the 14 emotions (using the final indication of a correct diagnosis or the user correction as a criterion). Column 2 shows in how many of these cases the first diagnosis was correct, and Col. 3 in how many cases the second diagnosis was correct. Column 4 shows the total number of misses. However, some of the latter cases can be considered as "dubious misses" as the input vectors not only deviate strongly from the predicted vectors but also from the empirically obtained mean vectors for each of the emotion (as shown in Table 5). It is highly probable, then, that the

TABLE 4
Results of Expert System Runs for 253 Emotion Situations

Emotion	Total Situat	1st Hit	2nd Hit	Total Misses	Dubious Misses	% Correct	Marked Diff	Profile Correl
Happiness/Feel good	27	21	1	5	2	88.0	3	0.76
Joy/Elation	34	30	3	1	1	100.0	3	0.63
Displeasure/Disgust	10	4	3	3	1	77.8	1	0.60
Contempt/Scorn	3	3	0	0	0	100.0	2	0.51
Sadness/Depression	34	19	3	12	3	71.0	2	0.24
Desperation/Grief	58	49	8	1	1	100.0	2	0.75
Anxiety/Worry	19	2	0	17	5	14.3	4	0.13
Fear/Terror	19	2	2	15	4	26.7	10	0.61
Irritation/Cold anger	11	3	4	4	1	70.0	3	0.30
Hot anger/Rage	19	10	4	5	1	77.7	6	0.74
Indifference/Boredom	3	1	0	2	0	33.3	3	0.36
Embarrassment/Shame	4	1	0	3	1	33.3	4	0.23
Guilt feelings	3	1	0	2	1	50.0	9	−0.10
Pride/Jubilation	9	6	0	3	1	75.0	6	0.75
Totals	253	152	28	73	22	77.9		

Notes: *Total Situat*, total number of situations clearly categorised by respondents; *1st Hit*, number correctly recognised on first attempt; *2nd Hit*, number correctly recognised on second attempt; *Total misses*, number missed as shown by user correction; *Dubious Misses*, cases in which the deviation of the input profile from the mean empirical profile exceeded half a standard deviation; *% Correct*, percentage of total hits (first plus second) on the basis of total number of situations minus dubious misses; *Marked Diff*, marked difference between predicted and empirically obtained vectors; *Profile Correl*, Pearson r between the mean empirical input profile and the theoretically specified prediction profile over $N = 15$ questions (0 in prediction vector treated as missing observation).

appraisal information was not provided in the correct manner. Twenty-two situations were considered dubious because the absolute value of the sum of the differences (deviations) obtained by deducting the individual values for each question from the mean value—Row 1 in Table 5 exceeded the value corresponding to a standard deviation for all difference scores. Column 5 shows the number of these "dubious misses" per emotion. Column 6 shows the percentage of correct diagnoses (excluding the "dubious misses" which are considered to be the result of incorrect input).

Table 5 lists, for each of the 14 emotions, the mean input vector (Row 1), the theoretically predicted SEC vector as represented in the knowledge base (Row 2), the difference between the two (Row 3), and the standard deviations of the empirical values in the input vector (Row 4). This table allows to compare the theoretically predicted SEC vectors in the knowledge base with the empirically obtained input vectors. Thus it permits to determine the stimulus evaluation checks for which the empirical values greatly differ from the predicted value and for which, in consequence, a revision of the prediction might be required (if there is reason to believe that the input value does not represent artifacts or errors). For this decision, the standard deviations of the empirical values are useful: High discordance of the values entered for a particular stimulus evaluation check can be taken to indicate that there may not be a standard appraisal pattern (or that the respondents did not understand the question).

The data in Table 5 generate a large number of interesting issues to be explored. A detailed discussion of these points would exceed the space available in this paper. However, some general trends can be inferred by doing a rough analysis of the size of the difference between theoretical and empirical patterns across stimulus evaluation checks and across emotions.[3] Counting the number of cases in which a difference score exceeds the value of 1 (absolute) for different emotions yields an indication of where the predicted patterns deviate most strongly from the empirically obtained patterns (these values are shown in Col. 7, Table 4). Another way of evaluating the fit between theoretical and empirical patterns is to correlate the two vectors for each emotion. Column 8 in Table 4 shows the mean Pearson correlation coefficients (over respondents) between the predicted profile or vector in the knowledge base, and the empirically obtained input vectors for each of the emotions across the 15 appraisal criteria (as shown in Table 5).

At first observation, although not directly pertinent to the questions outlined earlier, concerns the relative frequency of the different emotions which were presented to the expert system (Col. 1, Table 4). The categories mentioned most frequently are sadness/depression and desperation/grief, both of which are closely linked to some kind of permanent loss. Positive emotions, happiness/feel good and joy/elation are also mentioned relatively frequently. Anxiety/worry and fear/terror, both related to apprehension about impending dangers, are in third position with respect to frequency. Anger states (irritation/cold anger and hot anger/rage) are mentioned the least frequently of the four major fundamental emotion types. The remaining emotions are all relatively low in occurrence.

The most important question concerns the accuracy of the expert system in diagnosing the emotional state descriptions entered by the users. Column 6, Table 4 shows the percentage of correct diagnoses on either the first or second guess. The data in Cols 2 and 3 show that first hits are generally much more frequent (84.4% of all correct diagnoses) than second guesses. The accuracy percentage in Col. 6 is based on a comparison of all

---

[3] It should be noted that the differences should not be interpreted in cases in which the theoretical prediction is 0—not pertinent—as the difference score is not interpretable. Also, as explained in the description of the expert system design, the quantitative prediction vectors are based on but not identical to the patterns in the published prediction tables.

TABLE 5
Empirically Obtained and Theoretically Predicted Appraisal Vectors for 14 Emotions

Emotion	Nov	Time	Plea	Rele	Expec	Condu	Urgen	EgoC	OthC	ChaC	Cont	Power	Adjus	Ext	Int
Enjoy	2.59	2.19	4.41	2.70	3.59	2.96	1.52	3.11	3.41	2.19	3.22	2.37	3.33	3.85	2.93
	2.00	2.00	4.00	3.00	4.00	4.00	1.00	2.00	3.00	2.00	0.00	0.00	5.00	0.00	0.00
	-0.59	-0.19	-0.41	0.30	0.41	1.04	-0.52	-1.11	-0.41	-0.19	*	*	1.67	*	*
	1.18	0.86	0.70	1.57	0.88	0.87	0.95	1.38	1.29	1.06	1.55	1.20	1.21	1.09	1.44
Joy	3.29	2.97	4.26	3.76	2.85	3.97	2.62	3.12	2.97	2.71	3.32	2.59	3.53	3.97	2.88
	4.00	3.00	3.00	4.00	1.00	5.00	2.00	3.00	3.00	3.00	0.00	0.00	4.00	0.00	0.00
	0.71	0.03	-1.26	0.24	-1.85	1.03	-0.62	-0.12	0.03	0.29	*	*	0.47	*	*
	1.30	0.93	0.99	1.30	1.16	0.98	1.39	1.24	1.44	1.24	1.40	1.26	1.14	0.93	1.56
Disgus	3.10	2.30	1.70	1.60	1.90	2.40	2.40	2.00	2.70	3.30	2.30	1.70	2.20	2.70	1.50
	3.00	3.00	1.00	2.00	2.00	3.00	3.00	1.00	3.00	3.00	3.00	2.00	4.00	3.00	0.00
	-0.10	0.70	-0.70	0.40	0.10	0.60	0.60	-1.00	0.30	-0.30	0.70	0.30	1.80	0.30	*
	1.68	1.44	0.98	0.92	0.90	1.20	1.60	1.20	1.30	1.10	1.36	0.84	1.36	1.56	1.60
Contem	2.33	1.00	1.67	1.67	2.33	1.00	2.67	2.00	4.00	1.00	2.33	1.33	3.67	3.00	1.00
	2.00	2.00	2.00	2.00	2.00	3.00	2.00	1.00	5.00	1.00	3.00	4.00	4.00	2.00	0.00
	-0.33	1.00	0.33	0.33	-0.33	2.00	-0.67	-1.00	1.00	0.00	0.67	2.67	0.33	-1.00	*
	1.11	1.33	0.89	0.89	1.11	0.67	1.11	0.67	0.67	0.00	1.78	0.89	0.89	0.67	1.33
Sad	3.06	2.21	1.85	2.44	2.65	2.38	2.26	2.15	2.62	2.21	3.12	1.71	2.26	2.26	1.56
	2.00	2.00	2.00	4.00	2.00	2.00	2.00	2.00	3.00	3.00	3.00	0.00	2.00	0.00	0.00
	-1.06	-0.21	0.15	1.56	-0.65	-0.38	-0.26	-0.15	0.38	0.79	-0.12	*	-0.26	*	*
	1.24	1.15	0.97	1.58	1.39	0.94	1.27	1.07	1.46	1.25	1.59	0.91	0.87	1.17	1.12
Desper	4.12	2.74	1.79	2.90	2.17	2.00	3.34	1.95	2.53	2.38	2.52	1.50	1.69	1.90	1.47
	4.00	3.00	2.00	5.00	1.00	1.00	3.00	1.00	2.00	3.00	3.00	0.00	1.00	0.00	0.00
	-0.12	0.26	0.21	2.10	-1.17	-1.00	-0.34	-0.95	-0.53	0.62	0.48	*	-0.69	*	*
	0.88	0.91	1.05	1.98	1.07	0.93	1.51	0.98	1.42	1.53	1.41	0.72	0.54	1.27	1.27

Emotion	Nov	Time	Plea	Rele	Expec	Condu	Urgen	EgoC	OthC	ChaC	Cont	Power	Adjus	Ext	Int
Anxi	2.42	2.74	1.26	3.05	3.16	3.00	2.79	2.32	2.11	2.16	2.95	2.42	2.68	3.05	1.68
	2.00	5.00	2.00	3.00	2.00	2.00	3.00	1.00	4.00	3.00	3.00	2.00	3.00	0.00	0.00
	−0.42	2.26	0.74	−0.05	−1.16	−1.00	0.21	−1.32	1.89	0.84	0.05	−0.42	0.32	*	*
	1.43	1.10	0.49	1.42	1.11	0.74	1.51	1.28	1.39	1.25	1.64	1.07	0.58	1.41	1.35
Fear	4.32	2.79	1.42	2.79	2.05	2.11	3.53	2.11	2.11	2.37	3.42	2.26	1.47	1.00	1.58
	5.00	4.00	2.00	5.00	1.00	1.00	5.00	1.00	4.00	4.00	2.00	1.00	2.00	0.00	0.00
	0.68	1.21	0.58	2.21	−1.05	−1.11	1.47	−1.11	1.89	1.63	−1.42	−1.26	0.53	*	*
	0.94	1.05	0.71	1.80	0.82	0.88	1.44	0.99	1.20	1.48	1.30	1.36	0.97	0.84	1.51
Irrit	3.27	2.64	2.18	2.73	3.45	2.36	3.09	2.55	3.36	1.55	3.55	2.45	2.91	3.00	2.27
	3.00	2.00	3.00	3.00	2.00	2.00	3.00	2.00	4.00	3.00	4.00	3.00	4.00	2.00	2.00
	−0.27	−0.64	0.82	0.27	−1.45	−0.36	−0.09	−0.55	0.64	1.45	0.45	0.55	1.09	−1.00	−0.27
	1.21	1.19	1.02	1.70	0.96	0.76	1.02	0.96	0.76	0.69	1.21	1.14	0.84	0.91	1.16
Anger	2.63	2.05	1.32	2.79	2.11	2.21	3.26	1.53	2.89	1.63	4.21	2.68	2.42	1.74	2.11
	4.00	3.00	2.00	4.00	1.00	1.00	4.00	1.00	4.00	2.00	4.00	4.00	3.00	1.00	0.00
	1.37	0.95	0.68	1.21	−1.11	−1.21	0.74	−0.53	1.11	0.37	−0.21	1.32	0.58	−0.74	*
	1.37	1.10	0.60	1.51	1.08	1.13	1.09	0.93	1.39	1.15	1.00	1.17	0.88	1.01	1.29
Indiff	3.67	3.67	2.33	2.67	3.67	2.33	1.67	0.67	2.67	1.67	3.67	1.67	3.67	2.33	2.33
	1.00	3.00	3.00	2.00	5.00	3.00	1.00	0.00	0.00	0.00	3.00	3.00	4.00	0.00	0.00
	−2.67	−0.67	0.67	−0.67	1.33	0.67	−0.67	*	*	*	−0.67	1.33	0.33	*	*
	0.44	0.44	0.89	1.56	1.78	0.44	0.89	0.44	1.56	0.44	0.44	0.44	1.78	1.56	1.11
Shame	4.50	2.75	1.50	2.00	1.50	2.50	1.25	4.00	2.75	1.50	3.50	2.50	2.50	3.00	3.75
	2.00	3.00	2.00	4.00	2.00	2.00	2.00	4.00	2.00	1.00	2.00	2.00	3.00	2.00	2.00
	−2.50	0.25	0.50	2.00	0.50	−0.50	0.75	0.00	−0.75	−0.50	−1.50	−0.50	0.50	−1.00	−1.75
	0.50	0.38	0.50	2.00	0.50	1.50	0.38	1.00	1.25	0.75	1.50	1.50	1.25	1.00	0.75

(Continued)

TABLE 5
(Continued)

Emotion	Nov	Time	Plea	Rele	Expec	Condu	Urgen	EgoC	OthC	ChaC	Cont	Power	Adjus	Ext	Int
Guilt	3.33	3.33	1.67	0.33	1.33	1.67	3.33	3.33	2.33	1.00	3.00	2.00	1.67	3.67	2.33
	2.00	2.00	3.00	4.00	2.00	3.00	3.00	4.00	1.00	1.00	2.00	2.00	3.00	2.00	1.00
	-1.33	-1.33	1.33	3.67	0.67	1.33	-0.33	.067	-1.33	0.00	-1.00	0.00	1.33	-1.67	-1.33
	1.56	0.44	0.44	0.44	0.44	1.11	1.56	0.44	1.78	0.00	2.00	1.33	1.11	1.11	1.11
Pride	1.11	1.67	4.44	3.67	3.67	2.78	2.00	3.44	1.89	1.33	4.00	2.89	3.11	3.56	3.33
	2.00	3.00	4.00	4.00	4.00	4.00	2.00	5.00	2.00	2.00	4.00	4.00	5.00	4.00	5.00
	0.89	1.33	-0.44	0.33	0.33	1.22	0.00	1.56	0.11	0.67	0.00	1.11	1.89	0.44	1.67
	0.62	1.26	0.99	1.56	1.19	2.02	1.33	1.85	1.85	0.81	1.11	1.70	1.65	1.38	1.56

Note: First row: Mean empirical input vector. Second row: Theoretical predicted vector. Third row: Difference between empirical and theoretical vectors. Fourth row: Standard deviation for values in empirical vector. * signifies cases in which difference score is not meaningful because prediction is "0—not pertinent or open".

Abbreviations: Nov, novelty; Time, when did the event happen; *Plea*, intrinsic pleasantness; *Rele*, relevance; *Expec*, expectation; *Condu*, goal conduciveness; *Urgen*, urgency; *EgoC*, self as causal agent; *OthC*, other(s) as causal agent; *ChaC*, chance as causal agent; *Cont*, control; *Power*, Power to cope; *Adjus*, capacity to adjust; *Exr*, external; *Int*, internal.

346

hits with true misses (excluding the dubious misses because there is a very high probability that the information on the appraisal criteria was entered incorrectly). As shown in the row for the totals, the overall percentage of hits is 77.9% (180 first and second hits compared to 51 true misses). However, averaging the accuracy percentages in Col. 6 across all emotion categories yields a mean accuracy percentage of only 65.5%. This difference between the total accuracy percentage and the average percentage across the different categories is due to marked differences in the number of situations per category. Because the accuracy percentage is rather low in some of the categories containing a small number of cases, the average percentage drops. It is difficult to decide whether this lower accuracy is due to the small number of cases or to greater difficulties in predicting the respective categories. One has to assume that the true accuracy of the present version of GENESE lies somewhere between 65% and 80%. In view of the fact that with 14 emotion alternatives one would expect 7.14% accuracy if the system operated on chance level, this result seems quite respectable.

Closer inspection of the accuracy percentages for the individual emotions shows that the average across the emotion categories is reduced by very low percentages for anxiety/worry and fear/terror, on the one hand, and indifference/boredom, embarrassment/shame, and guilt feelings, on the other. With respect to the latter group, it is difficult to evaluate the lack of precision in the diagnoses, because only very few cases are involved and the results may not be very stable. However, it is possible that the low performance for indifference/boredom is due to the fact that the SEC profile for this state is not highly differentiated across the different stimulus evaluation checks (see Table 4). Shame and guilt are among the most complex human emotions and the current prediction profiles might well be too simplistic to differentiate these emotions. The comparatively low correlations between predicted and actually obtained profiles (shown in Table 4, Col. 8) suggest important divergences between prediction and empirical means. In consequence, it is not too surprising to find low accuracy for these emotions.

In contrast, the abnormally low accuracy percentages for anxiety and fear are quite unexpected. One possible explanation is the rapidity with which fear situations tend to change—particularly due to the occurrence of events that eliminate the danger or due to a re-evaluation of an event or stimulus as less dangerous. Because of the low accuracy in the anxiety and fear cases, the individual data files and particularly the input profiles were closely scrutinised. This qualitative analysis showed that in many cases subjects entered appraisal results from *both* the danger anticipation *and* the resolution part of the emotion process.

A concrete example may demonstrate this phenomenon: A man between 41 and 60 years of age describes a situation in which his daughter leaned over a burning candle in such a way that her hair started to catch fire. The input vector constituted by the answers to the SEC-based questions and the predicted fear vector are reproduced below (see Table 3 for the exact text of the questions corresponding to the vector entries):

Question	1	2	3	4	5	6	7	8	9	10	11	12	13	14	15
Criterion	nov	tem	ple	rel	exp	con	urg	ego	oth	cha	con	pow	adj	ext	int
Input	5.0	3.0	1.0	0.0	1.0	0.0	5.0	1.0	1.0	5.0	4.0	4.0	4.0	0.0	0.0
Prediction	5.0	4.0	2.0	5.0	1.0	1.0	5.0	1.0	4.0	4.0	2.0	1.0	2.0	0.0	0.0
Difference	0	−1	−1	*	0	*	0	0	−3	1	2	3	2	*	*

The comparison between the input and prediction vectors shows that for the first 10 questions there is rather good correspondence (the difference for "other responsibility"—question 9—is due to the cause of the event being exclusively seen in chance factors, which is of course possible in the present case). However, the answers concerning coping potential (control, power, and adjustment) are clearly related to a phase in the continuous appraisal process in which the danger has already passed (e.g. the flames having been extinguished) and the situation is under control. Otherwise it would be difficult to understand that "very intensive" fear results in spite of the strong ability to control and master the event (an input of 4—"strongly" for both control and power) and it being "quite easy" (4) to adjust to the cosequences of the situation. In this situation, fear was probably quickly followed by relief after realising that no serious consequences had ensued. Yet, the total situation was stored and referred to under the most prominent and distinctive label—in this case fear. Given that the appraisal results reported by the subject are likely to come partly from the fear phase and partly from the relief phase of this emotion episode, it is not surprising that the expert system does not correctly diagnose the target emotion—in this case fear.

Many other similar examples for the anxiety and fear cases could be listed. This probably reflects a tendency of the subjects to respond with respect to the *total situation* which may be characterised by a rapid change in the type of emotion—especially in the case of fear which has been empirically shown to be of very brief duration (Frijda, Mesquita, Sonnemans, & van Goozen, 1991; Scherer & Wallbott, submitted; Scherer, Wallbott, Matsumoto, & Kudoh, 1988; Scherer, Wallbott, & Summerfield, 1986; Wallbott & Scherer, 1986).

In consequence, some of the lack of accuracy may well be due to the respondents' tendency to report appraisals from *different phases* of an emotion situation rather than responding to all SEC appraisal questions with respect to a singular and well-defined slice of time. In addition, further refinement of the prediction profiles is required to improve the predictions for fear and anxiety. The correlation between predicted and obtained profiles is comparatively low for fear and particularly anxiety which would account for low accuracy. It is possible, then, that the theoretically predicted profiles for fear and anxiety are quite unrepresentative of reality and require major changes. Alternatively, it is possible that anxiety/worry situations, in particular, are very variable in their appraisal patterns which would imply that no clear-cut prototype profile can be defined. In this case, it could be one or more central criteria which determine the special nature of this emotion (one or all of which might be missing from the list of stimulus evaluation checks). Thus, the differentiation might hinge on one or more very central criteria which may not be contained in the list of stimulus evaluation checks or imperfectly measured by the questions.

This might imply the need for a revision in the theoretical underpinnings of GENESE, i.e. the list of stimulus evaluation checks. At present, the second question in the system (see Table 3) requires the subject to indicate whether the emotion-inducing event happened in the past, is about to happen, or is likely to happen in the future. This is not based on a particular stimulus evaluation check but is part of the facets of situations which are part of component process theory (see Scherer, 1984a). This particular facet was added to the prediction profile precisely because of the need to differentiate anxiety and fear, which imply threats of negative outcomes in the future, from other negative emotions. However, it may be necessary to go beyond the straightforward timing issue and include dimensions such as certainty (Frijda, 1987; Roseman, 1984, 1991; Smith & Ellsworth, 1985, 1987; see also Reisenzein & Hofmann, 1990). Although "outcome probability" was added to the prediction table in Scherer (1988) this check was not implemented as a question in the expert system (due to the reasons given above in the description of the expert system design). The present results could be interpreted to show that this appraisal dimension might be a major discriminating factor for fear and anxiety and thus needs to be added to the prediction vectors in the expert system.

These considerations demonstrate one of the major uses of the GENESE expert system, providing impetus and direction for theory development. The comparison between predicted and actual appraisal, as well as the precision of diagnosis, should help to identify the points where emotion-specific appraisals are badly represented in the theoretical predictions or where appropriate appraisal criteria are still lacking.

CONCLUSIONS

This paper illustrates how an empirical expert system approach to the study of emotion-antecedent appraisal can go beyond the established paradigms of obtaining correlational evidence between self-report of verbally labelled emotional experiences and inferred appraisal dimensions. In particular, the study examined the feasibility of using an expert system to empirically test the author's predictions on emotion differentiation as based on a limited number of stimulus evaluation checks. The results of a first major study reported here demonstrated an accuracy of *post hoc* diagnosis that substantially exceeds chance for many of the emotions studied and that lends support to the specific appraisal theory suggested by the author.

The present results might well underestimate the actual capacity of the system (and the support for the SEC predictions) as there is some evidence for incorrect input by some users. One particular problem is the reporting of appraisal results from different points in time during the emotional episode which may reflect different emotions (e.g. fear and relief). Because most real-life emotion episodes seem to consist of rapid sequences of changing emotional states (see also Scherer & Tannenbaum, 1986), it is necessary to make the requirement that appraisal reports need to be focused on one clearly defined point or time slice in the emotion episode more apparent to the users of the expert system. One possibility would be to ask the users to segment the recalled emotion episode into several clearly distinguishable segments and to report the appraisal process separately for each of these segments. In this case, GENESE could attempt to diagnose a sequence of emotions rather than an overall state.

One of the major sources for possible errors in reporting the recalled appraisal results is the wording of the questions. For example, even the use of the word "consequence" might have the effect of focusing the respondent's attention on the aftermath of the emotion episode rather than the crucial period of appraisal at the onset of an emotion-eliciting event. This would obviously lead to a reporting of appraisal results from totally different time periods in the emotion episode (and thus render an accurate expert system diagnostic impossible). This problem is one that the expert system approach shares with all other research paradigms in appraisal research that attempt to elicit verbal report of appraisal processes via questionnaires or interviewing. The process of appraisal is clearly non-verbal and probably occurs largely outside of awareness. Thus, the attempt to obtain a verbal report of many fine details from recall of a process that generally occurs in a split second is obviously fraught with many dangers. A particular problem is the conceptualisation of some of the major appraisal dimensions. In the process of developing GENESE it became clear that many subjects had great difficulty in understanding the concept of goal conduciveness (even in the simple formulation used in question 6, Table 3). In the further development of GENESE much attention will have to be paid to this problem. Providing copious HELP screens that the respondent can call up to get more information about a particular question are part of such efforts to avoid noise in the data that is due to incorrect responding to the questions.

The discussion of the results has attempted to show how the expert system approach yields precise suggestions as to where the theoretical assumptions need sharpening or modification. For example, the low accuracy for anxiety and fear clearly indicated the need to add a dimension or check likely to capture the future orientation of the respective appraisals. In consequence, the check of "outcome probability" (or certainty) has been added to the revised version of GENESE (and is given strong weight). First informal observation of some trial runs seem to show that the accuracy of GENESE in diagnosing these emotions has improved quite dramatically. Further studies like the one described here will be necessary to fine tune the prediction vectors with respect to the question of how many and which specific types of appraisal dimensions are required, and how they should be weighted, to satisfactorily diagnose the emotional states reported by the users of the system (see also Frijda & Swagerman, 1987).

Obviously, the expert system approach could provide a principled way of comparing rival appraisal theories and bring about further convergence. The requirement for using this approach in critical experiments opposing different theories is that pertinent questions for the hypothesised appraisal dimensions or criteria can be formulated and that explicit, quantified predictions for an overlapping set of emotion concepts are made by each of the respective theories. In principle, these requirements could be met by most, if not all, of the appraisal theories reviewed in the introduction. Although the present version of GENESE is based on the determination of Euclidian distance in a vector space, it is certainly feasible to implement a configurational, rule-based algorithm if that were to be preferable for a comparison between theories.

The automatic computer-based administration of GENESE allows for easy and economical administration of the procedure to large numbers of subjects, providing a high degree of anonymity. In consequence, the system seems to be well suited to collect large sets of data that would allow to base predictions at least in part on stable empirical patterns. Although some scholars in this area seem convinced that theoretical predictions should be made totally independently of empirical evidence, the present author believes that theory development and refinement must occur in a constant interactive process with empirical data collection. Thus, the predictions made on the basis of the stimulus evaluation check notion of the component process model (Scherer, 1984a,b, 1986, 1988) will change as a result of continuous empirical research. Concretely, the empirically found input patterns (as aggregated over many respondents) for the emotions reported in the study above, in so far as errors in answering the questions can be excluded, will be used to modify the theoretical prediction vectors in the standard version of GENESE.

The development and use of the expert system as a tool for refining theory has just started and new ways of making use of the information provided by the system are being explored. Although at present only the experienced intensity of the emotion is to be judged, future versions of the system will contain additional questions on the duration of the emotion episode and expressive and psychophysiological responding. This should allow to examine the relationship between appraisal patterns on the one hand and specific response patterning on the other. One possible use of this procedure might be to determine to what extent theoretical predictions only work in situations characterised by particular response profiles.

Such refinement may also help to study the issue of pure vs. blended emotions. More generally, GENESE might allow an empirical access to the issue of whether there are basic or fundamental emotions and how many there are of these. Users can specify new emotion concepts not contained in the "knowledge base" if neither of two attempts at a diagnosis have provided a satisfactory classification. The name given to this state is then associated with the input vector provided for the respective appraisal. One can determine, once a large number of such added emotion concepts has been obtained, which states (as defined by highly similar appraisal vectors) reoccur very frequently and ought to be added to the basic version of the system. In addition, these data allow to study the labelling used for specific appraisal patterns in a more inductive fashion.

GENESE also allows us to study individual differences in the appraisal process. Because information about age and gender is obtained, it will be possible, given a large number of respondents, to investigate the effect of these variables on the appraisal patterns reported for specific emotional experiences. More background information could be obtained to refine this kind of analysis. Even more importantly, as the system is able to learn, i.e. modify the appraisal vectors on the basis of the empirical input (see section on the design of GENESE earlier), it is also possible to determine user-specific emotion appraisal patterns. For example, a group of users could be asked to use the system repeatedly over a period of some months, entering each week some of the major emotions that occurred. It would then be possible to compare the resulting matrices, having been adjusted to the empirical appraisal pattern input for each situation in order to find interindividual differences in emotion-antecedent appraisal. This might provide interesting insights into the issue of habitual emotionality and may even lead to a better understanding of moods or affective disturbance.

Manuscript received 23 March 1992
Revised manuscript received 15 August 1992

REFERENCES

Arnold, M.B. (1960). *Emotion and personality*. Vols 1 and 2. New York: Columbia University Press.

De Rivera, J. (1977). A structural theory of the emotions. *Psychological Issues, 10* (4), Monograph 40.

Ekman, P. (1984). Expression and the nature of emotion. In K.R. Scherer & P. Ekman (Eds), *Approaches to emotion*. Hillsdale, NJ: Lawrence Erlbaum Associates Inc, pp. 319–344.

Ekman, P. (1992). An argument for basic emotions. *Cognition and Emotion, 6*, 169–200.

Ellsworth, P.C. & Smith, C.A. (1988). From appraisal to emotion: Differences among unpleasant feelings. *Motivation and Emotion, 12*, 271–302.

Folkman, S. & Lazarus, R.S. (1985). If it changes it must be a process: Study of emotion and coping during three stages of a college examination. *Journal of Personality and Social Psychology, 48*, 150–170.

Frijda, N. (1986). *The emotions*. Cambridge University Press.

Frijda, N.H. (1987). Emotion, cognitive structure, and action tendency. *Cognition and Emotion, 1*, 115–143.

Frijda, N.H., Kuipers, P., & ter Schure, E. (1989). Relation among emotion, appraisal, and emotional action readiness. *Journal of Personality and Social Psychology, 57*, 212–228.

Frijda, N. & Swagerman, J. (1987). Can computers feel? Theory and design of an emotional system. *Cognition and Emotion, 1*, 235–258.

Frijda, N.H., Mesquita, B., Sonnemans, J., & van Goozen, S. (1991). The duration of affective phenomena, or emotions, sentiments and passions. K. Strongman (Ed.), *International review of emotion and motivation*. New York: Wiley, pp. 187–225.

Gehm, Th. & Scherer, K.R. (1988) Relating situation evaluation to emotion differentiation: Nonmetric analysis of cross-cultural questionnaire data. In K.R. Scherer (Ed.), *Facets of emotion: Recent research*. Hillsdale, NJ: Lawrence Erlbaum Associates Inc, pp. 61–78.

Izard, C.E. (1977). *Human emotions*. New York: Plenum.

Johnson-Laird, P.N. & Oatley, K. (1989). The language of emotions: An analysis of a semantic field. *Cognition and Emotion, 3*, 81–123.

Lazarus, R.S. (1968). Emotions and adaptation: Conceptual and empirical relations. In W.J. Arnold (Ed.), *Nebraska Symposium on Motivation*, Vol. 16. Lincoln, NE: University of Nebraska Press, pp. 175–270.

Lazarus, R.S. (1984a). Thoughts on the relations between emotion and cognition. In K.R. Scherer & P. Ekman (Eds), *Approaches to emotion*. Hillsdale, NJ: Lawrence Erlbaum Associates Inc, pp. 247–257.

Lazarus, R.S. (1984b). On the primacy of cognition. *American Psychologist*, 39, 124–129.

Lazarus, R.S. & Smith, C.A. (1988). Knowledge and appraisal in the cognition-emotion relationship. *Cognition and Emotion, 2*, 281–300.

LeDoux, J.E. (1987). Emotion. In F. Plum & V. Mountcastle (Eds), *Handbook of physiology. Nervous system*, Vol. 5. *Higher functions*. Washington, DC: American Physiological Society, pp. 419–459.

LeDoux, J. E. (1989). Cognitive-emotional interactions in the brain. *Cognition and Emotion, 3*, 267–289.

LeDoux, J.E., Farb, C., & Rugiero, D.A. (1990). Topographic organization of neurons in the accoustic thalamus that project to the amygdala. *The Journal of Neuroscience, 10*, 1043–1054.

Leventhal, H. & Scherer, K.R. (1987). The relationship of emotion and cognition: A functional approach to a semantic controversy. *Cognition and Emotion, 1*, 3–28.

Manstead, A.S.R. & Tetlock, P.E. (1989). Cognitive appraisals and emotional experience: Further evidence. *Cognition and Emotion, 3*, 225–240.

Mauro, R., Sato, K., & Tucker, J. (1992). The role of appraisal in human emotions: A cross-cultural study. *Journal of Personality and Social Psychology, 62*, 301–317.

Mees, U. (1985). Was meinen wir, wenn wir von Gefühlen reden? Zur psychologischen Textur von Emotionswörtern. *Sprache und Kognition, 1*, 2–20.

Ortony, A., Clore, G. L., & Collins, A. (1988) *The cognitive structure of emotions.* Cambridge University Press.

Reisenzein, R. & Hofmann, T. (1990). An investigation of dimensions of cognitive appraisal in emotion using the repertory grid technique. *Motivation and Emotion, 14*, 1–26.

Reisenzein, R. & Schönpflug, W. (1992). Stumpf's cognitive-evaluative theory of emotion. *American Psychologist, 47*, 34–45.

Roseman, I.J. (1984). Cognitive determinants of emotion: A structural theory. In P. Shaver (Ed.), *Review of personality and social psychology,* Vol. 5. *Emotions, relationships, and health.* Beverly Hills, CA: Sage, pp. 11–36.

Roseman, I.J. (1991). Appraisal determinants of discrete emotions. *Cognition and Emotion, 5*, 161–200.

Roseman, I.J., Spindel, M.S., & Jose, P. E. (1990). Appraisal of emotion-eliciting events: Testing a theory of discrete emotions. *Journal of Personality and Social Psychology, 59*, 899–915.

Scherer, K.R. (1981). Wider die Vernachlässigung der Emotion in der Psychologie. In W. Michaelis (Ed.), *Bericht über den 32. Kongreß der Deutschen Gesellschaft für Psychologie in Zürich 1980.* Göttingen: Hogrefe, pp. 304–317.

Scherer, K.R. (1982). Emotion as a process: Function, origin, and regulation. *Social Science Information, 21*, 555–570.

Scherer, K.R. (1983). Prolegomina zu einer Taxonomie affektiver Zustände: Ein Komponenten-Prozeß-Modell. In G. Lüer (Ed.), *Bericht über den 33. Kongreß der Deutschen Gesellschaft für Psychologie in Mainz.* Göttingen: Hogrefe, pp. 415–423.

Scherer, K.R. (1984a). On the nature and function of emotion: A component process approach. In K.R. Scherer & P. Ekman (Eds), *Approaches to emotion.* Hillsdale, NJ: Lawrence Erlbaum Associates Inc, pp. 293–317.

Scherer, K.R. (1984b). Emotion as a multicomponent process: A model and some cross-cultural data. In P. Shaver (Ed.), *Review of Personality and Social Psychology,* Vol. 5. Beverly Hills, CA: Sage, pp. 37–63.

Scherer, K.R. (1986). Vocal affect expression: A review and a model for future research. *Psychological Bulletin, 99*, 143–165.

Scherer, K.R. (1988). Criteria for emotion-antecedent appraisal: A review. In V. Hamilton, G.H. Bower, & N.H. Frijda (Eds), *Cognitive perspectives on emotion and motivation.* Dordrecht: Nijhoff, pp. 89–126.

Scherer, K.R. (1993). Neuroscience projections to current debates in emotion psychology. *Cognition and Emotion, 7*, 1–41.

Scherer, K.R. & Tannenbaum, P.H. (1986). Emotional experiences in everyday life: A survey approach. *Motivation and Emotion, 10*, 295–314.

Scherer, K.R. & Wallbott, H.G. (Submitted). *Evidence for universality and cultural variation of differential emotion response patterning.* University of Geneva.

Scherer, K.R., Wallbott, H.G., Matsumoto, D., & Kudoh, T. (1988). Emotional experience in cultural context: A comparison between Europe, Japan, and the USA. In K.R. Scherer (Ed.), *Facets of emotion: Recent research.* Hillsdale, NJ: Lawrence Erlbaum Associates Inc, pp. 5–30.

Scherer, K.R., Wallbott, H.G., & Summerfield, A.B. (Eds) (1986). *Experiencing emotion: A crosscultural study.* Cambridge University Press.

Smith, C.A. & Ellsworth, P.C. (1985). Patterns of cognitive appraisal in emotion. *Journal of Personality and Social Psychology, 48*, 813–838.

Smith, C.A. & Ellsworth, P.C. (1987). Patterns of appraisal and emotion related to taking an exam. *Journal of Personality and Social Psychology, 52*, 475–488.

Solomon, R.C. (1976). *The passions. The myth and nature of human emotion*. Garden City, NY: Doubleday.

Tesser, A. (1990). Smith and Ellsworth's appraisal model of emotion: A replication, extension, and test. *Personality and Social Psychology Bulletin, 16*, 210–223.

Tomkins, S.S. (1984). Affect theory. In K.R. Scherer & P. Ekman (Eds), *Approaches to emotion*. Hillsdale, NJ: Lawrence Erlbaum Associates Inc, pp. 163–196.

Wallbott, H. & Scherer, K.R. (1986). How universal and specific is emotional experience? *Social Science Information, 26*, 763–795.

Weiner, B. (1982). The emotional consequences of causal attributions. In M.S. Clark & S.T. Fiske (Eds), *Affect and cognition. The 7th Annual Carnegie Symposium on Cognition*. Hillsdale, NJ: Lawrence Erlbaum Associates Inc, pp. 185–209.

Weiner, B. (1986). *An attributional theory of motivation and emotion*. New York: Springer.

Zajonc, R.B. (1980). Thinking and feeling: Preferences need no inferences. *American Psychologist, 35*, 151–175.

Zajonc, R.B. (1984). On primacy of affect. In K.R. Scherer & P. Ekman (Eds), *Approaches to emotion*. Hillsdale, NJ: Lawrence Erlbaum Associates Inc, pp. 259–270.

Zajonc, R.B. & Markus, H. (1984). Affect and cognition: the hard interface. In C.E. Izard, J. Kagan, & R.B. Zajonc (Eds), *Emotions, cognition, and behavior*. Cambridge University Press, pp. 73–102.

COGNITION AND EMOTION, 1993, 7 (3/4), 357–387

The Place of Appraisal in Emotion

Nico H. Frijda

Department of Psychology, University of Amsterdam, The Netherlands

The concept of "appraisal" has been used in the literature in a dual way: to refer to the content of emotional experience, as well as to the cognitive antecedents of emotions. I argue that appraisal in the former sense is what is contained in information in self-reports and that this information is of limited use for making inferences on emotion antecedents. This is so because emotional experience may contain appraisals that are part of the emotional response rather than belonging to its causes. They often result from elaboration of the experience after it has begun to be generated. Although in most or all emotions some cognitive appraisal processes are essential antecedents, these processes may be much simpler than self-reports (and the semantics of emotion words) may suggest. The appraisal processes that account for emotion elicitation can be assumed to be of a quite elementary kind.

INTRODUCTION

In the last several years a large amount of theory and data have been produced on the role of appraisal in emotions. Both theory and data make it desirable to evaluate this role, and to provide answers to questions regarding the place of appraisal in emotion: Whether it is indispensable for emotion elicitation, and what the process of appraisal consists of. The questions are of general relevance for the theory of emotion and, in particular, for determining the role of cognition (Lazarus, 1982, 1984, 1991; Zajonc, 1980, 1984). The evidence therefore deserves to be examined.

Appraisal occupies a pivotal role in much of present-day emotion theory. Emotions are considered to result from the appraisal of events with respect to their implications for well-being or for the satisfaction of goals,

Requests for reprints should be sent to N. H. Frijda, Department of Psychology, University of Amsterdam, Roetersstraat 15, 1018 WB Amsterdam, The Netherlands.

I am grateful to several people for helpful criticisms on earlier versions of this paper: Phoebe Ellsworth, Tony Manstead, Batja Mesquita, Reinout Wiers; and Keith Oatley who served as editor for this paper. A first version of the thoughts in this paper was presented at the 24th International Congress of Psychology in Sidney; see Frijda, 1989.

motives, or concerns (Frijda, 1986; Lazarus, 1991; Oatley, 1992; Ortony, Clore, & Collins, 1988; Roseman, 1984; Scherer, 1984; Smith & Lazarus, this issue). Different emotions correspond with different patterns of appraisal; there is ample empirical evidence for this assertion. Recall of instances of different emotions gives rise to different appraisal ratings (Davitz, 1969; Frijda, Kuipers, & ter Schure, 1989; Manstead & Tetlock, 1989; Roseman, Spindel, & Jose, 1990; Smith & Ellsworth, 1985; Tesser, 1990), and descriptions or recollections of events conducive to different appraisals give rise to different emotion ratings (Ellsworth & Smith, 1988a,b; Mesquita, 1993; Reisenzein & Hofmann, 1990; Roseman, 1991; Smith & Lazarus, this issue; Weiner, 1985). The results of both types of experiment closely correspond; appraisal patterns project on to emotion categories in a highly systematic fashion. The correlation between particular patterns of appraisal and particular emotion labels is fairly strong. In my own most recent study, discriminant analysis with appraisals as predictors and 29 Dutch emotion labels yields 38.6% correct predictions (Frijda & Wiers, in prep.). The results appear to hold cross-culturally, considering the work done with Chinese, Japanese, and Indonesian, as well as American and Dutch subjects (Frijda & Sato, in prep.; Markam, 1992; Mauro, Sato, & Tucker, 1992).

However, both the theory of appraisal and the empirical results harbour an important ambiguity. On the one hand, the patterns of appraisal appear to reflect the various emotional experiences. It can be argued that an emotional experience consists, in part, of the perception of the emotional event as appraised by the subject. One can say that an experience of joy is the experience of an event appraised in a joyful way, for instance as beneficial and within reach. The word "joy" may be regarded as just the verbal label for such an experience. Experiences of anger consist of the experience of an event as obstructing one's goals and as caused by someone else's blameworthy intent; "anger" is the word for such an experience. "Appraisal" thus refers to the *content* of emotional experience. It is true that emotional experience may consist of other contents as well (notably, awareness of modes of action readiness and bodily arousal, Frijda, Kuipers, & ter Schure, 1989), and the emotion words refer to these things, too; but awareness of the event as appraised is part of the experience.

On the other hand, appraisal theory holds that emotions *result* from a process of appraisal. Emotions are thought to result from a process that gives the actual stimulus event emotional significance, by linking it to the individual's concerns, and that detects the variables that cause the emergence of a particular emotion. In theory and in the discussions of the empirical results, the appraisal structures identified in self-report research tend to be interpreted as the causal conditions for the emotions. Joy is said to be *elicited by* the appraisal of an event as beneficial and within reach, anger by the appraisal of an event as goal-obstructive and due to someone else's blameworthy intent, and so on.

It is my contention, and that of others (e.g. Oatley, 1992; Parkinson & Manstead, 1992; Russell, 1987) that much of appraisal theory and research suffers from confusing these two roles of appraisal: those of content and of antecedent. This confusion has a serious theoretical consequence, blurring the whole issue of the relation between appraisal and emotions. It obscures the fact that, when discussing emotion antecedents, investigators of cognitive orientation often fail to specify what these antecedents are antecedents of. That is, they fail to provide independent definitions of the emotions concerned (e.g. Ortony et al., 1988; Smith & Ellsworth, 1985). When it is argued that a particular appraisal, for instance the perception of an event as beneficial and controllable, forms the antecedent of a particular emotion, say "joy", the meaning of "joy" is left unspecified, although it may well just refer to the experience of something being appraised as beneficial and controllable.

Of course, emotions involve more than the experience of the events-as-appraised. Emotions are multi-componential phenomena (Scherer, 1984), and affect (that is, pleasant or unpleasant feeling), state of action readiness, and bodily arousal are among the further components and the major determinants of how an emotion is named (Frijda, Kuipers, & ter Schure, 1989). One may argue that a process of appraisal is the antecedent of these other components. This is a reasonable position, and in fact the one I adhere to. I think that changes in affect, action readiness, and arousal result from a process of appraisal. Investigating the relationships between appraisals and these other components is meaningful research of independent variables, and so is research in the relationships between objectively assessed antecedents and appraisals as self-reported. But investigating the relationships between appraisals and emotion labels is research into emotion word meanings or into the structures of experience, as distinct from research that qualifies as investigation of emotion antecedents.

In the present paper, I argue that the appraisal content of emotional experience and the cognitive antecedents of emotion do not always coincide. I further argue that emotions can arise from cognitively relatively poor antecedents; that this is so even for emotions that are fairly articulate, in terms of behaviour or of experience, such as anger and guilt-feeling; that emotional experience often is the result of a constructive process extended over time. Finally, I give a tentative sketch of the process of appraisal that may be helpful in the ever-continuing emotion and cognition debate.

Appraisal as Content and as Process

Appraisal theory has been curiously silent about how appraisal is supposed to operate. Only a few authors have made explicit suggestions (Ellsworth, 1991; Frijda, 1986; Scherer, 1984, and this issue), based primarily upon research in which self-reports of recalled emotion incidents are collected, and appraisal data are derived from these recalls. The reported or derived appraisals are viewed as reflecting the antecedents of the recalled emotions. It should be obvious that this involves an interpretative step that is not necessarily correct or justified. The step contains an implicit assumption regarding the appraisal process that I will call the "linear model" of that process. Presumably, in this reasoning, emotional events elicit a number of cognitive appraisal steps, in fixed or variable sequence, or perhaps in parallel. The process is essentially linear: After the appraisal steps, emotion follows as their result.

Appraisal theory may be right in a general sense, yet the linear model may not be. Emotions may well result from appraisal processes, but these need not be those suggested by the self-reports. The appraisal structures manifest in experience do not necessarily reflect the appraisals that formed the actual antecedents of the emotion, nor need they stem from them. Emotion is not necessarily the end-point of the cognitive process.

It is indeed easy to confuse the contents and antecedents of emotional experience. It is easy to believe that one fell in love because of the beauty of one's beloved, but it would be hard to maintain that perceiving one's beloved to be beautiful always preceded the emotion and triggered it; there is, in fact, evidence for the reverse (Rombouts, 1992). Emotional experience, including its cognitive content, the awareness of the emotional event as appraised, belongs to the emotional *response*, that is, to the emotion itself. It is part of one's emotional reaction towards the eliciting event and stands in a complex and somewhat loose relationship to that event. This is particularly clear with respect to the perceived pleasantness or unpleasantness of the event, its valence. Experiencing someone's likeability or aversiveness *is* an emotional experience, and not its elicitor. Sense of helplessness has been shown often to be an expression of depression, rather than its cause. Judgements of life satisfaction vary with experimentally manipulated mood (Morris, 1989). These examples may for the moment suffice for giving credence to the claim that considering reports of emotional appraisals as reflecting emotion antecedents involves a nonself-evident interpretive step.

Discrepancies between Experiences and Antecedents

The interpretive step and the linear model assume an isomorphism between the appraisal content of emotional experience and the emotion antecedents. The reasons to doubt that such an isomorphism always applies are many; reports of emotional experience are not infallible cues to their causes. First, of course, the verbal reports are not infallible cues to experience. There are deep reasons for that. Apart from the general constructive nature of verbal report of emotional experience (e.g. Nisbett & Wilson, 1977), emotional experience in particular can be inarticulate for the very reason that it is emotional experience. "It is burning with a small flame, to be able to say how much one burns", Montaigne (1588/1965, p. 60, author's translation) quoted Petrarch; and I remember Goethe's dictum: "When the soul speaks, it is not any longer the soul that speaks". Secondly, Parkinson and Manstead (1992) have argued that there is no reason to believe that introspection is reliable in identifying the fine grain of the emotion antecedents, even when it might identify the fine grain of experience—for instance, precisely why anger rather than sadness resulted. Thirdly, extending the examples given previously, the contents of experience may be products of emotions as well as the other way around. Emotions can cause attributions, justifications, and belief changes; I will come back to this. The fourth reason to doubt that emotional experience gives valid cues to its antecedents, and in fact the major reason for that doubt, is that discrepancies exist between the contents of emotional experiences and what is known to have been their actual antecedents, or what can be reasonably inferred about them.

There are discrepancies of several sorts. Discrepancies exist between emotions and the accounts that individuals can give of the reasons for these emotions. Often, experience just lacks indications of what caused it. Animal phobias provide good examples. Most spider phobics know that their fears are unfounded; there often is no conscious awareness of what harm the spider might do, apart from that of evoking the fear (Rachman, 1990). The appraisal of the spider as dangerous or weird is a manifestation of the fear itself, and the accounts of what that weirdness comes from are mainly efforts at making sense of the feelings. Understanding phobia cannot rely on introspection.

Furthermore, there occur discrepancies between emotional experience or self-ascription of emotion, and the emotion suggested by the subject's behaviour (e.g. Furedey, Riley, & Frederikson; Lang, 1977). Behaviour may indicate that an event is being appraised in a particular way, although the subject's account of his or her experience does not reflect that appraisal. A person may manifest angry behaviour in response to an offence—reproaches, angry tone of voice, use of sharp words—but declare him- or herself sad or worried. A state of being upset or an angry response may follow an event usually considered jealousy-provoking (that is, an event representing an "outrage for the self because of a second person on whom one has some claim and in relation to a third person who could supplant one in the affections of that second person", Oatley, 1992,

p. 77), even though the subject does not report feeling jealous, or may even deny it. He or she may categorise the emotion differently, as fear, sadness or indignation (Bryson, 1991). Notice that the emotional upset, cognitive ruminations, and interpersonal behaviour can only be understood as the results of particular cognitive appraisals, but that the subject may not be aware of these (disregarding, for the moment, the possibilities of insincerity). Examples of such discrepancies abound in fictional literature (e.g. Tolstoy's *Anna Karenina*; see Oatley, 1992, pp. 196–197).

I will present some analyses that, I think, illustrate these discrepancies.

Illustration from the Analysis of Anger

The cognitive structure of anger is often considered to consist of an aversive event for which someone else is held responsible (Frijda, 1987; Scherer, 1984; Smith & Ellsworth, 1985). According to others, it consists of the perception of offence to a norm: An appraised wrong (Averill, 1982), something that "ought" not to be so (De Rivera, 1977), or someone's blameworthy action (Ortony et al., 1988). An additional appraisal feature is the unfair, arbitrary, or illegitimate nature of the inflicted harm. By implication, these features are generally assumed to form the cognitive antecedents of anger.

Are they? It all depends on how "anger" is defined. If it is defined as the feeling involving these features, or the feeling contingent upon events with those features, the assumption is trivially true. But if it is defined by how the subject labels his or her response, or by angry behaviour giving evidence of the attribution of causal agency or received harm, then the assumption is incorrect. Many experiences or responses of anger, defined in the latter way, are elicited by events that involve no blameworthy action, and sometimes not even a responsible agent, even according to the subject. Anger incidents of this type are mentioned rather frequently in diary studies (Averill, 1982) and comprise a separate and colourful section in Hall's (1899) large-scale survey of anger. They include simple frustrations: one's car refusing to start, finding one's bicycle has a flat tyre, seeing that it rains on the fifth day of one's holiday after four previous days of rain. Similar reactions appear upon unexpected pain or damage for which oneself rather than anybody else is to blame: hitting one's head on the kitchen shelf, dropping a needle for the third time in a row, hammering one's thumb. In some anger instances other people are indeed causally involved, but not as intending agents on whom responsibility falls. The target of anger may be a person who has fallen ill on the day of one's party, or one who just happened to be present when a plan failed.

The feeling, in the above instances, may be called "frustration" rather than "anger", but the point is that these frustration emotions often have the content of anger. That is, the subjects tend to treat the causes of their discomfort as intentional and responsible agents. Cars, bicycles, and rainy days are blamed; subjects may complain that it is unfair that they in particular always have to endure such misfortunes, as if indeed an unjust agent was responsible. Serious frustrations are blamed upon the garage mechanic, the person who borrowed one's bicycle last week, the producers of spray cans that harm the environment, or the unjustness of God; or, in the event, upon the hammer, the nail, or the kitchen shelf. The attributions also appear from the actions. The causal objects are treated as if they were to blame, physically as well as verbally, by scolding or hitting them. Hall (1899) gives convincing protocols: a carpenter who smashed his expensive tools, a man who hurt himself on a coil of barbed wire, and the next day walked a mile to dump the coil into the river, and a man who fell over a large stone, went into his barn, came back with a hammer, smashed the stone, and threw the fragments into a fire. The process appears to be quite basic: Rats attack nearby rats when receiving unexpected footshocks (pain-induced aggression; Laborit, 1969; Ulrich & Azrin, 1962). Often a "wrong" or norm transgression is perceived in the event: the kitchen shelf "ought not to have been there"; one "should" not be so stupid as to drop the needle. It appears undeniable in all these instances that the blame-worthiness of agents and the unfairness of the events are invoked after an angry emotion has already been elicited, and because of that emotion. There is no reason to assume that the same sequence is not followed in many events where an intentional agent is in fact involved: First the anger, then the causal attribution. In fact, there *is* reason to assume such a sequence, because of the evidence that anger does enhance such attributions (Ellsworth, 1991; Schwarz, Bless, & Bohner, 1991).

Emotions of Guilt and their Antecedents

Further illustrations that the cognitive content of an emotion is not always a cue to its antecedent come from an analysis of guilt emotions.[1] The analysis is based upon a study conducted by Kroon (1988). The data consist of self-reports of serious guilt emotions by 42 subjects who came to our laboratory in response to a newspaper advertisement requesting participation in a study of such feelings. The subjects were asked to report in detail

---

[1] Because "guilt feeling" sometimes may suggest the awareness of a guilt that has been established independently, I will use "guilt emotion" whenever there might be a risk for misunderstanding.

the event or events that had produced the emotions, and to describe the precise circumstances, the relationship to the victim, if any, and what they felt guilty about. The subjects gave their accounts while seated alone in a dimly lit room by speaking into a microphone placed close to them, so that they only needed to whisper. After signalling to the experimenter that they had finished their account, they filled out an extensive questionnaire in her presence.

The analysis of the spontaneous accounts and the questionnaire probed for the elements assumed to cause guilt emotions, according to current theories, and to determine their appraisal structure. Guilt emotions are supposed to originate in blameworthy acts by the self, that is, norm transgressions for which the subject feels he or she carries responsibility. For instance, Izard (1977, pp. 423,424) says: "The phenomenological determinants of guilt are perhaps easier to explain than the determinants of any of the other negative emotions. Guilt results from wrongdoing. The behaviour that evokes guilt violates a moral, ethical, or religious code. Usually people feel guilty when they become aware that they have broken a rule and violated their own standards or beliefs. They may also feel guilty for failing to accept or carry out their responsibility" and "Guilt occurs in situations in which one feels personally responsible"; and Lewis (1971, p. 81) states: "Guilt . . . is evoked by . . . the acceptance or acknowledgment of moral transgression." The content of guilt feeling is supposed, and found, to consist of these same elements (Roseman, 1984; Scherer, 1984; Smith & Ellsworth, 1985), together with the felt action tendency to undo what happened, to atone or compensate for it, or to comply with the victim's wishes (Freedman, 1970). Kroon's questionnaire contained questions asking for these various aspects as felt at the time of the guilt emotion, for action tendencies felt and for behaviours shown. Questions about responsibility, causality, and blame were taken from a guilt emotion study by McGraw (1987). The analysis suggests that whereas the emotional event is almost invariably appraised in the way just indicated, this appraisal appears in many cases to be a result of the emotion rather than its cause. Considering the events that precipitated the emotion, it appears unlikely that the emotion was always precipitated *because* the event was perceived in that way.

Here are the results. Almost all 42 accounts concerned intense guilt emotions; the average intensity rating on a 7-point scale was 5.9, with only 3 of the subjects indicating a "weak" or "moderate" emotion (scale values 1 or 2). Seventy-four per cent indicated that they had been quite overcome, and 81% had been "truly gripped" by guilt feeling (scale values 5 to 7). The structure of the emotions corresponded to the hypothesis; true and serious guilt emotions were involved. Ninety per cent of the subjects indicated that the harm they had inflicted was serious to very serious (this and the following percentages in this paragraph refer to rating scale values of 5 to 7). Self-blame was considerable. Seventy-five per cent of respondents considered themselves to have been egoistic, 75% considered themselves to have acted badly or wrongly, which we take as evidence of felt moral transgressions. Furthermore, 70% of the respondents considered themselves to have been responsible for what happened, and 60% considered themselves strongly guilty. Behaviours and thoughts were indeed of the undoing or compensating type. Seventy per cent had often had thoughts like "if only I had . . .", 60% were angry with themselves, 80% had been ruminating and turning things over in their minds; 80% had tried to be helpful and agreeable to the person about whom they felt guilty, 60% had wanted to apologise, and 54% had tried to accommodate the other person's wishes.

However, there are inconsistencies in the data. The feelings of responsibility often tended to conflict with more objective assessments by the respondents themselves of what had happened. Only 28% of the subjects considered themselves to have been the cause of whatever had happened. Thirty-one per cent considered the event to have been caused by someone else; 59% indicated that they had indeed felt themselves to have been the cause while they knew this had not in fact been the case (the percentages are non-exclusive). As regards norm transgression: 40% estimated that what they had done had been the right thing to do, the feeling of guilt notwithstanding; 64% judged that they could not have acted otherwise. Only 7% admitted to any evil intention; 30% had felt provoked. One may doubt the honesty or reliability of these responses; there would however seem little reason to do so, considering the strength of the feelings of guilt reported, and the nature of the detailed accounts of the events. The data, moreover, accord with the finding of McGraw (1987) of a negative correlation between having intended the victim's misfortune and the intensity of one's guilt feeling. The data cast doubt upon a linear relationship between a prior appraisal process involving one's blameworthiness, one's responsibility, or a norm transgression, and a subsequent guilt emotion. Of course, considerations of responsibility enter somewhere into the appraisal process, as they figure in experience. What is doubtful is that they necessarily are among the elements eliciting the emotion in the first place.

That doubt is sustained by a close examination of the precipitating events. In several instances, appraisal of own responsibility or of norm transgression prior to emotion arousal appears implausible—implausible, that is, unless one holds to the a priori assumption that wherever there is an emotion of guilt there should be some sort of guilt, at least subjectively. There often are discrepancies between the cognitive content of the emotion and the presumed structure of the antecedents.

TABLE 1
Antecedents of Guilt Emotions ($N = 42$)

Antecedent Category	N	%
Intentionally caused harm; neglect; morally reprehensible behaviour	14	33
Harm or grief to others as an unavoidable consequence of following one's desires or goals	13	31
Unintended harm or grief to others (other than previous)	19	45
Misfortunes suffered at the hands of others	4	10
Falling short of one's expectations or those of others	4	10
Reproaches suffered	9	22
Having obtained or received some advantage	3	7
Serious sequel to one's unrelated act	10	24

The events that led to the guilt emotions, as reported by the subjects, were categorised. Sixty assignments to the various categories were made, because some accounts led to more than one assignment. Table 1 lists the numbers and proportion of cases in each category. Fourteen cases (33%) were assigned to the categories of guilt by commission or omission (morally reprehensible behaviour such as in sex guilt or having committed sexual assault, having intentionally caused discomfort, or having been neglectful in one's own eyes) that clearly form appropriate causes, in terms of theories of guilt emotion such as that of Izard (1977). Four other subjects (10%) mentioned events that also suggest transgression of norms: The subjects had fallen short of their expectations or of those of others. The remaining instances did not, or at least did not clearly, seem to involve something that could meaningfully be called norm transgression or the subject's responsibility, or both. Nineteen (45%) of these cases concerned having caused unintended harm to some loved person; in 13 of these the harm to a loved one was the unwanted consequence of following one's desires or goals. The nature of the harm, and the motivations of the subjects, varied widely. One subject felt badly towards her parents because she had made them suffer by abandoning her vocation as a nun; another because of the pains she had caused them when in a psychotic period; a third because of the lack of understanding he had shown his parents during his puberty; a fourth because she loved her foster parents more than her true mother; a fifth because she had left her mother to live an independent life; a sixth felt guilty towards her ex-boy-friend because she had fallen in love with someone else; a seventh felt guilty because she did not love her husband any more; an eighth because she refused her husband sexual intercourse, and he showed how he suffered. The last-mentioned subject commented: "The strange thing is that, deep down, you know you're not guilty." It is remarkable that many of the subjects said that they did not regret what they had done, and that they would do it again in the same situation, albeit pehaps in a somewhat different manner.

In 10 (24%) of the cases the guilt emotion was provoked by a serious event that happened to the person they felt guilty towards, but that did not stand in a causal relationship to the act they felt guilty about. For instance, one woman felt guilty when, after she had left him, her former boy-friend suffered a serious accident. Four subjects (10%) mentioned guilt emotions after having experienced harm at the hands of others; examples are having been left by one's partner and having suffered abuse from one's parents when a child. In fact, guilt feelings appear quite frequently in victims of child abuse, sexual or otherwise.

Norm violation does not seem prominent in the causation of guilt emotions that emerged after serious loss for which the subject is not responsible; for instance, when a relative has died, towards whom they felt they should have been more kind or caring. The contingency is known from mourning therapy (Ramsey, 1979), and occurs among Kroon's (1988) subjects. Norm-violation seems entirely absent in those cases of strong guilt emotion (not occurring among Kroon's subjects, but described in the trauma literature) that result from having been an active participant in a traffic accident in which someone was gravely hurt or killed. Particularly if the victim was a child, and even if the accident was clearly the victim's fault, the guilt emotions can be long-lasting and lead to intense ruminations and vain efforts in thought to undo what happened. And as regards responsibility: Would one have felt responsible if one had managed to narrowly avoid the child who jumped into the road without looking? No, the blame would fall entirely upon the child itself. All these latter cases strongly suggest the sense of responsibility to result from some sort of secondary cognitive elaboration.

The main issue is the role of appraisals of having been responsible for a harm and of having transgressed a norm. They certainly are components of the experiences, but the accounts make it doubtful that they are always components of the antecedents. It is true that in many of the above instances one may suppose culpable aggressive or sexual wishes to have been present. Why, however, should one make this supposition, except on a priori grounds? And even if the presence of such wishes can be demonstrated, are they indeed responsible for the guilt emotions? Can it be blindly assumed that aggressive wishes, in subjects like those described, were against their norms?

The issue carries weight because an alternative account of many of the instances of guilt emotions is possible and plausible, even if it does not fit the moral, normative connotations of the concept of guilt. One aspect appears common to almost all accounts in Kroon's (1988) study. It is an aspect that indeed figures prominently in some analyses of guilt feeling

(Hoffman, 1976, 1984; Manstead & Tetlock, 1989), namely, that harm has been caused by the subject. It seems that almost all the emotions of guilt are elicited by an event in which the subject was causally involved in inflicting harm, whether this was against a norm or not, and whether he or she was responsible or not. It seems that one feels responsible in being involved in the causation of harm, whether this is warranted or not. That appears to be the invariant. As with anger as discussed previously, it appears that a distress about being causally involved with harm comes first, and the attribution of responsibility second.

In fact, it is quite plausible to consider distress contingent upon having inflicted harm upon someone else as the basic root of guilt emotion. Such distress may well represent a fundamental human propensity. It would result, in part, from elementary empathy (Hoffman, 1984). It may well constitute an original and unlearned stimulus for correcting one's behaviour, and for efforts at undoing the harm or compensating for it. Such an unlearned propensity is, of course, biologically plausible: It renders the individual careful in her or his dealings with fellow individuals, and diminishes the chances of reprisals. Guilt can be seen as a mechanism for the regulation of interpersonal behaviour (Baumeister, Stillwell, & Heatherton, in press).

An elementary propensity for suffering distress upon having inflicted harm is as plausible as a propensity to inflict harm upon someone who inflicted harm upon you. It may be recalled that McGraw (1987) found an inverse correlation between the intention to inflict harm and subsequent guilt-feeling. This finding is contrary to Heider's (1958) theory claiming that level of intentionality should correspond to degree of experienced guilt; it also is in conflict with current assertions in cognitive emotion theory (e.g. Roseman, 1984; Scherer, 1984). McGraw explains her finding by assuming that an intention to harm justifies having done the harm and thereby reduces the blameworthiness or guilt; having harmed unintentionally or accidentally cannot benefit from such reduction. However, this presupposes that harming others is necessarily felt to be blameworthy, and there is little evidence to that effect. McGraw's explanation can be plausibly and parsimoniously rephrased by way of the assumption that causing harm to others can be both a source of distress and a source of satisfaction; it all depends upon who the others are, whether or not the harm one did was elicited by having suffered harm, and what the outcomes were of the harm one did: Loss of threat or loss of love.

It should be noted as perhaps one of the most salient facts about guilt emotions that their object is not just any person, but usually someone with whom one maintains an intimate relationship. That is not only so in the cases examined by Kroon (1988). It appears to hold generally. Baumeister et al. (in press), found that in 85% of the recalled guilt episodes the protagonist was regarded highly or favourably. For that reason they suggest that one of the main functions of guilt emotion is to contribute to good relationships. One may infer that a major source of guilt emotions is not an appraisal of norm transgression or own responsibility for harm, but an appraisal of risk of loss of love.

Note, if all this is true, that the cognitive antecedents of guilt emotions are much simpler than the content of the guilt emotion suggests. They even may be quite different.

The Antecedents of Shame

Shame is generally supposed to involve fairly complex cognitive appraisals. Shame is "about the self", it is thought to be an expression of superego functioning, and to result from discrepancies with the ego-ideal (Lewis, 1971, pp. 82, 83, 87). Its development is held to depend upon an awareness of the self. It is supposed to be triggered by perceived inconsistency with personal standards or by falling short of expectations of others (Manstead & Tetlock, 1989, Scherer, 1984), and to involve a sense of responsibility for the shameful act (Manstead & Tetlock, 1989). Ample evidence exists that these appraisals are, indeed, part of most experiences of shame (Manstead & Tetlock, 1989; Frijda, Kuipers, & ter Schure, 1989).

Analysis of shame antecedents often traces these appraisals back to what elicited the emotion but, as with anger and guilt emotion, this is not always appropriate. There exist instances of shame where inconsistency with the ego-ideal and with one's norms does not appear to play a role; there exists nonmoral as well as moral shame (Ausubel, 1955). Most noticeable nonmoral instances are those in which shame is evoked by social ridicule on issues that the subject did not consider shameful before that ridicule occurred. Our own material (from self-reports by volunteers from a non-student population; Terwijn, 1993) contains the example of a girl called Johnny,[2] who suffered each time her name was called out and she saw the surprised faces. The case is representative of those many instances in which children are shamed, and felt ashamed, because of some morally neutral attribute singled out as a basis for rejection by others, such as red hair or racial characteristics. Whatever norm or ego-ideal might be argued to be involved, it concerns a norm or ideal only because one is shamed by not conforming to it. This would seem to apply also to many instances where shame is aroused by an act rather than an attribute of the self. Take another example from Terwijn's (1993) data. The subject had felt ashamed because she tried to jump a ditch and fell into it, much to everyone's

---

[2] The Dutch name was different, but also a name usually reserved for boys.

merriment except hers. Perhaps the subject held a norm that one should not make mistakes in public; more likely the shame stems from the dislike of social ridicule.

Social rejection appraised as due to an attribute or act of the self appears sufficient as an elicitor of shame. The "self" has here no more cognitive content than that of being the carrier of the attribute leading to rejection. "Shame" here means the painful emotion so labelled by the subject or a witness, and that gives rise to blushing and to hiding behaviour (Scheff, 1988). Its cognitive content may involve the self, as something that should change in order to escape the ridicule, but if this is so it can well be the product of the painful emotion rather than its source; and the same may well apply to the norm of not to be red-haired, black, or called Johnny. In fact, Terwijn (1993) advances evidence that the subject's moral or other rejection of the shameful act or property is part of the shame response, rather than the cause of that response: it helps to decrease the distance caused by rejection. As with anger and guilt emotion, one may argue that a painful emotion caused by social rejection and leading to hiding behaviour is to be called "distress", because "shame", by definition, implies a more elaborate sense of norms and self; but as is the case with anger and guilt emotion, these latter appraisal attributes cannot be said to explain anything, except a certain word use. They are relevant in analyses of semantics (e.g. Johnson-Laird & Oatley, 1989), but not for the analyses of emotion elicitation.

It is not unlikely that the elicitation of shame may even be simpler than just sketched. The trigger of some shame (as defined by crying, hiding, blushing, and avoidance) may well be the felt disruption of social joining behaviour. Nonmoral shame may easily be seen in this way (disruption of social joining is the reverse side of rejection), and many instances of moral shame may be similar. This explanation would make (some) shame similar to (some or all) embarrassment, when the latter is understood as due to the disruption of social role behaviour, as in the "dramaturgic theory" of embarrassment (Parrot & Smith, 1991).

All this does not deny that the antecedents of shame may always include important cognitive elements. However slight the notion of self may be in attributing the rejection to the self, some attribution is involved. The laughter of the others in social ridicule, as with the girl who fell in the ditch, must have been understood as implying social rejection. But those cognitive elements are low-level ones that may be available at an early age, long before the development of a true sense of self and of an ego-ideal.

Of course, typical emotions of shame are elicited by norm-incompatible behaviour and by offences against the ideal self; and, of course, the role of these cognitive aspects grows during emotional development. Shame caused by having offended one's norms is not the same and feels different from shame caused by simple social ridicule; for one thing hiding from others does not really help. But still: One may wonder about the precise contribution of such cognitive elements to emotion elicitation. That is to say: One may wonder whether, in such cases of shame, it is the norm incompatibility that elicits the shame (that is, the painful emotion, the blushing, the hiding), or the appraisal of threat of social rejection implied by the incompatibility. In other words: Is the emotion elicited by the appraisal of norm incompatibility, or by the fact that norm-incompatible behaviour makes one foresee social rejection? To put it yet another way: Is the triggering role of public exposure of one's mistakes or misdeeds peripheral or central to shame emotions? The question has a deeper implication: Is shame primarily an inner state and evaluator, or is it a regulator of social relationships?

Cognitive Elaboration

The discrepancies between the appraisal processes that elicit emotions, and the experience of events-as-appraised suggest that appraisals as may appear in consciousness only partly reflect the emotion antecedents. How events are appraised *during* emotions appears often to result from a cognitive elaboration of the appraisal processes *eliciting* the emotion. The products of such elaboration are often what provides the characteristic flavour of the experience. In anger, the eliciting appraisal may be that of sudden, unexpected pain, but the experience is that of an evil-doing and responsible agent. Guilt emotion may be precipitated by the appraisal of having caused harm with a risk of loss of love; the experience includes one's sense of responsibility and blameworthiness. If this is so, why do these elaborations occur, and where does their content come from?

Why are the elaborations made? I think that their main source lies in the very mechanisms of emotion. Emotions involve attributions, belief changes, changes in attention and in sensitisation for particular classes of stimuli. It is not for nothing that emotion has been defined as a change in activation "which being given, the mind is thereby determined to think of one thing rather than another" (Spinoza, 1677/1989, III, General definition of the emotions). These cognitive processes can themselves be seen as instrumental in accomplishing the aims of the action readiness that forms a core component of the emotion (Frijda, 1986). Modes of action readiness represent the activation or deactivation of sets of response mechanisms for dealing with emotional contingencies. Attribution, belief change, and the like belong to these sets of response mechanisms. Anger, for instance, involves the action readiness to remove an obstacle or a wrong; attributions can be understood as efforts to identify a responsible agent at which the actual removal efforts may be directed. Guilt emotion involves the urge to undo a harm or forestall a loss of love; beliefs concerning one's actual guilt identify a reason for the loss of love, which may make undoing or forestalling possible. Shame is directed at preventing social rejection; identifying some feature as the ground for rejection—an inconsistency with a norm—may help in such prevention. That emotions have cognitive consequences, as well as causes, is generally accepted. That they are elements of the emotional response mechanisms is a plausible conclusion from several lines of research. Mood and memory research indicates that sadness activates memories of previous misfortunes (e.g. Teasdale & Spencer, 1984) and failure outcomes (Johnson & Tversky, 1983); mood and attention research suggests that anxiety leads to enhanced attention to potentially threatening information (e.g. Matthews, 1988); emotion and belief change studies indicate that anger leads to a search for intentionally acting causal agents (Ellsworth, 1991; Schwarz et al., 1991). I mentioned pain-induced aggression in rats as showing such search in an entirely different research context. Sensitivity changes in cats seeing a mouse (Flynn, 1973) show at what elementary levels the cognitive response mechanisms may operate.

Some cognitive elaborations result from a somewhat different cognitive emotion mechanism: That of the cognitive monitoring of emotion. Under normal circumstances, humans continuously monitor their emotions, in order to be able to regulate them and to adapt them to circumstances, such as the seriousness of the eliciting event or the likelihood of retaliation or support—in general to fit pragmatic, social, and normative requirements (Carver & Scheier, 1990; Diener, 1980; Frijda, 1986). Justifications for one's emotion or emotional act are among the considerations influencing emotion regulation. In anger the background of such processes is clear in the elaborate prescriptions and proscriptions for what is proper as a cause for anger, as a target of anger, or as angry behaviour (Averill, 1982).

Close to justification is the desire to understand and make sense of one's emotions. Emotion monitoring occurs simultaneously at several different levels, including that of integrating the emotion into one's self-standards (Carver & Scheier, 1990).

Then there are what psychoanalytic theory calls defensive functions. Cognitive elaborations may help to maintain the emotion when it provides the subject with some sort of gain, or to transform the emotion into another one that yields a higher gain or less discomfort (Frijda, 1986, 1988; Frijda & Zammuner, 1992). The gains follow closely the functions of emotionally motivated cognition mentioned earlier. Attributing one's misery to a responsible agent, whether in anger or in guilt emotion, provides an object through which change can be affected and, in addition, it can produce some appraisal of controllability: If what has happened was due an intending agent it might not have happened, and it may be possible to undo it or make up for it. Thoughts like "if only I had not done that . . ." after loss or accidental harm play with possibilities of the situation, as if these were still in some measure open, or as if time could be turned backwards.

There may be further, more subtle gains in elaboration. For instance, having caused distress may well be more acceptable, more bearable, when it is seen as coming from a norm transgression and reflecting upon one's self-image, as someone who did wrong. The act is thereby placed within a causal nexus and it clarifies one's position towards the offended party. Also, emotions differ in the social roles they imply, or the effort they cost. Guilt emotion aims at restoring ties with others (Baumeister et al., in press), and anger sometimes aims to disrupt them, and sometimes to renegotiate them (Averill, 1982). Instructive, in this regard, is the account of one of Kroon's (1988) subjects, a 35-year-old woman who had been abused by her father. She sometimes feels guilty, she reported, because as a 13-year-old child she had refused, her mother's urgings notwithstanding, to say goodbye to her father when leaving for school; in the course of the day someone came to the school to tell her that her father had died from a heart attack. Now, 20 years later, she occasionally feels a strong compulsion to visit his grave. One may easily suppose various sorts of unconscious processes (guilt for wish-fulfilment when the father died, or for her anger as such), but these do not seem to be the main issue, considering the points of emphasis in her story: Being rejected by her family for her coldness towards father, and her own interpretation of her guilt emotions: "He has spoilt my life, because he . . . he vented his sexual hang-ups upon me. It is . . . eh . . . I think my guilt feeling is a form of anger. But because I have no means of expressing my anger, because there is nothing I can do with it. For me, guilt feeling is easier to express than anger."

Quite clearly, the motivations for cognitive elaboration, their effects, the variables that determine them, can only be pointed at, in this section. Cognitive elaboration is too vast a topic to be truly treated here. But it seems important, if only because individuals, genders, and cultures may well differ in major relevant variables.

Where does the material for cognitive elaborations come from, and why is the content of these elaborations often fairly consistent over individuals, different propensities notwithstanding? The answer appears to be simple, in principle at least. The cognitive elaborations are rendered possible both by additional uptake of information from the stimulus event, and from memory, that is, from cognitive schemata (Fiske, 1982) or "emotion scripts" (Fischer, 1991; Russell, 1987). Emotion scripts or schemata are learned structures that embody event types, their associated affect, the possible causes and consequences of associated emotions, and their social and personal significance, and so on. Scripts and schemata allow experienced appraisal patterns to deviate from appraisal based upon the actual input that triggered the emotion in the first place (Parkinson & Manstead, 1992; Russell, 1987). But the scripts tend to reflect correlations between event features that are present in reality. For many inflictions of harm one *is* responsible, social rejection often *is* the consequence of having deviated from a group norm, and is often paralleled by rejection by the self because of deviation from ego-ideals.

Cognitive elaboration is described in this section from a strategic perspective. I think that, indeed, cognitive elaborations are controlled processes, even if most of the time one is not very much aware of them. They continue, presumably, until a stable cognitive state is reached, that is, until experience corresponds with the subject's norms for acceptability. More importantly, one may expect elaboration to be engaged in only if the subject has reasons to do so, and has time and other resources for it. If time and resources are lacking or if the subject does not bother (as in high excitement or "deindividuation"; Diener, 1980), elaboration may never be undertaken. Emotional experience remains diffuse or inarticulate, as emotional experiences often are. It may remain a perception, like the perception of a foul deed or a dangerous event, an experience of mere pain or distress.

Emotion Antecedents

The above considerations imply that even emotions like anger, guilt, and shame, that have cognitively complex definitions, can result from rather elementary stimulus constellations, and through rather elementary appraisal processes. That is to say: hostile behaviour, atonement behaviour and compliance, or hiding behaviour and blushing, and self-labelling as "anger" or "guilt" may result from much simpler cognitive antecedents than are usually associated with those emotion concepts. The more complex cognitions result from elaborations motivated by the emotions.

One may argue that the subjective experience, before such elaboration, is "really" one of distress or pain, rather than of anger or guilt; and of course cognitive elaborations use some sort of appraisal process. To some extent, my distinction between emotion-eliciting appraisal and the processes underlying elaboration parallels Lazarus' (1966) early distinction between primary and secondary appraisal, the first responsible for emotions *per se*, and the second for what specific emotion it will turn out to be. But the point here is precisely that the specific emotion, in terms of articulate, differentiated behaviour, as well as in those of self-ascription, results from the "primary", automatic, and relatively simple appraisal.

Let me suggest what, in the simplest cases, might be the eliciting conditions for anger, guilt emotion, and shame.

As for anger: The most elementary elicitors, as in the examples given earlier, are acute goal interference (the interruption of ongoing goal-directed behaviour, as when a nail slips from your fingers while hammering, or because of sudden movement obstruction; Watson, 1929), acute frustration (not getting what you firmly had expected to get; Dollard et al., 1939), and acute aversive stimulation (pain and startle stimuli—hitting your head on the kitchen shelf; Berkowitz, 1989). The qualification "acute" refers to the occurrence of an event clearly delineated in time. Acute interferences engender that peculiar feeling that they "ought" not to be there, but not in a socially normative sense: One is geared to coming closer to one's goal, and the acuteness of the interference underscores that it in no way fits that what one was set for, that one reckoned that the goal situation would in fact be obtained. The qualification does not require much cognition; it is implicit in the very fact of being oriented towards one's goal, even if perception of animate agency would seem strongly to facilitate the ought-not. At the same time, an elementary cognitive condition *is* involved, even without perception of animate agency: namely, in the orientation towards the goal, its prominence, the effort with which it is held.

Not all events that arouse anger embody this elementary constellation. The interferences, frustrations, and pains causing anger often are not acute at all, and these may well involve more cognitive intervention. A class of anger antecedents that seems quite remote from the elementary condition is that of perceived norm transgression. Norm transgressions by others often evoke vehement anger, even when no personal injury is involved. Averill's (1982) subjects frequently mentioned norm transgressions as anger antecedents. Hall (1899), in his survey, found a number of anger causes that are best understood as perceived norm transgressions: "Personal antipathies based on physical forms and features", "Personal antipathies based upon peculiar acts and automatisms", "Dress and ornament", and "Injustice". The causes collected in the category "Dress and ornament" included such things as earrings worn by men, abhorrent to 130 out of Hall's 679 female respondents.

Perception of a norm violation of course implies knowledge of some norm. Even so it may not be so different from acute goal interference. It may well be that norm violations incite anger only when the subject feels that the other person's behaviour renders customary social interaction unfeasible, or upsets one's view of the world. It may not be so different, as an elicitor of anger, from the thwarting of desires for power and control over the environment, that even enrages a dominant chimpanzee, just as does deviation from customary behaviour (De Waal, 1982).

It is important to notice that a number of cognitive variables involved in emotional arousal do not so much represent additional cognitive conditions for a given emotion, but additional meanings of the eliciting event. They increase the number of concerns the event is relevant for; and it is known (Sonnemans, 1991) that emotional intensity depends on the number of relevant concerns. Arbitrariness and unfairness of an injury, for instance, that have been found to strengthen anger (Berkowitz, 1962; Pastore, 1952), seem to do so not because anger is a response to suffering arbitrary harm (rather that to suffering just any harm), but because they add insult to injury.

The previous analysis of guilt emotion indicated that the antecedents for that emotion, too, can be fairly simple and elementary: Having caused harm to someone else and, particularly, when that entails risk of loss of love or of retaliation. "Guilt" as felt norm-transgression, in this view, often is only a codification and elaboration of the sensitivity to that elementary appraisal. Evidently, awareness of another's distress, of having caused harm, and of risk of loss of love, result from cognitive appraisals. They are low-level appraisals, however, requiring no more than an innate sensitivity, a perceptual capacity, and simple anticipation learning (I shall come back to this).

Shame, as I said, often needs no more antecedent appraisal than is involved in the perception of actual or incipient social rejection—jeering, mockery, and exclusion from the group of playmates—with a property of the self, something one walks around with, causing that rejection. Developmentally, acquisition of the sense of covariation between those latter features would seem to be a sufficient condition for wishing to hide from the jeering others and anticipatory avoidance, with a more articulate sense of self building upon that.

Even a complex emotion like jealousy may, on close scrutiny, be found to have fairly elementary eliciting conditions; here, too, norms about rights of possession or the notion of claims one has upon someone else are in a sense secondary, and this even applies to the involvement of a third party. These latter variables form essential conditions for a person to label his or her emotion as "jealousy", but that is only because the label is reserved for this particular subclass of loss responses, or for the awareness of third-party involvement. They are also essential for particular events (say, the partner kissing a third party, or looking at her/him) to be construed as personal losses or threats of such loss. But what elicits actual emotion is the loss or threat of loss of an attachment figure. Emotionally, much of what we call jealousy often is just an instance of the reactions to loss or threat of loss: Loss of love or loss of attention (Hupka, 1991; Parrott, 1991). The emotional core of much jealousy is anguish or pain or "emotional devastation" (Bryson, 1991), usually with attribution of this to the partner or the third party (Bryson's "anger" factor). The third party is merely what causes the loss or forms the signal for threat. People share such causal attribution, as well as sensitivity to loss, with primates; both sexual jealousy and grief have been well documented in chimpanzees (De Waal, 1982; Goodall, 1986).

A case can be made that most emotions are elicited by appraisal of events with regard to a quite restricted set of event features—more restricted perhaps than the set discussed in current appraisal theory. I will venture some guesses. Anxiety, it would seem, can be evoked by any uncertainty of some magnitude, that is, by any condition that involves uncertainty about whether one's coping repertoire will suffice. Fear can be evoked when such uncertainty is caused by an unfamiliar or aversive source localised in space or time. Distress may be the general response to aversive events when further cognitive appraisals are not made. Sorrow occurs in response to negatively valued events when one's repertoire of actions to remedy the situation appears, or has been, exhausted. The emotion labels, here, refer in the first place to states of action readiness as inferred from behaviour (behavioural inhibition, expectant behaviour interruption and self-protective behaviours, apathy, and so on), together with whatever reflections there are in experience of the antecedents, the response tendencies, and their elaboration.

It is clear that the antecedents of most emotions of anger, guilt, fear, and so on involve more cognitive processes than those indicated above. Emotion elicitation can occur at quite different levels, the sensorimotor, schematic, and cognitive ones (Leventhal & Scherer, 1987). What I have tried to show is that the more complex cognitive processes are not indispensable for arousal of emotions, even those of the kinds discussed. Moreover, it needs to be emphasised that most cognitive activity involved in emotion antecedents has to do with what makes an event emotionally relevant, rather than with the process of emotion generation when an event recognised as relevant is encountered. The cognitive activity has to do with establishing the link between certain kinds of event and the individual's concerns, or with establishing a concern. For instance, having broken a promise is an elicitor of remorse because it is understood as norm transgression, and such a norm transgression is understood as incompatible with high self regard or with social acceptance, or whatever the emotional source (the example is discussed by Oatley & Johnson-Laird, 1987). However, the cognitive activity involved does not take place in an appraisal process. It does not occur at the time of emotion arousal. As Parkinson and Manstead (1991) have convincingly argued, most of it has occurred in the past, through social and other learning, and operates through affective schemata in the sense of Fiske (1982). One knows that breaking a promise is bad. At the same time, when an emotion is aroused these schemata function in a true appraisal process. The event of just having broken a promise elicits an emotion because, on the basis of that schema, it is appraised as of negative valence, as something that cannot be easily undone, that involves one's agency, involves no uncertainty, and whatever other appraisal components may be responsible for an emotion of a given intensity. One cay say that in the case of cognitively complex antecedents the elementary emotion-eliciting conditions are embedded in a larger cognitive context. One can also say that the complex antecedents derive their emotive force from the elementary conditions; and that if they do not, they remain mere cold cognitions.

The last point is relevant for a very basic problem for appraisal theory, namely, to specify what it is, in the information that elicits emotion, that differentiates appraisal from knowledge. The distinction between those two has often been made, notably by Lazarus and Smith (1988; Lazarus, 1991) without, however, sufficiently specifying what differentiates one from the other. "Appraisal" is described as including the personal significance of events, and mere knowledge as consisting of "cognitions about how things are and how they work" (Lazarus & Smith, 1988, p. 282). However, this would not seem to be enough, because there may be knowledge about the personal significance of an event without true appraisal or emotional arousal. This in turn is linked to the facts, almost untouched in the literature, that emotionally relevant information may fail to elicit emotions: For instance, verbal warnings and events not believed to be true or likely. Also, negative emotions often fail to be modified or disappear even when the stimulus events are clearly innocuous, as in the animal phobias (Bandura, Adams, & Beyer, 1977). The question is, of course, what in the information or their processing it is that makes information believable or likely, or emotionally impacting. I have tentatively referred to this problem in what I called the "Law of Apparent Reality": emotions are elicited, and only elicited, by events appraised as real (Frijda, 1988). "Apparent Reality" is but a poor and provisional indication of the factors that might be operative. The hypothesis may be proposed that emotions are elicited when, and only when, elementary conditions are involved, either directly, or by association, or through vivid imagination. But what, precisely, is the nature of those conditions?

The Appraisal Process

The preceding analyses asserted that the appraisal processes responsible for emotion elicitation can be relatively simple. Still, they are cognitive processes that are interposed between the stimulus and emotional response. In addition, it is a core supposition of appraisal theory that the cognitive processes involved in appraisal are nonconscious, having nothing to do with reasoning, with rational considerations or with conscious deliberation. Is this a plausible assertion?

In principle, it certainly is. There is no necessary incompatibility between cognitive processes and their nonconscious nature or the fastness and automaticity that characterise many emotional reactions. Recently, there has been extensive discussion of the existence of nonconscious cognition (Loftus & Klinger, 1992), with general agreement that there is abundant evidence for it, albeit that such cognition is essentially simple. There also is clear evidence of quite complex cognitive processes that occur nonconsciously, provided they are built from simple, modular components. The clearest demonstration is offered by speaking. It has been shown to involve a series of complex cognitive acts: thought evocation, sentence frame formation, lexical retrieval, morphological shaping, and motor programming (Levelt, 1989). Yet, most sentences come without effort, as if by themselves.

Then, how should one conceive of the basic processes of emotion elicitation? First, it must be admitted that it hinges upon a noncognitive step. Recall that emotions involve primary appraisal, the assessment of an event's affective valence or its relevance for some concern. As discussed in the last section, primary appraisal often involves elaborate steps of inference and the intervention of knowledge. Ultimately, however, all emotional valence derives from the anticipation or actual presence of primary satisfiers or annoyers: pain, pleasure, proximity of an attachment figure, unhampered bodily activity, unrestrained movement, feeling in command, or whatever the sources of the various concerns. Ultimately, all emotionally valent events point back to events that are instrinsically pleasant or unpleasant, without possibility of further cognitive justification. Certain contingencies just evoke positive or negative affect.

Still, there is a sense in which even such elicitation of affect by direct confrontation with a primary satisfier or annoyer involves an appraisal process. I hinted at the issue of the "reality" of emotional information. Such information, which includes primary satisfiers and annoyers, has to be appreciated as such, and this does not necessarily or always happen. Pain stimuli are not felt as aversive by analgesic persons or by people after frontal lobotomy; traumatic events are not felt as unpleasant during "numbing" (Parkes, 1972) or in "denial states" (Horowitz, 1976). LeDoux (1989) has summarised extensive evidence that the amygdala is responsible for the affective appraisal of stimulus events. Certain damage to the amygdala abolishes affective response; and, as numbing strongly suggests, the processes in the amygdala can be blocked in the intact organism. This most basic appraisal process may perhaps not meaningfully be called cognitive, as it may not always involve comparison between two representations, which might be taken as the minimal attribute of "cognition". Still, it involves some "computation" (LeDoux, 1989, p. 271), and an appraisal process thus is a necessary condition for emotional experience and major aspects of emotional response.

But notice, in addition, that only part of the elementary occurrences of affect involve contingencies that are intrinsically affective. Emotions are not only elicited by the presentation of some satisfier or annoyer, but also by the withdrawal or loss of one of these, as in sadness and relief (Arnold, 1960; Frijda, 1986; Lazarus, 1966). Such withdrawal or loss necessarily involves a process of comparison and mismatch with an expectancy, as has extensively been argued by Mowrer (1960). Even at a quite basic level of emotion, certain cognitive processes play an essential role.

Additional cognitive variables are involved in the arousal of true emotion, that is, in the elicitation of action readiness change, and not merely of affect. Occurrence of true emotion would seem to depend on the involvement of variables like how close in space the event is, and how close in time its anticipated outcome; how serious its consequences are supposed to be; and how difficult coping with the event is felt to be. No difficulty, no emotion, or so one may suppose; and the variables indicated may belong to those that are essential for turning cold cognition into hot cognition. Moreover, even the simplest stimuli that elicit emotions pre-suppose some comparison with stored information. These simplest stimuli include unexpected intense stimuli; unexpected stimuli in unfamiliar surroundings; unfamiliar stimuli close by, or of some size; body restraint and other movement interference; pain that persists after one has tried removing its source; loss of balance. They all involve comparing a stimulus against schemata or expectations, or termination of an activity with its prepared termination. The only exception I can find is that of startle by intense stimuli. The suddenness required to elicit emotion may not be a cognitive condition but the absence of such a condition, and function as a default value in the emotion process; but then startle may not be considered an emotion (Ekman, Friesen, & Simons, 1985). The implied assertion is, of course, that pain *per se*, and similar stimuli, do not evoke emotion; which is plausible.

At the same time, cognitive processes such as those determining proximity, seriousness, etc. readily pass the test of being simple. This also applies to the appraisal checks proposed in the current appraisal literature (Frijda, Kuipers, & ter Schure, 1989; Scherer, 1984; Smith & Ellsworth, 1985; Smith & Lazarus this issue). These appraisals can all occur at the perceptual level. Most of them can be seen as implied by the very perceptual processes by which stimulus events are taken in. For instance, the appraisal of novelty can well be nothing more than an output of the process by which input is matched to a schema or "neuronal model" (Sokolov, 1963); the same applies to familiarity. Unexpectedness cor-responds to the registration of an event not fitting an expectancy. Uncertainty corresponds to the output of a partial failure in the process of generating expectations. Appraisal of agency is, in its simplest form, no more than perceptual causality combined with perceived intentionality, which categories of perception have both been demonstrated by Michotte

(1950; see also Thinès, Costall, & Butterworth, 1991). Involvement of the self, as in shame, may merely mean that a property or act perceived as belonging to one's physical appearance is perceived as the cause of some event.

A major source of appraisals is the monitoring of action planning and action execution. Appraisal of controllability can be considered as implied in the outcome of a successful match of means to ends in the process of action planning. Uncontrollability, helplessness, or despair, is the outcome of finding one's actions unsuccessful and the repertoire of untried actions exhausted. Frustration is the output of finding that actions prepared or underway cannot be carried to completion. In the dramaturgic theory, embarrassment results from "lacking a coherent or acceptable way to behave" (Parrott & Smith, 1991, p. 468), and similar reasoning may apply to shame, to the extent that a meaningful distinction between these emotions can be upheld.

All these appraisals involve perceiving the "affordance" (Gibson, 1979) (or lack of affordance) of stimulus elements for one's coping activities, that is, the anticipated fit between potential actions and perceptual features. In this vein, the cognitive bases of frustration and the sense of "ought not" in anger were traced, above, to the interaction between expectations implicit in one's actions and events.

If this analysis of appraisal processes is correct, these processes are simpler than would appear from their logical descriptions in the analyses of people like Scherer (1984), Smith and Ellsworth (1985), and myself (Frijda, 1986). Familiarity, expectedness, absence of agency are not really appraisals; they do not represent outcomes of cognitive processes or checks, but default values.

CONCLUSION

What are the conclusions to be drawn from the preceding discussion? First, that emotions in all instances involve a process of appraisal, and cognitive appraisal at that. Subject-dependent processes intervene between stimulus and emotional response. These processes relate to the appraisal of the event as emotionally meaningful (primary appraisal) as well as to the kind of emotion that results (secondary appraisal). Secondly, the cognitive appraisal processes can be minimal in complexity. They can be of elementary kinds, bound to general processes of information intake and action monitoring. These often involve factors that can indeed scarcely be called cognitive. "Acute interference" is not a cognition but a fact that happens: One is progressing towards some goal, and bang! one cannot go further; although of course the plan and its interruption are compared and found to clash.

Thirdly, the thesis of the simplicity of cognitive conditions sufficient for eliciting emotions holds for some of the conceptually complex emotions as well as for allegedly simple ones. The conditions sufficient to evoke the pains or distresses which on the basis of behaviour, and upon elaboration, are called guilt feeling, remorse, and jealousy are fairly elementary; they seem to require little in the way of socio-cultural norms. This is not to deny that the occurrence of most emotions presupposes elaborate cognitive antecedents. However, most of these have to do with prior learning by which the objects or events have acquired emotional significance, and they do not necessarily involve cognitive processes at the time of emotion arousal. They may, incidentally, involve controlled processes of conscious deliberation and reasoning, in contrast to the appraisal processes actually responsible for emotion arousal that can be held to be nonconscious and automatic.

A major argument of this paper has been that self-report is valuable in providing access to the cognitive content of emotional experience, and thereby provides cues to what differentiates one type of emotional experience from another. However, it is of limited value in determining emotion antecedents and, in particular, in determining appraisal processes leading to emotional arousal, experience, and response.

From the analyses given, emotion can be seen to result from an automatic, essentially simple basic appraisal process that may subsequently be cognitively elaborated. The basic process is sufficient for emotion arousal, and for instigating elaboration.

But note: This process is usually, though not always or necessarily, squeezed between much more complex cognitive activities. At the one side, the elicitor of the basic appraisal process itself is often the product of extensive prior cognitive events; it is often the result of cognitive activities that have been going on for a long time. In fact, this explains rather than contradicts the speed and immediacy with which emotions may arise. Guilt, anger, shame, and sadness rarely fall upon an unprepared mind. They build from previous doubts, irritations, ruminations, and apprehensions, that themselves are the precipitates of earlier relevant experiences. These doubts, ruminations, etc., and the earlier experiences form the background for what actually triggers the emotion. Emotions indeed rarely have the one-shot, immediate, and fast character of the paradigmatic case of being startled by a crackle in the solitary woods. And even there one has been walking around with all sorts of expectations against which the crackle is perceived.

At the other side is the sequel to any given basic emotion process. Elaboration provides information that may itself elicit new emotion, or modify the prevailing one; and information uptake from the environment continues, often modified by the previous response. Emotions usually are processes over time. They usually are not one-shot responses, from that perspective too. Most emotions have the form of protracted transactions (Lazarus, 1991) or emotion episodes (Frijda, Mesquita, Sonnemans, & Van Goozen, 1991). And articulate emotional experience, as Ellsworth (1991) and Parkinson and Manstead (1992) have argued, is quite generally the outcome of successive steps of information pick-up that gradually build up that experience. Each step is determined by the outcomes of the preceding steps; elaborations are among those outcomes.

But these outcomes as well as previous doubts, ruminations, and relevant experiences coalesce, as it were, into a cognitive structure that serves as the input of the emotion-governing appraisal process at any given moment of time. In that structure, emotion-relevant stimuli are represented, together with their meanings as these have accumulated over time ("this is the fifth insult I had to endure!"), contextual elements ("he did it on purpose, to show his contempt for me"), results of previous elements in the interaction ("these efforts are hopeless!"), gleanings of the consequences of potential responses, as these control emotion regulation (see Frijda, 1986, Ch. 8; Gray, 1982), and so on. Emotion generation can best be viewed as governed by a blackboard control structure: What is on the blackboard is continuously incremented or modified by additional uptake of information from the stimulus event, from activated schemata, and from feedback from preceding emotional response phases, including elaborations. These, as I say, coalesce into sense of reality, sense of imminence, of certainty or uncertainty, agency, and all the basic appraisal components. And for that sense of reality, agency, etc., it makes no difference whether the cognitive road to them was a long or a short one.

That emotions result from appraisal processes of a relatively simple kind, involving elementary cognitive processes is, of course, a hypothesis, and this also applies to suggestions as to which these elementary processes are, and which ones are responsible for which emotions. These hypotheses can only be tested by careful experimental study of antecedent-emotion sequences of which self-report data are unreliable reflections.

What I have suggested is tentative, an effort to see clearly. This holds most strongly for the suggestions concerning the elementary stimulus aspects and appraisal processes, the reasons for cognitive elaboration, and these last remarks on the temporal development of emotional experience. There still is very much work to do.

Manuscript received 5 January 1992
Revised manuscript received 10 November 1992

REFERENCES

Arnold, M.B. (1960). *Emotion and Personality*. Vols I and II. New York: Columbia University Press.

Ausubel, D. (1955). Relationships between shame and guilt in the socializing process. *Psychological Review, 62*, 378–390.

Averill, J.R. (1982). *Anger and aggression: An essay on emotion*. New York: Springer.

Bandura, A., Adams, N., & Beyer, J. (1977). Cognitive processes mediating behavioural change. *Journal of Personality and Social Psychology, 35*, 125–139.

Baumeister, R., Stillwell, A.M., & Heatherton, T.F. (In press). Interpersonal aspects of guilt: Two studies using autobiographical narratives. In J. Tangney & K. Fischer (Eds), *Self-conscious emotions*. New York: Guilford.

Berkowitz, L. (1962). *Aggression: A social psychological analysis*. New York: McGraw-Hill.

Berkowitz, L. (1989). Frustration-aggression hypothesis: Examination and reformulation. *Psychological Bulletin, 106*, 59–73.

Bryson, J.B. (1991). Modes of response to jealousy-evoking situations. In P. Salovey (Ed.), *The psychology of jealousy and envy*. New York: Guilford, pp. 178–207.

Carver, C.S. & Scheier, M.F. (1990). Origins and functions of positive and negative affect: A control-process view. *Psychological Bulletin, 97*, 19–35.

Davitz, J.R. (1969). *The language of emotion*. New York: Academic Press.

De Rivera, J. (1977). *A structural theory of the emotions*. New York: International Universities Press.

De Waal, F. (1982). *Chimpanzee politics*. London: Johathan Cape.

Diener, E. (1980). Deindividuation: The absence of self-awareness and self-regulation in group members. In P.B. Paulus (Ed.), *The psychology of group influence*. Hillsdale, NJ: Lawrence Erlbaum Associates Inc.

Dollard, J., Doob, L.W., Miller, N.E., Mowrer, O.H., & Sears, R.R. (1939). *Frustration and aggression*. New Haven: Yale University Press.

Ekman, P.E., Friesen, W.V., & Simons, R.C. (1985). Is the startle reaction an emotion? *Journal of Personality and Social Behaviour, 49*, 1416–1426.

Ellsworth, P.C. (1991). Some implications of cognitive appraisal theories of emotion. In K. Strongman (Ed.), *International review of studies on emotion*. New York: Wiley, pp. 143–161.

Ellsworth, P.C. & Smith, C.A. (1988a). From appraisal to emotion: Differences among unpleasant feelings. *Motivation and Emotion, 12*, 271–302.

Ellsworth, P.C. & Smith, C.A. (1988b). Shades of joy: Patterns of appraisal differentiating pleasant emotions. *Cognition and Emotion, 2*, 301–331.

Fischer, A.H. (1991). *Emotion scripts. A study of the social and cognitive facets of emotions*. Leiden: DSWO-Press.

Fiske, S.T. (1982). Schema-triggered affect: Applications to social perception. In M.S. Clark & S.T. Fiske (Eds), *Affect and cognition: The 17th Annual Carnegie Symposium on Cognition*. Hillsdale, NJ: Lawrence Erlbaum Associates Inc, pp. 55–78.

Flynn, J.P. (1973). Patterning mechanisms, patterned reflexes and attack behaviour in cats. In J.K. Cole & D.D. Jensen (Eds), *Nebraska Symposium on Motivation, 1972*. Lincoln, University of Nebraska Press, pp. 125–154.

Freedman, J.L. (1970). Transgression, compliance, and guilt. In J. Macaulay & L. Berkowitz (Eds), *Altruism and helping behaviour*. New York: Academic Press, pp. 155–162.

Frijda, N.H. (1986). *The emotions*. Cambridge University Press.

Frijda, N.H. (1987). Emotion, cognitive structure and action tendency. *Cognition and Emotion, 1*, 115–144.

Frijda, N.H. (1988). The laws of emotion. *American Psychologist, 43*, 349–358.

Frijda, N.H. (1989). The different roles of cognitive variables in emotion. In A.F. Bennett & K.M. McConkey (Eds), *Cognition in individual and social contexts*. Amsterdam: Elsevier, pp. 325–336.

Frijda, N.H., Kuipers, P., & ter Schure, L. (1989). Relations between emotion, appraisal and emotional action readiness. *Journal of Personality and Social Psychology, 57*, 212–228.

Frijda, N.H., Mesquita, B., Sonnemans, J., & Van Goozen, S. (1991). The duration of affective phenomena, or emotions, sentiments and passions. K. Strongman (Ed.), *International review of emotion and motivation*. New York: Wiley, pp. 187–225.

Frijda, N.H. & Sato, K. (In prep.). *Appraisal and action readiness in emotion: Comparison between Japanese and Dutch subjects*.

Frijda, N.H. & Wiers, R. (In prep.). *The relationships between appraisal, action readiness, and emotions: A replication with modified materials*. Report, Institute of Emotion and Motivation, University of Amsterdam.

Frijda, N.H. & Zammuner, V. (1992). L'etichettamento delle proprie emozione. *Giornale Italiano di Psicologia, 19*, 1–22.

Furedey, J.J., Riley, D.M., & Frederikson, M. (1983). Pavlovian extinction, treatment resistant phobias, and the limits of the cognitive paradigm. *Pavlovian Journal of Biological Science, 18*, 126–135.

Gibson, J.J. (1979). *The ecological approach to visual perception*. Boston: Houghton-Mifflin.

Goodall, J. (1986). *The chimpanzees of Gombe: Patterns of behaviour*. Cambridge: Belknap.

Gray, J.A. (1982). *The neuropsychology of anxiety: An enquiry into the functions of the septo-hippocampal system*. Oxford University Press.

Hall, G.S. (1899). A study of anger. *American Journal of Psychology, 10*, 516–591.

Heider, F. (1958). *The psychology of interpersonal relations*. New York: Wiley.

Hoffman, M.L. (1976). Empathy, role-taking, guilt and development of altruistic motives. In T. Lickona (Ed.), *Moral development and behaviour: Theory of research and social issues*. New York: Holt, Rinehart & Winston, pp. 124–143.

Hoffman, M.L. (1984). Interaction of affect and cognition in empathy. In C.E. Izard. J. Kagan, & R.B. Zajonc (Eds), *Emotions, cognition, and behaviour*. Cambridge University Press, pp. 103–131.

Horowitz, M.J. (1976). *Stress response syndromes*. New York: Jason Aronson.

Hupka, R.B. (1991). The motive for the arousal of romantic jealousy: Its cultural origin. In P. Salovey (Ed.), *The psychology of jealousy and envy*. New York: Guilford, pp. 252–270.

Izard, C.E. (1977). *Human emotions*. New York: Plenum.

Johnson, E. & Tversky, A. (1983). Affect, generalization and the perception of risk. *Journal of Personality and Social Psychology, 45*, 20–31.

Johnson-Laird, P.N. & Oatley, K. (1989). The language of emotions: An analysis of a semantic field. *Cognition and Emotion, 3*, 81–124.

Kroon, R.M. (1988). *Aanleidingen en structuur van schuldgevoel*. Masters Thesis, Psychology Department, University of Amsterdam. No. psy.11.8.88.225.

Laborit, H. (1979). *L'inhibition de l'action: Biologie, physiologie, psychologie, sociologie*, Vol. I. Paris: Masson.

Lang, P.J. (1977). Physiological assessment of anxiety and fear. In J.D. Cone & R.P. Hawkins (Eds), *Behavioural assessment: New directions in clinical psychology*. New York: Brunner/Mazel, pp. 178–195.

Lazarus, R.S. (1966). *Psychological stress and the coping process*. New York: McGraw-Hill.

Lazarus, R.S. (1982). Thoughts on the relations between emotion and cognition. *American Psychologist, 37*, 1019–1024.

Lazarus, R.S. (1984). On the primacy of cognition. *American Psychologist, 39*, 124–129.

Lazarus, R.S. (1991). *Emotion and adaptation*. Oxford University Press.

Lazarus, R.S. & Smith, C.A. (1988). Knowledge and appraisal in the cognition-emotion relationship. *Cognition and Emotion, 2*, 281–300.

LeDoux, J.E. (1989). Cognitive-emotional interactions in the brain. *Cognition and Emotion, 3*, 267–289.

Levelt, W.J.M. (1989). *Speaking: From intention to articulation*. Cambridge, Mass.: MIT Press.

Leventhal, H. & Scherer, K.R. (1987). The relationship of emotion and cognition: A functional approach to a semantic controversy. *Cognition and Emotion, 1*, 3–28.

Lewis, H.B. (1971) *Shame and guilt in neurosis*. New York: International Universities Press.

Loftus, E.F., & Klinger, M.R. (1992). Is the unconscious smart or dumb? *American Psychologist, 47*, 761–765.

McGraw, K.M. (1987). Guilt following transgression: An attribution of responsibility approach. *Journal of Personality and Social Behaviour, 53*, 247–256.

Manstead, A.S.R. & Tetlock, P.E. (1989). Cognitive appraisals and emotional experience: Further evidence. *Cognition and Emotion, 3*, 225–240.

Markham, S. (1992). *Dimensi pengalaman emosi: kajian deskriptif melalui rama-emosi berdasarka teori kogniif*. Ph.D. Thesis, University of Indonesia.

Matthews, A. (1988). Anxiety and the processing of threatening information. In V. Hamilton, G.H. Bower, & N.H. Frijda (Eds), *Cognitive perspectives on emotion and motivation*. Dordrecht: Kluwer, pp. 265–284.

Mauro, R., Sato, K., & Tucker, J. (1992). The role of appraisal in human emotions: A cross-cultural study. *Journal of Personality and Social Psychology, 62*, 301–317.

Mesquita, B. (1993). *Emotions in people from different cultures*. Ph. D. Thesis, University of Amsterdam.

Michotte, A.E. (1950). The emotions as functional connections. In M. Reymert (Ed.), *Feelings and emotions: The Mooseheart symposium*. New York, McGraw-Hill, pp. 114–126.

Montaigne, M. de (1588/1965). *Essays, I*. Paris: Gallimard Editions Folio.

Morris, W.N. (1989). *Mood: The frame of mind*. New York: Springer.

Mowrer, O.H. (1960). *Learning theory and behaviour*. New York: Wiley.

Nisbett, R.E., & Wilson, T.D. (1977). Telling more than we can know: Verbal reports on mental processes. *Psychological Review, 84*, 231–259.

Oatley, K. (1992). *Best laid schemes: The psychology of emotions*. Cambridge University Press.

Oatley, K. & Johnson-Laird, P. (1987). Towards a cognitive theory of emotion. *Cognition and Emotion, 1*, 51–58.

Ortony, A., Clore, G., & Collins, A. (1988). *The cognitive structure of emotions*. Cambridge University Press.

Parkes, C.M. (1972). *Bereavement: Studies of grief in adult life*. New York: International Universities Press.

Parkinson, B. & Manstead, A.S.R. (1992). Appraisal as a cause of emotion. In M.S. Clark (Ed.), *Emotion. Review of personality and social psychology*, Vol. 13. Newbury Park, CA: Sage, pp. 122–149.

Parrott, W.G. (1991). The emotional experiences of envy and jealousy. In P. Salovey (Ed.), *The psychology of jealousy and envy*. New York: Guilford, pp. 3–30.

Parrott, W.G. & Smith, S.F. (1991). Embarrassment: Actual vs. typical cases, classical vs. prototypical representations. *Cognition and Emotion, 5*, 467–488.

Pastore, N. (1952). The role of arbitrariness in the frustration-aggression hypothesis. *Journal of Abnormal and Social Psychology, 47*, 728–731.

Rachman, S.J. (1990). *Fear and courage* (2nd edn). New York: Freeman.

Ramsey, R. (1979). Bereavement: A behavioural treatment of pathological grief. In P.O. Söden, S. Bates, & W.S. Dockens (Eds), *Trends in behaviour therapy*. New York, Academic Press, pp. 217–248.

Reisenzein, R. & Hofmann, T. (1990). An investigation of dimensions of cognitive appraisal in emotion using a repertory grid technique. *Motivation and Emotion, 14*, 19–38.

Rombouts, H. (1992). *Echt verliefd*. Amsterdam: Boom.

Roseman, I.J. (1984). Cognitive determinants of emotion: A structural theory. In P. Shaver (Ed.), *Review of personality and social psychology*, Vol. 5. *Emotions, relationships, and health*. Beverly Hills: Sage, pp. 11–36.

Roseman, I.J. (1991). Appraisal determinants of discrete emotions. *Cognition and Emotion*, 5, 161–200.

Roseman, I.J., Spindel, M.S., & Jose, P.E. (1990). Appraisals of emotion-eliciting events: Testing a theory of discrete emotions. *Journal of Personality and Social Psychology, 59*, 899–915.

Russell, J.A. (1987). Comment on articles by Frijda and by Conway and Bekerian. *Cognition and Emotion, 1*, 193–197.

Schwarz, N., Bless, B., & Bohner, G. (1991). Mood and persuasion: Affective states influence the processing of persuasive communications. In M. Zanna (Ed.), *Advances in experimental social psychology*, Vol. 24. San Diego: Academic Press, pp. 161–199.

Scheff, T. (1988, April). *Hiding behaviour: Toward resolving the shame controversy*. Paper presented at the Conference on Shame Research, Asilomar.

Scherer, K.R. (1984). Emotion as a multicomponent process: A model and some cross-cultural data. In P. Shaver (Ed.), *Review of personality and social psychology*, Vol. 5. Beverly Hills: Sage, pp. 37–63.

Smith, C.A. & Ellsworth, P.C. (1985). Patterns of cognitive appraisal in emotion. *Journal of Personality and Social Psychology, 48*, 813–838.

Sokolov, J.N. (1963). *Perception and the conditioned reflex*. Oxford: Pergamon Press.

Sonnemans, J. (1991). *Structure and determinants of emotional intensity*. Ph.D. Thesis, University of Amsterdam.

Spinoza, B. (1677/1989). *Ethica*. Amsterdam: Rieuwertsz [English translation: G.H.R. Parkinson. London: Everyman's Library].

Teasdale, J.D. & Spencer, P. (1984). Induced mood and estimates of past success. *British Journal of Clinical Psychology, 23*, 149–150.

Terwijn, H. (1993). *A study of shame experiences*. Masters Thesis, Psychology Department, University of Amsterdam.

Tesser, A. (1990). Smith and Ellsworth's appraisal model of emotion: A replication, extension, and test. *Personality and Social Psychology Bulletin, 16*, 210–223.

Thinès, G., Costall, A., & Butterworth, G. (Eds). (1991). *Michotte's experimental phenomenology of perception*. Hillsdale, NJ: Lawrence Erlbaum Associates Inc.

Ulrich, R.E. & Azrin, H.N. (1962). Reflexive fighting in response to aversive stimulation. *Journal of the Experimental Analysis of Behaviour, 5*, 511–521.

Watson, J.B. (1929). *Psychology from the standpoint of a behaviourist* (3rd edn). Philadelphia: Lippincott.

Weiner, B. (1985). An attributional theory of achievement motivation and emotion. *Psychological Review, 92*, 548–573.

Zajonc, R.B. (1980). Thinking and feeling: Preferences need no inferences. *American Psychologist, 35*, 151–175.

Zajonc, R.B. (1984). On the primacy of emotion. *American Psychologist, 39*, 117–123.

Subject Index